THE BOYS FROM BULAWAYO

Copyright © 2023 by Barry John Cohen

The right of Barry John Cohen to be identified as the Author of the Work has been asserted in accordance with the Copyright Act 98 of 1978.

All rights reserved. No portion of this book may be reproduced, stored in a retrieval system, or transmitted in any form or by any means, electronic, mechanical, photocopying, recording, or otherwise without the prior permission of the copyright owner.

First Edition October 2023 in print

ISBN: 978-0-7961-3009-9

THE BOYS FROM BULAWAYO

THE BIGGEST POLICE INVESTIGATION IN AUSTRALIAN HISTORY

BY BARRY JOHN COHEN

BY THE SAME AUTHOR

Blazing the Trail: This sport collector's volume chronicles the impact black golf had on overcoming discrimination, their history, and how they broke down the apartheid barriers.

Let me Play: This is the story of Papwa Sewgolum who rose from humble beginnings to challenge the might of the golfing titans on an equal footing, and after winning three Dutch Opens and two Natal Opens beating Gary Player, he was banned from playing in white tournaments and his passport was withdrawn.

Let The Storm Burst: 1895. A group of trekkers travel by wagon through the bushveld to the goldfields. Romance, adventure and a plot to overthrow the Boer Republic.

Mike West: South Africa's Super Soldier - Co-written with Hannes Wessels: Mike West is heading for a life of crime. Then he manages to be accepted to fight in the Rhodesian war where he learns the art of survival, tracking and killing, before joining the SANDF where he must fight both the Afrikaner internal prejucie and the terrorists for survival.

PAPWA: Against all odds, discovered at 27 and taken abroad, he wins the Dutch Open 3 times, 2nd in the SA Open, and wins the Natal Open 2 times beating Gary Player and becoming the figurehead of the anti-apartheid movement only to be banned from playing in white tournaments and takes away his passport.

By the Same Author

AN UNEXPECTED LIFE: Fighting apartheid, music, video, sailing America Cup boat, scratch cards, Supersport television gaming, touring with the Springboks, CANSA in transition, the Golf Hall of Fame, finally becoming an author and film possibilities, all go to make up a life interacting with giants on the world stage. From treachery to hope, and life's lessons. Barry John Cohen, my unexpected journey.

The CEDRIC KUSHNER Story: Cedric Kushner broke the mould by following his passion insofar as organising and promoting music and boxing events abroad at the highest level and ignoring the naysayers who look at school reports to gauge potential. We are all good at something. We just have to find our passion. What matters in life and what you achieve and the memories you leave behind. Cedric was such a man.

CONTENTS

PREFACE	8
OVERVIEW	9
PROLOGUE	12
Introduction	12
Background	15
Freda Briggs discusses Lizzie and the Twins	17
Professor Freda Briggs' emails Russell.	19
The Family Law Act	21
CHAPTER 1 – THE EARLY YEARS	25
A Brief History of Rhodesia	25
Patrick Finbar McGarry O'Dea - My Early Life.	32
Life after the War	68
William Russell Massingdon Pridgeon – My Early Life	88
CHAPTER 2 – THE ARRIVAL	112
Russell arrives in New Zealand	112
Russell arrives in Australia	116
Debbie and Christopher	117
CHAPTER 3 – PROTECTING MY CHILDREN	131
Desperation	131
Lizzie takes the Twins	134
Russell and Patrick enter the fray	135
The Search for Lizzie and the Twins	140
On the Run	141
Conclusions and Recommendation	156
Response from the meeting	157
CHAPTER 4 – RUSSELL TAKES ACTION	160
The Australian Anti-Paedophile Party is formed	160

Plankton Sues	167
The Bugging	173
Ann and Christopher Gordon	174
Lizzie (Morris) Weber arrested	188
CHAPTER 5 – THE LAW COMES CALLING	**202**
Arrest of Russell and Patrick	202
The Media	209
Prime Minister Scott Morrison apologises	215
The AFP responds	219
Plankton defamation case	222
Charges laid	223
The Charges	223
The Yacht Saga	229
Medical License Withdrawn	230
CHAPTER 6 – THE LEGAL ARGUMENTS	**233**
Trials	233
Medical License Appeal	240
Russell requests for evidence withheld	244
Plankton: Health Care complaint	248
Serena Teffaha and Ann Gordon	251
Graeme Bell and Pastor Paul	257
CHAPTER 7 – THE TRUTH IS REVEALED	**276**
Trials continue	276
Justice Clare	278
Child abuse in Australia	281
Relief At Last: Medical License Returned	285
Review	295
CHAPTER 8 – FORWARD LOOKING	**301**
Where to now?	301
The AFP's Conundrum	307
Showdown with the Devil	311
BIBLIOGRAPHY	**319**

PREFACE

This ongoing story is in no way intended to embarrass any person, legal authority, AFP, the Family Court or the ongoing trial, nor have the potential to influence any jury members, or interfere with the administration of justice. Nor should this be seen as a threat to the capacity of the Federal Court to dispense justice in this case.

This is a legal drama, but more than that, hopefully, it will clarify the law insofar as Family Court rulings, and when such rulings where children are concerned, may be circumvented, if at all, especially where there is probable cause concerning acts of paedophilia, especially when evidence received from a young child.

Names have been changed to protect the identity of most of those involved aside from the two main characters, Nor has the narrative, insofar as the second half of the story, been taken from anywhere other than public domain from reports in the print and other mediums, as well as comments made by the main parties. Further, there is no attempt to pass judgement on this case which is still ongoing after nearly six years at the time of writing.

This is potentially a very important legal ruling as it may have ramifications far beyond Australian law.

OVERVIEW

With the moving of time and the changing of attitudes, laws are sometimes reviewed, change, or confirmed when challenged. This is especially so as more sophisticated methods are employed and where even after spending 48 years in jail for murder, they are released such as in the case of Glynn Simmons in the USA

Yet it is instinct that sometimes must be overlooked, especially where children are concerned. "They are too young for their evidence to be taken seriously" when all the data suggest otherwise. At the same time, reports must be handled with the greatest care supposedly to protect these children, and at times, even to their detriment.

So how does the expert stack up against the law? Like all other instances without actual proof, it is merely supposition. And yet.... do you do nothing until you find the proof to the detriment of a defenceless child?

Then you may be faced with conflicting laws, How do you challenge a ruling when it appears wrong as not all the evidence is provided in order to protect the child?

It is the duty of the parent and the child minder, such as a doctor, to protect the child at all times, yet Family Court rulings may put this at odds with the child protection law. Which comes first? Is it always the official legal ruling? And if it is challenged in good faith, does the same degree of penalty apply?

Such is the situation two Australian immigrants from Rhodesia, one a doctor, found themselves when the Australian world authority Professor Emeritus Freda Briggs, a child protection advocate and 2000 Senior Australian of the Year for her pioneering work on child protection requested their help concerning two twins before she passed on.

But tackling the legal authority comes with consequences as they have the ability to wield the power their authority entrusts to them, similarly the court authorities. This is the situation Dr. Russell Pridgeon and Patrick O'Dea found themselves in.

Rarely do we see anyone kind enough to help others in distress, even more so when they do not know the person. Maybe it's because these two men had been through hard times and didn't want others to also experience such difficulties, or possibly because someone they admired asked for their assistance, but probably because they believed these young children were being abused. They did this out of the goodness of their heart, spending substantial amounts of their own funds with no expectations of anything in return.

But the law is very clear. Obey a court order which can only be superseded by the welfare of children in certain circumstances. These men thought they were being called to act given these circumstances.

Could this will be the test case the law requires for all who find themselves in similar situations?

The shadow of paedophilia runs deep, and those in authority are exposed to its deadly tentacles, and sometimes succumb, enticed by participants and dangled benefits. Sadly there are bad apples within these organisations, especially those who do not like seeing their authority being challenged.

Overview

The story you are about to read is true! This case has been ongoing since 2018 with no end in sight.

Why? Because one after another of the seven charges collectively representing a possible 50 year sentence have been dropped when challenged, and in the case of Dr Pridgeon, only two charges are left.

Meanwhile, charges are reconfigured to get around technicalities. Should this seventh charge not be upheld it will have major ramifications for the Townsville Children Services and the court who appear to have done everything possible to bury certain evidence, using 'protection of the children' as their weapon, thereby preventing the full facts from being tested, as were they wrong, heads no doubt would roll.

In so doing, they have attempted to bankrupt the defendants by preventing them from working, feeding nonsense stories to the press, and possibly even committing perjury. Legal aid was denied despite the fact that they appear to have qualified for such assistance, but these fellows are resourceful and swotting upon the law with some outside unlikely assistance, they have put up their own excellent defence.

Now the shoe maybe on the other foot, as if they cannot convict them, and it would appear there may be pressure from higher up to obtain a conviction, it could be them in the dock, and the likely recipients of the stripped uniform.

Let the cards fall where they may. In a wider sense, this story is actually about the Rule of Law. It is possibly a test case to determine whether the Family Court's ruling can be ignored, and if so, is there a defence sufficiently strong which can override this court ruling, and when can it be used?

PROLOGUE

Introduction

I grew up a little in awe of Australians. I remember listening to my father tell stories about some of the great Aussie fighter pilots he met in the Western Desert in WWII. Rhodesia was rugby and cricket-mad, so we were all steeped in the legend of Don Bradman. One of the first cricket books I read was about the great Aussie all-rounder, Keith Miller, who flew Mosquitoes during the war. One of the first Australians I came to know was John Cheffers, who came to the country to coach athletics and became a house-guest. His trip was sponsored by a sports-body of which my dad was a member. He was a big, jovial guy with a smiling face and a hearty laugh, and I so enjoyed the time I spent with him. I remember reading books about the Outback and the rugged ranchers who lived in those remote places; they looked very much like my countrymen, and I thought they must be kindred spirits. Some Aussies came to Rhodesia to fight in our war and all the guys I met were tough blokes I liked. Ten years ago, my wife and I went to Australia with a view to emigrating. Apart from the natural beauty, I was struck by the orderliness, compared to the disorder we have become used to in Africa. I liked the idea that this was a country where the rule of law was applied without fear or favour.

Against this backdrop, writing this book has been a sad shock because this is a horrible story about 'good guys' being beaten. It would be comforting to believe this narrative is speculative, but as

Prologue

you will see from the references, it is verifiably true.

In trying to get a message across I wanted to find a way to persuade the reader that the two 'Bulawayo Boys' were indeed the 'good guys' and so I pleaded with them to tell me their stories before they got themselves into trouble in Australia. Both were reluctant because they were adamant that this should be about the children and not them, but I prevailed upon them to understand they needed to reveal themselves, warts and all, to the public who will ultimately decide whom they believe. And because I am of the view it might be interesting and instructive, I decided to detail a little of the history of the country in which they grew up because I know the ethos and character of the country shaped them. They learned early, from their parents and their countrymen, that men do not walk away, least of all children in distress. Today, 'the Rhodesian way' would be lampooned for being patriarchal, and maybe it was, but with that male dominance came responsibility and a commitment to help others, no matter the risk. This commitment has landed Patrick O'Dea and Dr Russell Pridgeon in terrible trouble.

In following the saga in Australia once they involved themselves in assisting abused children, fair-minded people will be left asking why the system appears to favour the miscreants rather than the children?

After all, this book is about one of the longest, most complicated, most expensive investigations and trial processes in Australian legal history. It is about two men who believe they simply did their duty in helping people in trouble when they believed the system failed them. In so doing, they have essentially given the last ten years of their lives to helping people they never knew, impoverished themselves and wrecked their lives. To have been charged with 'profiting from the proceeds of crime', is at once laughable and preposterous and tells us more about the investigators than the accused.

At the time of writing, after all the hype and hullabaloo about the police 'smashing child-stealing syndicates', all but two charges against Russell (namely conspiracy to defeat justice) have been dropped, whilst Patrick still faces eight charges (namely 2 x conspiracy to defeat justice, 3 x using a carriage service to menace and harass, and 3 x exposing section 121). And this, too, is surprising, as the indictments appear to be contingent on the more serious charges which have been withdrawn.

To the reader we leave the question hanging as to how this ridiculous sham could go on for so long when it now appears there was no crime committed in the first place unless it is to protect a Family Court ruling, right or wrong? How could the mighty Australian Federal Police have seen the need to mount the huge investigation derisorily referred to known as "Operation Noetic", employ massive force to arrest and hound two good men while feeding the country's media a story that portrayed them to millions of people as monsters dealing in child trafficking. To their utter discredit, this same press has maintained a sullen silence in lieu of reporting the dropping of the charges they announced with such abandon.

There is worse news: this case looks like it is the tip of the proverbial global iceberg, where innocents are abused, their lives ruined forever, where unspeakable acts of depravity and cruelty are a regular reality.

All this happened because upon one fateful day, the late Mrs. Freda Briggs (AO), one of Australia's most celebrated human rights activists, asked Dr Russell Pridgeon to help with what she described to him as 'one of the worst cases of paedophilic abuse she had ever seen'.

Prologue

In spite of what they had to endure, the long-term goal of these two brave men remains true to that of Freda; to devote the rest of their lives to protecting Australia's greatest resource – its children.

If they prevail, Australians can surely sing again with pride; "Advance Australia Fair".

Thomas Burke, the renowned Irish philosopher, summed it up: 'All that evil needs to prosper, is that good men do nothing'.

Background

Having escaped the savage and cruel despotic regime of Zimbabwe's Robert Mugabe and the hurt of apartheid, how would Dr Russell Pridgeon have known a chance interaction with Professor Freda Briggs would dramatically change his and Patrick O'Dea lives such that they would face potentially sixty years in jail, and lead to a challenge to Australia's Family Court legal system, and the integrity of the Australian Federal Police (AFP)

These authorities seem blissfully (or studiously?) unaware that child sexual abuse is a crime of secrecy: it is perpetrated behind closed doors, in the privacy of the family home. The injuries to the child (anal or vaginal tears) heal quickly, unless the crime is videotaped and the video falls into the hands of the police, there is no evidence. If the DPP refuses to prosecute then they create the perfect crime, the get out of jail card for the majority of abusers. The present Royal Commission into institutional child abuse has been absolutely clear about this: CHILDREN HAVE TO BE BELIEVED. If the DPP will not prosecute after there has been clear, articulate and detailed testimony from an intelligent 13-year-old boy, it is reasonable to ask: under which circumstances would they prosecute? People often wonder why victims of sexual abuse take decades before they finally come forward to disclose; part of the answer is that the word is out; their disclosures are invariably dismissed by the Police and the prosecuting authorities, making it almost impossible to initiate a successful prosecution for child sexual abuse in Australia as things stand presently. The outcome of the DPP's failure to prosecute Dave Plankton has had appalling repercussions in all of our lives.

- Christopher and Debbie live in hiding from this man.
- Christopher is devastated by the apparent refusal of the authorities to believe his brave testimony.
- Any reminder of his father, even a birthday card, causes a recurrence of his terrible nightmares.
- Debbie, who has unflinchingly protected her son, has paid a very high emotional and physical price.

"It was after my move to Grafton in 2010," remembers Patrick, "that I came to know about the problems Russell was having with his stepson and the alleged abuse by his biological father David Plankton. When I heard the story I was furious and quickly climbed on board to help Russell and the youngster. Initially I was conscripted to drop the boy off for meetings with his father at the local park and then I would set up surveillance on him and set about trying to expose Plankton. On one occasion I took Christopher to See Park where the PI videoed the interaction. I drove off and watched Christopher running from his father and refusing to get out of the tree and, when he did, watched Plankton frog march the boy to the car and bundle him into the back seat. I followed Plankton but he saw me and when I pulled over, the little wanker got out of the car abusing me but because Russell had begged me not to put him in hospital I ignored his abuse and put my window up."

Prologue

Freda Briggs discusses Lizzie and the Twins

Russell: "In an effort to understand this grotesque perversion of justice, towards the end of 2013, I sought assistance from the non-governmental National Child Protection Alliance and was introduced to Professor Freda Briggs, Australia's preeminent authority on child protection. This, as it would turn out, was a watershed moment.

Few people cope with the in-your-face details of sexual abuse, yet Freda did; she went into jails, spoke to convicted paedophiles, and learned what and why they did what they did. She was able to explain to us the significance of Sasha's grossly distressed behaviour and helped interpret his graphic drawings which depicted his father's actions. She also explained to us, in distressing detail, the malfeasance of the courts in dealing with child abuse.

But it did not end there, and she then turned to me for assistance; more specifically for assistance with someone unknown to me at the time by the name of Lizzie Morris (née Weber whose twin girls had been removed from her and returned to their allegedly abusive father by the Family Court. She believed that this was one of the worst cases of sexual abuse she had ever seen. On hearing the details I was simply unable to decline the request for help. Nothing in my 30+ years of medical practice prepared me for what was to come.

Freda told me the children had made over 40 disclosures to 13 different people when they were between ages of four and five. But only one of the people who had witnessed and reported the twin's disclosures of abuse was interviewed by the police. These witnesses included an IAPT (Improving Access to Psychological Therapy) trained psychologist, teachers, social workers and occupational therapist, as well as other family members and family friends.

Report by the girls' grandfather Arthur Weber:

23rd Oct 2011. I phoned the girls this morning and they were waiting for their father to arrive for an access visit. They wouldn't talk. Made me think that they were obviously nervous as they are normally very chatty whenever we phone.

2nd Nov 2011. approx. 7:30pm. Lizzie and the girls arrived home after David had access. The girls were both in very pretty nighties which were nylon and completely unsuitable for sleeping in through Townsville's warm nights. These nighties were on the girls when David dropped off the girls to the Hermit Park State school where a Prep. Orientation night was being held. Lizzie changed the girls into cotton nighties. Charlotte complained about being sore in her 'toushka' and when Lizzie looked, she had quite a severe rash. When asked what had happened Charlotte said that she had wet her pants as she didn't want to go to the toilet at dad's as he would start 'playing with her private parts' while she sits there.

3rd Nov 2011 7.55am. Charlotte said that she didn't want to go to school today as she is scared that her dad will be picking her up after school (as he had the day before) and she wanted Lizzie to stay with her if she had to go to school. Lizzie took her and stayed for a while as Charlotte was crying and Lizzie waited for her to settle.

10:44 am. Arrived at solicitors just as Lizzie received a call from the school that Charlotte had cried again after Lizzie left for work but had settled and was very quiet and clinging to her teacher Miss Cawood.

4th Nov 2011. Met Lizzie at work by 11.00am to pick up girls from school. Returned home for lunch then girls went off to work with Liz. David to pick up girls for overnight access from there at 4.30pm. Liz phoned and Charlotte still not in David's car by

Prologue

5.20pm. Charlotte had left a message on our phone pleading with Poppy to come and get her and bring her back to our place. Just so heart-wrenching. David phoned at 5:46pm asking us to take Charlotte's toy dog out to the car which Arthur did at 5:48pm. Both girls were very subdued.

5th Nov 2011. Girls arrive back from their overnight access visit just after 5.00pm and they both look extremely tired and so quiet and when Poppy went out to have a chat with them Charlotte ran around the side of the house and hid, and they would not talk to me. We had all spent a sleepless night worrying about these precious little girls and wonder all the time why they have to be made continually scared and upset.

That night, at about 10.30pm, Jane was crying and so distressed with pain which she said was in her 'touska' and also in her bowel. She could not be comforted or cradled. She has had these 'attacks' quite often over the past few months and upon investigation with doctors and ultra-sounds, nothing seems to be found. Why? What is causing these attacks as she is just so distressed that they could not be just 'make believe' surely? These 'sessions' are just so upsetting for all in the house as Jane cries out in such pain and is obviously feeling 'real' pain."

Professor Freda Briggs' emails Russell.
Wednesday, 28 November 2012 9:26 AM
Subject: Townsville

Dear Russell

After receiving all my work I received a message via Lizzie that I am not needed. She said that the arrogant, bullying sexist police officers who said that the children (who reported sexual abuse to 13 people were only dreaming, that the father was wholly safe and always had been - and if she reports more abuse they won't investigate it but will jail her) – are highly regarded and impressive whereas I was saying that they needed to be discredited.

I had to cancel appointments for the whole week because they didn't know how long the trial would last.

Charles thinks the lawyers have been "got at".

They have the same judge who said that Lydia's children aged 4 and 3 were behaving normally when they were caught on 100 mins of CCTV obsessed with trying to have anal and oral sex and ejaculate, saying this was what daddy did. J. Bell gave daddy custody and sent Lydia for psych treatment.

Five psychs say she is sane so she breached a court order. She is a uni lecturer in social work so a judge said I had convinced her that her children had been abused when they hadn't so I was responsible for the decision to deprive them of their mother.

The case started in 2006. I became involved in Nov 2010 and the contradiction was dismissed when she appealed.

Given that the solicitors sent me 360 pages which I had to print and read and respond to, how much should I charge them?

Kind regards

Freda

"As the reader can see from this email, the response from the authorities was to accuse the mother of training the children to make these allegations," writes Russell. "This, despite the fact that the mother's only contact with the twins had been strictly supervised for a long time before this. No evidence was produced to prove this training ever actually occurred, although it remained the underlying assumption of the Police and Child Safety. The investigating officers were satisfied all these allegations had been the result of bad dreams. One has to ask how could four-year old girls even begin to know this sort of detail?

"Records show Detective Senior Sergeant David Miles was involved in the failure to investigate the abuse of the twins. Miles certainly appears to have made false reports to the courts, stating that the abuse of the children was 'unsubstantiated' in both cases.

"Police interview tapes were leaked via WikiLeaks that were shocking to view and which thus caused a collective shout of outrage among activists and advocates and even saw two investigators involved with the initial, corrupt investigation that failed the twins in the first place sent for retraining and facing restrictions on engaging with minors 'in the system' until further notice. Despite all the disclosures to 13 different adults only one of them was interviewed by the police.

"Despite that, the first judge presiding, Judge Foster stated in 2013: 'There is sufficient evidence for the proposition that the children were and would be in danger of being abused sexually were they placed in custody of dad.'"

Freda Briggs: "In my professional experience, the fact that the children made consistent disclosures of sexual abuse by their father to a number of people additional to their mother suggests that (a) these disclosures are credible and (b) they persisted in making reports because none of the trusted adults responded and stopped the abusive behaviour."

The Family Law Act

Issues associated with all children fall under the *Family Law Act 1975* (Commonwealth) and when a court makes a parenting order, it is this Act that makes it a requirement to regard the best interests of the child as the most important decision.

The Act underscores the **rights of children** along with the responsibilities that each parent has towards their children. This presents a shift away from parental rights, the aim of which is to ensure that children can enjoy significant relationships with their parents and also be protected from harm. Accordingly, there is also a presumption that arrangements encompassing shared cooperation and responsibilities between parents are in the best interests of the child.

When family law orders are made, despite being on an interim or final basis, they are binding on all parties involved. Breaching a Family Law order is a serious offence.

A person breaches an order if they deliberately choose not to observe the order or make no reasonable attempts to comply with it. Should they help someone else to avoid compliance or prevent someone else's compliance, then they can also be in breach of an order.

In most circumstances, courts and their decisions are accessible to members of the public. This policy of 'open justice' is reflected in section 97 of the *Family Law Act 1975*, which provides that all proceedings should be heard in open unless a court decides otherwise. The principle of open justice is fundamental to ensuring that courts remain transparent and accountable for their decisions.

However, the special nature of Family Law proceedings, which often involve children, requires that a balance be struck between the need for open justice and a family's right to privacy.

The Family Court, and the Children's Court are therefore secret courts, whose procedures are closely guarded secrets. The secrecy is enforced by application of Section 121 of the Family Law Act makes it an offence to publish proceedings that identify persons or witnesses involved in family law proceedings. This prohibition also extends to the publication of any picture.

However, Section 70NAE of Australia's Family Law Act 1975 clearly provides for a "reasonable excuse for contravening an order; A person is taken to have had a reasonable excuse for **contravening a parenting order (putting the kid in a different home than the one on the order)** … if (the person (a) believed on reasonable grounds that the actions constituting the contravention were necessary to protect the health or safety of a person (including the respondent or the child)…"

CHAPTER 1 – THE EARLY YEARS

A Brief History of Rhodesia

Cecil John Rhodes was born in Bishop's Stortford in Hertfordshire on the 5th July 1853. One of 11 children born to the local vicar, he was educated at the Grammar School in the village before sailing for Africa in 1870 with £2,000 given to him by an aunt. Arriving in Natal he joined his brother Herbert on a cotton farm before moving to Kimberley in 1871. A shrewd operator, he quickly amassed a small fortune before returning to England and Oxford where he gained a BA. After graduating from Oxford he returned to South Africa, where he quickly immersed himself in the politics of the day before being elected to the Cape Parliament. Determined to further British interests he struck a blow for Empire when he successfully brought Bechuanaland (now Botswana) into the British realm to the dismay of acquisitive Boer 'freebooters'.

In 1887, with the discovery of gold on the Witwatersrand, Rhodes formed Goldfields of South Africa and soon thereafter took control of the Kimberley diamonds simultaneously becoming the dominant figure in the world diamond trade. Money and power was only incidental to Rhodes' grand design, which was to do no less than bring Africa under British control.

To this end Rhodes arrived in London in April 1888 brandishing the Rudd Concession which he had wheedled out of Lobengula, Chief of the Matabele Tribe, through his emissaries. His immediate goal was to convince Prime Minister Salisbury that it was in Britain's interest to give his expansionist plans a Royal stamp of approval through the granting of a charter, but he was frustrated by the timidity of a British government that was reluctant to share his expansionist zeal. Undaunted, he decided to do it himself, with his own resources and his own men. A key ally was Lord Nathaniel Rothschild, one of the richest and most influential men in England. He liked Rhodes, believed he was a sensible investment and particularly liked his grand plan which would, in the full course of events, bring the coveted gold-fields of the Witwatersrand under the British flag. In Rhodes' favour was Salisbury's wish to extend British hegemony as long as his government's political and financial exposure was limited.

Having secured the money and support of the British government, Rhodes switched his attention to finding the right men. Over lunch at the Kimberley Club in the diamond capital of South Africa, he explained his thoughts to Frank Johnson, the man he asked to lead his force. The two agreed most recruits would be from a military background, but Rhodes wanted more. Tough and resolute, he insisted they must be, but also gentlemen in the classical sense of the time and possessed of the eclectic array of skills required to build a country[1]. It has been suggested that the same qualities he would later mandate for those applying for his scholarships were applied to selection of the chosen few who would be deployed in the extension of Empire. As a result, top Cape families were invited to contribute their sons, and doctors, lawyers, pharmacists and farmers filled the ranks of this elite body of men who rode north and colonised the

---

1   A more cynical rationale suggested is that Rhodes wanted well-to-do families involved so there would be a stronger response in the event the men got themselves into trouble.

1 – The Early Years

country that came later to bear its founder's name. The seeds of future conflict were sown.

In a harbinger of what was to come, on the day the column camped on the Shashi River, the first activity engaged in had nothing to do with conquest; it was a game of rugby. Then they crossed into the territory that would become Rhodesia and into a dangerous new land. Lives would later be lost in battle, to disease, wild animals and other natural calamities, but the tide of history was swiftly turning and for better or worse, the white man had arrived. On 13 September 1890, some 200 men stood at attention as the Union Jack was raised at a place they called Fort Salisbury. The claim had been staked.

While the initial occupation had been surprisingly peaceful, it was not long before hostilities broke out and the Pioneer Column was called on to show its mettle. On the battlefield, Lobengula's Matabeles fought with courage and fortitude. Mostly dissolute Zulus on the run from Shaka's tyranny in the south, they were also recent arrivals north of the Limpopo, but they had got there first and the white man was shaping up to become a nuisance. As warriors, they earned the respect of their white adversaries, but the same could not be said of the motley collection of tribes that came to be known as the Mashona, who were found in the main to be cowering in caves and crevices on the rocky hills of the central Highveld, where they resided in perpetual fear of marauding Matabele impis.

Frederick Courteney Selous, the great hunter-adventurer, was particularly scathing about them: "… for no one who has lived long amongst the various peoples generically known as 'Mashunas' [sic] whose principal characteristics are avarice, cowardice, and a complete callousness to the sufferings of others, will be inclined to doubt that were they governed by an angel from heaven, they would infallibly kill that angel if his wing feathers were of any value to them, provided that they believed at the same time that the crime might be committed with impunity.[2]"

Ultimately, the native rebellions were suppressed with a mixture of force and diplomacy, but with conquest, the white interlopers put an end to the endemic tribal genocide and quickly insisted upon changing the mindset that killing another human being was a right of might. This was anathema to the blacks but he was forced to live with it on pain of punishment. The irony following from this is the Zezuru people (one of the six or seven tribes making up the Mashona) who would probably have been wiped out by the Matabele in the course of time, were saved by white intervention. Had this not happened, a Zezuru child by the name of Robert Gabriel Mugabe might never have been. His journey into the living world was made safe by the white man he would grow to revile.

Frontiersmen in the classic sense, the pioneers were essentially magnanimous in victory and, unlike their counterparts in North America and Australia, they refrained from further attacks on the natives who now fell under their authority. Once in control of their domain they in fact nurtured the indigenous populace rather than annihilated it, and, in a feat of nation-building unmatched anywhere, they took a barbarous land by the scruff of the neck. By 1923, when self-rule was granted, they had transformed it into an orderly polity with a diverse and dynamic economy capable of generating real wealth and lifting the living standards of all its inhabitants. Relishing a period of unusual peace, population growth among the black people was spectacular: from an estimated 300 000 at the point of occupation to six million by the middle of the century.

But it was never a settled and easy existence for the Rhodesians. Right from the start there was tension between them and the Afri-

---

2   F.C. Selous. "Sunshine and Storm in Rhodesia". Books of Rhodesia.

1 – The Early Years

kaners of the republics of Transvaal and Orange Free State, who had also been studying the northern reaches with acquisitive eyes. To the east, the Portuguese were wary of their cocky new neighbours who were limbering up to block the expansionist plan being plotted in Lisbon that would have absorbed the vast hinterland between the colonies of Angola and Mozambique, thereby establishing a Lusitanian empire of massive proportion in Africa.

Unsurprisingly, it was not long before the Portuguese problem escalated into fighting, and following several skirmishes on the eastern frontier, a bold young captain by the name of Patrick Forbes decided to take matters into his hands. With pluck, daring and less than a dozen troopers, he invaded Mozambique and attacked the Portuguese garrison in Vila de Manica. Determined to seize the port of Beira for the Crown, his plan was thwarted by British Prime Minister Salisbury who wasted no time in ordering Forbes to desist and return to British territory immediately. Unbeknown to Forbes, the attack was a breach of a non-aggression pact between Portugal and Britain that had not been violated in several hundred years but the world had seen an early indicator of the fighting talents of the Rhodesians.

As the new century entered its teens, however, events in distant places were spinning out of control. No sooner had the pioneers established order and basic government in the colony than the First World War broke out. Nation-building had to be put on hold while most of the able-bodied men left Rhodesia to battle the Germans in Tanganyika and the bogs of Belgium and eastern France.[3] Many did not return, but in the years between that war and the next, great progress was made, albeit again in the face of much adversity. The Rinderpest and Foot and Mouth disease took a heavy toll on

---

3   Over 5,000 whites, some 25% of the population volunteered for the war.

livestock, added to which a series of crippling droughts devastated farmers, throwing the nascent agricultural economy into turmoil. Malaria killed hundreds of settlers and the global depression of the 1930s ended the hopes of many aspiring businessmen. The added challenge of distance to the sea made it costly to get export goods to the ports.

But in spite of all the obstacles, a spirit of enterprise and endurance prevailed and most of the problems were tackled and eventually overcome. Against this backdrop, a parsimonious British government merely looked on, offering little more than moral support. With the advent of self-rule in 1923 the settlers were largely masters of their own destiny. For better or for worse they were pretty much on their own, but that was how they liked it.

The 'Spirit of Rhodesia' was summed up by an anonymous writer when the country was divided over whether or not to forsake self-rule and become part of the Union of South Africa: "We have experienced a Native War, a Native Rebellion, the Boer War, The Great War, the Rinderpest, and East Coast Fever, drought and floods, adversity and prosperity. From these the Spirit of Rhodesia has been compounded; and everyone who has been touched by the magic wand of the spirit of Rhodesia is a 'Rhodesian'. Our people have come from the four corners of the earth, mostly British but no matter what nationality they were; if they were of the fit the country took them unto herself and gave herself unto them and they became Rhodesians. That is what we mean when we say 'Rhodesia for the Rhodesians'[4]."

When the Second World War erupted, Rhodesia had an infrastructure and governmental organisation that could compare favourably with any nation in the world. Across the country schools

---

4   A. P. DiPerna: "A Right to be Proud." Books of Rhodesia 1978

1 – The Early Years

and hospitals had been built, roads and bridges constructed and a modern telecommunications system installed. An extremely professional police force, the majority of its members black, brought peace and security.[5] Courts presided over by highly-qualified judges and magistrates dispensed justice fairly and firmly without any hint of political interference. 'Native administrators' worked in tandem with chiefs and other traditional leaders in administering the Tribal Trust Lands, reserves set aside for exclusively black habitation. Not even the Rhodesians' most virulent critics could see their way clear to accuse the civil administration of being corrupt, incompetent or inefficient.

With war looming, such was the enthusiasm of the men to enlist, that steps were taken to compel a proportion to remain at home for fear that the colony would collapse due to lack of manpower. Nevertheless, as a pro rata percentage of the white population, Rhodesia contributed more manpower to the Second World War and suffered greater casualties than any other country in the Empire, including Great Britain herself. Because so many volunteered, there was a real fear at official level that big Rhodesian losses would decimate their numbers to such an extent the future of the colony would be in jeopardy. As a result the Rhodesian volunteers were deliberately distributed throughout the various services to spread the risk as widely as possible. All served with great distinction.

Being men who had weathered a variety of challenges in the wilds of an untamed continent, they adapted easily to the rough realities of war and took the responsibilities of leadership in their stride. A large number were quickly assessed as officer material and

---

5   It is noteworthy that from the time of the formation of the British South Africa Police until 1963, this excellent force did not kill a single person in the course of exercising their duties. Through the war years patrolmen and woman carried out the bulk of their duties unarmed.

found their way to playing distinguished roles in a variety of services, ranging from flying in the Battle of Britain to becoming specialised operatives in the Long-Range Desert Group which provided the platform for the formation of the SAS.

With Hitler vanquished, the post-war period saw the colony enter a golden era. The soldiers, sailors and airmen returned. They brought with them a considerable number of ex-servicemen who decided to leave Britain and build a new future in a new country. But true to Rhodes' ethos, the Rhodesian immigration authorities were selective and high standards had to be met to gain entry. The new arrivals were deemed to be people of stature and means, who were prepared to take a chance and work hard. With an inflow of capital and expertise the country grew and prospered at a rate matched only in South Africa. The future looked brim-full of promise.

Patrick Finbar McGarry O'Dea - My Early Life.
I was born in Salisbury, Rhodesia, on the 29th of January, 1974. My father John McGarry O'Dea was born in Lanarkshire, Scotland in 1926, and was a train driver during World War II. He came out to Rhodesia soon after the war ended when he was about 21 and joined the Rhodesia Railways as a train driver. I loved my dad. He was a wild man, and there was never a dull moment around him. But he had a drinking problem he struggled to overcome.

After school, my first job in 1973 was with Grindlays Bank in Bulawayo in 1974, where I was the waste-clerk, tasked with putting country cheques into a machine registering different pigeonholes for country cheques, which was very boring. To liven things up, I decided to be a nuisance by placing the same cheques in the wrong compartments, but this resulted in me having to stay there until midnight cross-balancing. Not a good plan.

1 – The Early Years

My nemesis was a lady who looked like she had been underwater for six months, and who had an equally ugly girlfriend with whom I did not get along with, so I knew my days at Grindlays were numbered. One of my few friends there was Frank Napa, then the bank and country's first black teller, who I got along with well. Every day he and I and another friend Mike Eltringham (Mike has since died) used to go into the basement. We were meant to be filing but it was really to drink the brandy Frank had brought to work for all of us.

Back in Bulawayo a month before national service – for which I'd volunteered – I was on the tear with a mate of mine by the name of John Kirwan with whom I had been at school. John was on a break from the seminary in Durban where he was in his 4th year of studying to become a Catholic priest! He obviously needed relief from different pressures because we had been 'hitting it with a whip' at The Terrace in the Selborne Hotel and we were on a borrowed motorcycle, a 250cc Yamaha, loaned to me by my mate Jimmy Jeans who later became famous for hitting three landmines!

A new helmet law had been introduced the week before, making it compulsory to wear a helmet on a motorbike. Neither John nor I had one on and were painfully aware of this fact. John, being a God-fearing, strictly law-abiding citizen went into panic-mode when we mounted the bike. This went to a higher level when a police 'B Car' cruised past us along Grey Street and stopped at the traffic lights a block away on Selborne Avenue. The driver of the car, a smartly uniformed white policeman, stepped out of his car at the traffic lights, blue lights flashing, and shouted and waved at me to approach him which we did slowly. Bearing in mind the amount of alcohol that we'd already imbibed, John was babbling away in my ear from behind, stating the obvious: we were in for it! As we slowed approaching the police car, the traffic light turned green and something in my head shouted GO, and I accelerated past the police car at full throttle. John immediately grabbed my sides, gripping on tightly and begun screaming in my ear 'Stop stop I'll pay the fine' but my now addled mind was set, and I responded by opening up full throttle while laughing loudly.

So off we raced down Grey Street at over 160 km/h speeding through those huge drainage dips which were in our roads, ramping high into the air as we came out the incline with John's arms wrapped tightly around me while screaming, 'Stop stop, for God's sake stop and I'll pay the fine'! This carried on all the way down Grey Street until we reached 'L and L Motors' where we turned right, speeding through the drift into Paddonhurst and then onto the Salisbury Road and past the Military Police standing guard at the Brady Barracks entry-boom with the B car in hot pursuit, siren wailing. Looking in my mirror, I swear I could see the black constable in the passenger seat turning white. Then I pulled a hard right into George Avenue but missed the turn off and ploughed my way through the flower beds and back on to the road. On the straight now towards the Holiday Inn, I began to pull away from the cop-car, so I decided to cut through Kumalo suburb in order to try and lose him. Then I turned left and then quickly left again, entering a circle from which I could see no exit. I proceeded to just go round and round at speed as the B car was now parked at the entrance to the circle blocking my exit. I was now going nowhere.

Realising the game was up, I stopped the bike and, being pissed, we both promptly fell flat on our faces. The cop, calmly beckoned John to approach him, handcuffed him and placed him on the back seat. The black – now white – constable ordered me to remount and follow them to the main Bulawayo Police Station but to my surprise, at the Holiday Inn, where we should have turned right, the cop-car went straight, and I saw John staring back at me with an odd look on his face. To my further surprise, the car continued towards John's house on Cecil Avenue where they turned left into his yard.

My bewilderment increased when I watched John being gently removed from the car, spoken to and then ordered into his home. He had been simply told to go to bed, get some sleep and avoid my company for a while. John must have thought his divine connections had intervened because he had a look of disbelief on his face.

By this time, with the adrenaline receding and my eyesight returning, I recognised the white cop was Simon Parkin, a mate. He'd recognised me on the chase and John had confirmed it was indeed me. When we recognised one another, we both burst into laughter. We hugged each other, laughed some more and went our merry ways. Such was the joy of life in war-torn Rhodesia.

Prior to my going into the army in May 1974 I acquired an undeserved reputation (or so I felt) for being a street fighter as a result of an incident that occurred when I attended a house party at a friend's place in Suburbs, Bulawayo. Attending the same party was a well-known Rhodesian sportsman with somewhat of a reputation behind him as being Mr Rough and Tough (especially with less physically endowed, or inebriated individuals) and was generally considered not one to mess around with! As I only found out afterwards, he was having an affair with a petite, vivacious, much older lady who had a liking for young studs and who was married to one of the local jewellers. The 'gentleman' I refer to was a very good rugby player and all round sportsman who was well known around town. During the course of the evening I had attracted a young lady who I knew from before and had a couple of dances with her and figured we would move on to town and grab a coffee at 'Fritz's', the all night burger and snack venue where youngsters my age ended up after late-night parties. While making my way out, this 'gentleman', who was a couple of inches taller than me, started swearing at me whilst pushing his finger into my face, so the hand I was using to push the young lady away from the altercation came from way back and landed squarely on his nose and jaw! As he went down I did only what my father had taught me, which was to make sure he stayed down! And so he ended up with two more fists in the face against an unforgiving ground which did not do his future in the beauty stakes any good whatsoever. My father had also taught me that if anything like this happened I was to leave the area as soon as possible to prevent any additional problems. Whilst doing so and leading the young lady away, looking for my vehicle, I heard footsteps running up behind me on the tarmac and upon turning around encountered the brother of the fellow I had just hit, who was in the process of taking a running swipe at me. He also received a '*klap*' for his troubles. The mate who I had attended the party with climbed into him for good measure and my mate received a small hiding for his troubles. By this time a free-for-all had developed. I ended up with a fat lip and blood running down the front of my shirt!

Two months after this fracas and after five months in the bank I volunteered for National Service. I was inducted into Intake 139 which started in May 1974. The Rhodesian bush war, which at that time was being fought against the Chinese trained terrorists of Robert Mugabe, and the Russian and Cuban trained terrorists of Joshua Nkomo, was escalating significantly. Our intake, like all the others before and after us, proceeded to Llewellyn Barracks where many a Rhodesian schoolboy began the tough transition to soldier.

Soon after induction and getting all our kit, we were informed there was a team there from the School of Infantry in Gwelo looking for suitable candidates to attend their Officers' Course. They ran a selection course for volunteers and I 'jimmied' my way through and passed. I was one of 16 in with a chance of becoming an officer. All

Patrick's officers' course at School of Infantry in Gwelo. Back row: Wynand Viljoen, Gordon Wuinton, Marcus De Bertadano, Patrick Finbar McGarry O'Dea, Arthur McLeod, George Carew, Alan Spence, Raymond Van Wyk, Front row: Keith Searle, Stanley Barrance McArthur, George Lambert-Porter, Terence Miller, Neville Williams, Billy Cooper

of us selected went on to the School of Infantry in Gwelo.

Our commanding officer was Major Lambert-Porter and our two instructors were Colour Sergeant Terence Miller and Corporal Theo Kruger. It was a tough course which I enjoyed but my sometimes unruly behaviour probably led them to conclude I was not ready for higher office, and so I passed out as a corporal in the infantry. I would honestly say I was not up to being officer material, so wasn't unhappy at the result. Twelve of the sixteen finished the course. Whilst I came out top at nearly all the physical and endurance-related exercises together with my mate Wynand Viljoen, I believe I was too young for the responsibility expected of an officer.

My first posting as an operational soldier was to 3 Independent Company based at Inyanga in the country's Eastern Highlands, close to the Mozambique border. Our OC was Major Wellburn and his 2IC was Captain Buttenshaw from the Rhodesia Light Infantry (RLI). One of the senior NCO's, a 'regular', was Winston Pullen, who we nicknamed 'Ring a ding ding', after the sound his car made when he drove off. Our company Medic was Sergeant Jimmy May.

The big surprise for me though was a lone soldier still in the camp when our company arrived at Inyanga. It was the same 'gentleman' I had had the punch-up with in Bulawayo. As it turned out, on the fight-night previously described, he was actually Absent Without Leave (AWOL). After he came out of hospital, he ended up going to DB ((Detention Barracks) for 28 days. As a result, he was having to stay on for the extra 28 days that he had served in DB. The irony of it!

Mozambique was still a Portuguese colony at the time, but incursions by the terrorists had commenced and soon the situation would worsen with the coming to power of a new government under Samora Machel, who was a hard-line Marxist. We were deployed in small sections called 'sticks', normally numbering anything between four to eight men, to patrol, occupy high features (called OPs, short for observation points) at times and watch for movement below, and also to ambush suspected infiltration routes. Generally, the enemy moved at night, so we were often active after sunset. To curtail their nocturnal activities, a curfew was introduced, making it illegal for anyone to move from 6pm in the evening to 6am in the morning. Anyone breaking the curfew was to be shot on sight.

Whilst entering an ambush position one night, my section of four

1 – The Early Years

came across a group of four youths who, upon seeing us, buggered off at a high rate of knots. One of my guys opened fire with his shotgun as they disappeared into the night. A deathly hush came over the nearby business centre and village. Even the dogs stopped barking. We moved into a different ambush position as a result and a few hours later, a candlelight came on in one of the buildings, so we approached said building where we found the storekeeper treating one of the miscreants who had an arse full of buckshot! Feeling guilty at what had happened we fed the youngster 24 'Cafenol' (a popular mixed analgesic that would 'make you well'), a packet of biscuits and a Coke to help with the pain as he was not going to get any of our morphine. The following morning a truck arrived to collect him, and the platoon medic removed SSG pellets from his backside using forceps. Not a pleasant sight and the youngster screamed all the time. He was lucky, as he could have been dead. Two nights before, another one of our guys, a lieutenant, had killed a few curfew-breakers alighting from a bus. The 'gooks' always used '*mujibas*'[6] to scout for them, and to spy on the security forces.

After four months at Inyanga we were given our first leave: a five-day pass, but as Bulawayo was the other side of the country it was a long way home, and we had to get there and back in five days as well. Our only chance was hitch-hiking and that was not easy either. On this occasion I was stuck in Gwelo, 164 kms from Bulawayo, desperate to get home, so I called dad and he came to fetch me at 2.00 am in the morning. On the way back to barracks at the end of my pass, I boarded a bus with my rifle and kit and was the only white man aboard. It was so full I had to stand and, as I had been on the piss for days, I was severely lacking in sleep. I kept falling asleep on my feet and falling down, much to the amusement

---

6 Young male enemy collaborators who assisted the insurgents.

of my black compatriots.

If we were late back to camp, we were in trouble. Upon returning to barracks and not having had a regulation haircut I was charged, together with Derek Hatch, the platoon medic, and had to do extra duties. On another occasion, we were had up for relieving one of the chefs at Troutbeck Inn of his bicycle and riding it back to camp, a distance of many kilometres. All downhill. How we did not kill ourselves, God only knows.

One day at the barracks, in-between patrols, we received an urgent call from Inyanga village. It was Jimmy May our esteemed Battalion Medic phoning reverse-charges from a call box in Inyanga Village sounding like he was under attack, shouting over the phone for someone to 'come and get me quickly'. Derek and I raced into town not knowing what to expect and found Jimmy in our headlights, sprinting stark naked down the road towards us, carrying his clothes under his arm. His distress had nothing to do with the gooks; he had been getting leg-over with the shop-keeper's wife while her husband was in Salisbury; he had come home early and caught them in *flagrante delecto*. He had grabbed his clothes and leapt off the first-floor balcony above the shop, and run for his life to the nearest call box to phone us to save him from a beating.

Across the border, Frelimo were becoming more aggressive, and I had some Portuguese guys in my stick who were not happy about what was happening in their former homeland. The new regime had stripped the Portuguese of everything they had worked for in Mozambique, except for what could be carried in one suitcase, and were told to leave within 24 hours or be killed. We were patrolling the Gaerezi River which formed the border with Mozambique when Frelimo started hurling abuse at us from across the river. One of my soldiers took offence at what was being said and opened up on

1 – The Early Years

the bastards which put them to flight, but we were uplifted by helicopter soon thereafter, returned to base where we were castigated for causing an international incident.

When I saw what the enemy tactics involved, it came as a huge shock. I also found out the priests and missionaries were actually helping the terrorists. Suddenly I realised that people whom I had looked up to all my life and who could do no wrong in my eyes, were now guilty of helping the enemy who were instrumental in the mutilation and murder of thousands of innocent civilians. I saw what I believed was an evil agenda. I found this fact alone very hard to reconcile with my religion, and as a result became temporarily estranged from the church and the scriptures.

After completing my National Service we were allowed to return to our civilian lives with the future prospect of call ups being six-weeks in and six-weeks out (also called 'continuous call up'). I went back to Bulawayo where, thanks to my father, I was employed by Guardian Royal Exchange Insurance Company. Having the attitude, quite current at that time, of 'live for today, for tomorrow I die,' I did not exactly hit it off with the senior lady members of staff. The manager, Mr Clarke was one of God's own gentlemen, who called me into his office after a year of ongoing altercations with the ladies, and very politely informed me that my services were no longer required.

Moving on once again, my father found me employment with National Employers Mutual (NEM) in Salisbury via a mutual friend Graham Hancock whose father was a partner in Hancock and Ward Plumbers. The manager of NEM at the time was Geoff Todd, an elderly gentleman, who employed me without ever having met me. My employment contract started on the first of the month, which happened to fall on a Saturday and as I was called up on the third for another army call up. I ended up being employed officially (and getting full pay) but not having to report for work for the first six months of my employment because by that time we were doing six weeks in and ten days out, reflecting the seriousness of the war situation. So, gainfully employed, I returned to the army and proceeded with my company to Operation Hurricane in the northeast of the country. Our Officer Commanding was Major Mike Glenshaw, and the 2IC was Captain Greg Watson.

On this, my first call-up with C Coy 2RR, I was blown up in a landmine in October 1975. This was an unusual occurrence as the mine had been laid on good tar road, leading out of Bindura into the Madziwa TTL (Tribal Trust Land). We were travelling along at around 60 kph when our troop carrier detonated the mine, which resulted in the truck rolling and injuring a number of us. I was knocked unconscious but only briefly and ended up with a minor injury to my leg and hip. It felt like someone had taken a 20-yard run up and booted me in the hip. The truck was upside down with the driver Kevin Sutton, uninjured, hanging also upside down but held in place by his seat belt. There were a couple of other minor injuries with the only serious one being a broken leg and hip for Johnny Nel.

An ambulance came from Bindura to come and collect the wounded. On the way back to hospital the ambulance had a back left blow-out which resulted in us veering off the road into the bush. We all almost soiled our pants as a result of the bang! A pantechnicon on its way into town was waved down and we were loaded onto the flat-bed, and ended up being delivered to hospital that way. After a two-hour wait, with all of us being attended to, most of us were released to go back to the JOC (joint operational command) where we pissed it up, regaling others with our recently experienced war stories. My father, meanwhile, had a visit from the army chaplain and a captain from Brady Barracks to inform him I was injured but they were not in a position to tell him to what extent. My old man frantically tried to get more information and finally got hold of me on the phone at the pub in Bindura JOC. When I answered the phone, I was totally smashed and dribbling out of both sides of my mouth. The fact that I was alive but inebriated did not please him at all.

Johnny Nel, who had broken his leg and hip when the truck rolled, was our platoon cook. He used to carry his little black cooking pot everywhere. On patrol-breaks and on basing up in the evenings he used to make up tea or cook up lunch and dinner, which we all enjoyed. That is until one morning one of the guys caught him squatting over the black pot washing his piles! He never cooked for us again.

Jimmy Jeans, otherwise known as JimBob, washing the bosses back whilst in the fresh meat box

Me washing in the box our fresh meat was delivered in. Minutes later there was a contact which we all were called to 2km from that spot. Russell Harding, gunner who carried the MAG machine gun shot a gook in the leg and ankle and we caught the gook almost 2km later, but he died. When we lifted him to put him in the truck his foot/ankle fell off as it had basically been held on by the flesh and skin and yet he ran 2km - Adrenaline charge from hell!

While operating in the Shamva area later we received 'hot int' that gooks were hiding on a granite '*gomo*' (a.k.a. small hill) which we pinpointed on a map. A number of us were despatched to look into the possibility of the gooks being there and upon arrival at the village, situated at the bottom of the hill in the treeline, we came across an elderly back lady with her head covered in a blanket, wailing loudly. We took this to mean the gooks were around, and half of us quickly did a sweep up the gomo, finding nothing. At the crest we moved across the top and started sweeping our way down. We could

1 – The Early Years

Speaks for itself. Same area where guy had foot shot off

see the rest of our troops along the road at the bottom, sweeping through the kraal line. All of a sudden, the gooks who happened to be between us and the road opened up on the guys below. I still have a vision in my head of a little Hungarian guy, George Moscatar rolling over and over in the dirt on the road with bullet strikes everywhere around him, just like you see in the movies. We overran the gook position, firing as we went, and then took cover below the embankment lining the road. There was still a machine gunner giving us hell, so we stayed beneath cover and called in Fireforce who happened to be RLI at the time. The helicopters came in dropping off stop-groups and a section which swept its way through the gook position firing as they went. About a kilometre away, one of the 'stop-groups' encountered a group of the gooks fleeing the contact at a distance. The section that was doing the sweep were then picked up by chopper again to follow up on the tracks of the gooks who had run into the stop-group. With Fireforce having left, we again swept through the enemy position coming across the RPD gunner who had been wounded. 'Wild Bill Stanbury,' the 'Old Man' as we referred to him because he was a great deal older than us, opened up with his MAG and the gook got a good snot-squirt (normally refers to a short, sharp blow to the nose, but in this case a well-deserved bullet or three) whilst he set off a grenade. We took off downwards again with the grenade exploding behind us. When all was said and done, my mate Jimmy Jeans and I returned to collect the body of the RPD gunner. His appearance will stay with me for the rest of my life. It looked as if someone had removed the top of his head from above his eyes and ears and taken his brain out and laid it next to his body. Jimmy and I dragged the body down with the empty head bouncing off the rocks and loaded it into a body bag and onto the helicopter which then delivered it to the police camp. During the contact I came across a woman who upon seeing me took off. I screamed at her to stop and fired two warning shots, and because she did not stop, I put two rounds into her, killing her.

At the police camp later I was so distraught at my killing of the woman that I hid when her two sons came to collect her body. Upon my return to Bulawayo I went to my local church at Christ the King Parish and confessed to Father Kevin about my shooting of the civilian. He granted me absolution but none of this sat well with me, and the thoughts of it have haunted me forever.

Whilst on another call up we were based up at a Sabi Valley mining camp on the banks of the Sabi River. My section settled in for the night close to a cave where we discovered a grave that had been disturbed by animals leaving bones and a skull strewn outside in the sand. We took the skull with us back to camp, attached some sticks covered in overalls and a cap on the skull so from a distance it looked a little like a person. At the time, we were hungry because we had no resupply for a few weeks, so we attached a large sign with the words, WHERE ARE THE RATIONS. The message eventually got through, and the re-supply vehicle finally arrived, whereupon we had a group photograph taken with our very welcome fresh rations.

On the same deployment, whilst returning to Brady Barracks at

Rest break in deserted kraal

the completion of our call up, we were not the best behaved soldiers, but tough times take their toll and we had been drinking. One of my good mates Ricky Laurent fell off the truck travelling ahead of

Just a photo of me fooling around

us and went under the wheels of the ammunition trailer and those of our vehicle. He was severely injured and unconscious with blood coming out of his mouth and ears and blood and snot coming out of his nose. A passing vehicle took me, the platoon medic Bert Storey, and Rick from Filabusi to the Bulawayo General Hospital, a distance of 98 km. The whole way I gave him mouth-to-mouth, and Bert pumped his chest until we got him to hospital. He died. Another tragedy that should never have happened.

Back in Salisbury between call ups it was hard to leave the war behind; the young men were living it up because guys were going down fast, and there was no telling how long life was going to last. We had all been affected in some way or another and it was hard to settle down and live again like normal people.

I stayed in a 'mess', a sort of communal flat or house, with other

1 – The Early Years

guys from the same school as I who were serving in various units. Darryl Squance was a member of this mess and was a helicopter pilot. He had been on an external operation into Zambia where his helicopter had been shot down, luckily no injuries, but he was badly shaken. The rest of us were partying hard between call ups and greeted Darryl, who then went through to his room. The next minute we all hit the ground as he let go with his Uzi 9 mm, emptied a full magazine which blew holes in the roof over the veranda where I slept. After that I had to use an army-issue poncho to cover my bed and myself as it was rainy season and I needed to stay dry. We couldn't inform the estate agent to get repairs carried out, otherwise we would have been evicted.

Alan Brooke, another school mate and good friend who was also part of the mess, let rip one night with his FN and a stray bullet went through the window into a block of flats across the way. This brought the estate agent round to visit but Alan managed to talk his way out of it saying he had a faulty weapon; she was quite cute, and I think Alan was more concerned about his other 'weapon', the sweet talking '*sumbish*'.

Mike Austin, yet another classmate, was getting married, so at his stag party we proceeded to get him very pissed and stuck him on a train to Umtali with no clothes and no money after he flaked out. Needless to say his future wife was not pleased.

On Saturdays, a popular spot for a lunchtime piss-up for the troops between call-ups, was the Oasis Motel; there was always a band, lots of women, and where matters almost always got out of hand. I ended up in an altercation with two policemen, one white and one black who were there for some disturbance or the other and who decided I was fair game as they came at me with their riot batons. Having now gotten my attention I proceeded to get theirs, whereupon an ambulance was called, and they were taken to ICU at Andrew Fleming Hospital. Police reinforcements were called, which included a dog section which ended up in my leaping on the car rooftops outside the Oasis and running down the whole line of cars leaping from roof to roof to avoid the two German Shepherds from having me for lunch.

I went to jail that night and Sunday night and was presented at court Monday morning to account for my sins. As it turned out I was convicted of two counts of Grievous Bodily Harm, (GBH), fined $50.00 and given a two-year suspended sentence. I was extremely fortunate, as the magistrate pretty much found in my favour as I was the one initially beaten by the two policemen, and with them being in hospital in ICU it could have been a great deal worse.

We had all gone a little off the rails I suppose. Blokes used to come and go at our place, the mess; whoever was in town always had a place if they needed it. It was a wild time and we lived for the moment.

Back in the bush again in the south-east part of Rhodesia, we were based at Boli airstrip, my stick was ordered onto on a very high gomo next to and overlooking Battlefields Ranch, owned by Ben Stander, where we acted as a relay station for a number of sticks operating under companies of 2RR. The road to Boli was known as 'landmine alley' – vehicles were hitting mines on almost a daily basis.

While on my shift operating the radio, one of the sticks on patrol became involved in a serious contact. As it turned out I recognised the voices on the radio as good friends of mine. One was Sixpence Kinleyside (he was to become an in-law of mine as my son Luke married his daughter Megan) who was shot through his hand. Another pal, Lawrence Cooper, a swimmer at the same club I was a member of prior to the war, was shot in the leg. A third soldier, by the name of Knott was shot in the arse and my really good mate Mike Collington had two fingers shot off in the contact. It was said by the others that he was running around after the firefight pointing his two finger-stumps at all and sundry and shouting 'spot the mistake' whilst laughing like a maniac! When all this was happening, I was trying to call in helicopters and relaying contact details to the local JOC in an attempt to casevac the wounded to hospital. Sadly the helicopters were on external operations in Mozambique so these poor buggers needed to be evacuated by vehicle.

After our relay-stint my stick and I joined Boet Boshoff, a local farmer and Selous Scout in going around villages looking for labour to work on his farm as the gooks operating in the area had intimidated the youths into not working for the whites. We entered one village, Boet shot the two dogs who came for him, we burnt the huts in the village and took away four young men to go and work on Boet's farm. For this little foray we were subsequently charged with kidnap, arson and assault for which we needed Prime Minister Ian Smith to intervene to get the charges dropped. It was a full-blown war, but we still had to play by the rules and stay within the law of the land; the same did not apply to the enemy, which was why the populace was terrorised into submission.

During a period of 'R and R' (Rest and Retraining/Recuperation) C Company was on a full charge in the bar at the Terrace Selborne Hotel and a few of us, including my mate Chris Jonker, walked up to Lancaster's Coffee Tavern on 9th Avenue to collect my car. On the way, a group of aggressive black youths came out of the alleyway and started abusing us to the point that I belted one a telling blow and left him lying unconscious in the middle of the street thus preventing vehicles from driving past. This triggered the arrival of an angry crowd. Realising a full-blown riot was about to happen, I went inside Lancaster's and promptly called the police, telling them to get there immediately. I then went back out onto the pavement to face the angry mob who were shouting and screaming at me whilst their mate was still lying in the street not moving. Figuring I would be safer inside than outside, I turned to go back in when one of these idiots grabbed my collar. I turned around and hit him square in the face. He dropped like a stone and began twitching uncontrollably on the pavement – I thought he was going to die. Just then the police arrived, put handcuffs on me, and hustled me into the back seat of the 'B Car', and then proceeded to disperse the mob. While I was sitting there one of the mob came up to the window screaming at me and spat in my face.

This was too much for me, so even though handcuffed, I jumped from the car and took off after him and only caught him by the High Court where I cornered him. Before I could give him the hiding he so richly deserved, the police arrived and took me back into custody, and arrested him as well.

We were taken back to the main Charge Office where both of us were now behind the counter giving our statements with me the only one in handcuffs. Whilst giving my statement this illustrious gentleman piped up and said "You are a liar." By the time the police managed to pull me off him you could barely recognise him and so off he went to hospital. During this time just about all of my platoon was filling the charge office with their large frames, as Chris Jonker had gone back to the Terrace to tell them what was happening and to call for support.

Standing there now and with many more members of the police appearing, my father stormed into the charge office, took one look at all of us and said to one of the policemen that he did not care

1 – The Early Years

what I had done but that if they did not take the handcuffs off me, he and the rest of C Coy were going to tear that police station apart. The threat worked – the cops were not in the mood for a bunch of battle-hardened boozers running amok, and I was let free.

Back in the bush, we were based up at the airstrip in the Gona re Zhou Game Reserve, near to a lodge owned by a popular South African band called the 'Four Jacks and a Jill'. We arrived at the camp late afternoon passing by a Coloured Protection Unit who were there to protect the personnel and equipment belonging to Gulliver's Construction working on the roads. As we drove in the soldiers already based there all shouted out in unison, 'Welcome to Malapaaaaaattiiii (Malipati), the place what gets mortared once a week'. Well, bugger me, we were mortared that night. The only person injured was one of our soldiers by the name of Pete – while running for cover he ran into a mechanic's pit and broke one of his legs. None of the mortar bombs even landed close.

As it turned out this particular camp was to be my most eventful in the short span of my army life. Having survived the mortars on the first night, the day after we arrived we were deployed on our first patrol with my great pals Mark Sommer (now the late – murdered by 'dissidents' on his farm after the war), Jimmy Jeans (commonly known as JimBob, still going strong here in Australia), and Eddie Grey (now late, as alcohol got the better of him), all of them good soldiers.

We were collected at the end of the patrol by one of the trucks and were being taken back to our camp. Whilst on deployment Eddie had fitted a '32 Zulu' rifle grenade on the end of his rifle and suddenly fired it at God knows what in the distance. He told us after we had taken cover that he had seen a gook in the distance – this was tough to believe – it turned out he was tired of carrying around the grenade on the end of his rifle.

At the time the army was going through a phase of 'winning the hearts and minds of the local populace' so when we saw a family walking along the road carrying all their possessions, we stopped to offer them a ride, but they were reluctant to accept the offer which struck me as strange. Our view in those days was 'grab em by the nuts, or the short and curlies, and their hearts and minds would naturally follow', but orders were orders.

Carrying a MAG (light machine gun) because I had been demoted, I was sitting over the back right wheel when we struck a mine. The machine gun bounced off the edge of the truck, flew over my head and hit my best mate JimBob seated behind me, over the head, embedding the foresight in his cranium.

I still have the picture in my mind, of Eddie flying into outer space as the blast blew him upwards. Jimmy had only that second finished crapping on him to put his seat belt on in case we hit a mine. I figured this was just punishment for his misdeeds and did not have him charged (as I was going to do) when we returned to camp. Clearly the blacks on the truck knew something was going to happen before it happened and after hitting the mine they took their hearts and minds and were last seen kicking up dust, buggering off into the distance. Amazingly, other than Jimmy's head, there were no other injuries. On our next patrol along the Nuanetsi River we were involved in another contact with the net result of one dead gook.

Going through a quiet patch, our platoon literally had nothing happening for the next two weeks, during which time 'D Company', led by Boet York, had the pleasure of killing ten gooks in assorted contacts and for our sins, we being C Coy, ended up cutting off and keeping the hands for identification purposes together with

1 – The Early Years

JimBob and I on the ambushed vehicle where Bill and Gavin were shot. Note bullet hole on strut under my left elbow. Bill Cullen was sitting just left of there and the hole you see is the one that caused the bullet to shred with pieces going into his head and neck. Pieces remain in him today. On the far right of the picture there is a bullet hole on the corner about half inch from top of photograph

This is a better picture of the ambush truck showing the bullet holes more clearly in the strut, level with my tummy and in the corner of the spare wheel compartment behind me level with my backside

The Boys from Bulawayo

The truck where we hit a mine where the gun bounced up and hit JimBob in the head

Truck we were ambushed in where Bill on back was shot and Gavin in front seat who got the bullet in his thigh Note four bullet holes in windscreen (how they missed Gavin God only knows) and bullet hole through the engine (hole barely noticeable) which was armour piercing, and which went through the motor into Gavin. Soldier standing in front of truck is Rick Scott-Roger the driver who screamed Paddy I've been hit!

1 – The Early Years

Moi with the gun that hit JimBob on head. I was seated above that wheel when mine went off and JimBob directly behind me

their weapons for forensic investigation, and then disposing of the bodies in a fire pit.

From the same camp, we were heading back home as our stint had been completed when on that very Chikombedzi road we were ambushed by a large number of terrorists. The immediate action upon encountering an ambush was for all of us to open up firing at will, and to clear the ambush zone. We were heading down towards a river-crossing when the terrorists opened fire on us and in amongst all the weapons going off I heard the driver, Rick Scott-Roger scream, 'Paddy I've been hit!' and I had visions of us being wiped out in the kill-zone, but as it turned out it was the guy sitting next to him who was hit in the leg which as a result spewed blood all over Rick. The chap hit in the leg was Gavin Smith, a Rhodesian baseballer. An amour piercing round went through the engine area and dashboard and entered his leg just above the knee and lodged in his thigh up near the hip. On the back of the truck, my mate Bill Cullen was shot through the neck and shrapnel from a round that hit the upright strut pierced his neck and head in numerous places. Even during the middle of the contact I looked at Bill who had that enquiring look in his eyes pointing at his neck saying, 'am I going to live Patrick?' I am sure he was not impressed with my response – all I saw was blood pissing out of his neck spraying everywhere whilst I shook my head saying, 'No Bill I don't think so'. Sitting next to me was Chris Jonker, brother of Cedric Jonker, the Rhodesian cricketer. A bullet passed through the sleeping bag which he was using as a cushion, fusing all the nylon in the bag. How that bullet got where it did without hitting any of us is still a mystery to me.

On the follow-up immediately after the ambush, I ended up shooting a duiker that I thought was a gook when it bolted out of the bushes just ahead of me. We spent a very nervous night after Billy and Gavin had been casevaced by helicopter and the following day we proceeded to the Beit Bridge road. As we reached the tar road, behind me was sitting Frank Tuohy, the MAG gunner and next to him a black policeman that we were giving a lift to Beit Bridge. Frank laid his gun down and when he did this, he had what is known as a 'runaway gun' which essentially is an AD (accidental discharge) which fired off a belt of 50 rounds in no time at all. Needless to say, all of us promptly fell through our backsides. The policeman threw himself across Frank's gun and there was nothing Frank could do to stop the gun firing.

The third mine incident happened not long afterwards. It also took place near Chikombedzi, where we were heading for the main road to Beit Bridge when we hit the 'tin'. Fortunately no serious

1 – The Early Years

Vehicle after hitting mine on Chikombedzi Road

Moi same landmine

injuries. Clearly our 'hearts and minds campaign' was not working.

My worst landmine experience was my fourth and last. It happened on 20th September 1977. My stick had been on patrol operating from Beit Bridge. I had missed an external attack into Mozambique which was a big operation involving the air force, elements of RAR and RLI as well as some of the Territorial units like us. As my stick and I were on patrol when the external was called, I missed being a part of it, which really pissed me off. Subsequently we were assigned as a protection unit escorting Ministry of Water Development vehicles and personnel to a 'Keep' (Protected Village) based on the Limpopo River at Chicualacuala.

We were about an hour from Romeo Base which was the Police Post in the area, when we detonated a boosted mine. I was driving. The front right wheel beneath me struck the mine. The steering column simply exploded into the cab through the back of the truck behind where I was sitting. Fortunately it did not go through me or injure anyone in the back of the vehicle. Dave Adlam, a mate from Bulawayo sitting next to me, was uninjured. I was not as fortunate as the explosion broke my left leg, causing a compound fracture of the talus in the right ankle and foot, resulting in a bone protruding out of my foot below the ankle, four broken ribs, and a split skull. I was black from top to bottom from the cordite. Dave dragged me from the truck into the bush while someone tried to radio for help but the only radio undamaged was the 'Big Means' TR 48. As I was the only guy who knew how to operate this radio it was left to me to give the necessary instructions on how to set it up. I was in so much pain and in such a mess I was struggling to think clearly, but I managed to focus on the job and explained to them the process of setting up the radio for transmission.

A call went through directly to Colonel Cedric French at JOC in

1 – The Early Years

Dave Adlam above and myself after he pulled me from the mined vehicle

Chiredzi, but he was unable to help as all the choppers were on the external raid into Mozambique. I know Cedric would have helped if he could have as I was friends with the family, and my mate Derek Hatch (the bicycle thief at Inyanga) was dating Cedric's daughter Janet, whom he ended up marrying.

The only individual who could help was Ken Gault at the Police Camp and he came in a Land Rover with a truck following. Unfortunately he had no medic pack, and I was desperate for morphine. The drive in the back of his truck to the police airstrip were the most painful hours of my life. Upon arrival at the airstrip Balfour Chandler, a Bulawayo architect, collected me in his aircraft. I was given morphine, which was heavenly. He flew me to Chiredzi hospital for treatment. At the hospital a nurse came to attend to my injuries and wash off all the cordite. I knew the morphine was working when I got a hard-on. She was not impressed.

Next day I was flown by Air Rhodesia Viscount to Bulawayo for hospitalisation and specialist treatment. Between the morphine and the numerous whiskys purchased for me by the passengers, I was off my nut when we arrived at the Bulawayo airport and once again was dribbling out of both sides of my mouth, whilst sitting in a wheelchair awaiting an ambulance from Brady Barracks to collect me. Due to some administration debacle at Brady Barracks no ambulance was sent, so after an hour of waiting for the ambulance to arrive a kind lady who worked at the airport took pity on me and came to ask me what was happening. I was so smashed I couldn't respond, so she took it upon herself to arrange the necessary, and an hour later an ambulance arrived to collect me.

When I arrived at Bulawayo Hospital the back doors of the ambulance opened and there was my dad who jumped in to greet me upon which the dam broke, and all I could do was cry. This ankle injury put an end to any hopes of playing rugby again. A week before, I had been picked to play at fullback for the 'Probables' to play the 'Possibles' in a trial for the Rhodesian Under 21 team which had always been a dream of mine. I couldn't make it because I was needed in the army, and now I knew it would never be.

The funny part was when I was being wheeled into X-Ray at Bulawayo General Hospital I was met by this black orderly who greeted me with this big cheesy grin showing a mouth missing several teeth. To my great surprise he seemed to know me: 'Hello Baas, remember me,' he said cheerily. He was one of the blokes I had smacked outside Lancaster's when I was arrested. We became big buddies.

Whilst recovering at home, I had my car stolen by some bastard

1 – The Early Years

who attended a house-party at our place one night. At the time I was having physio on my leg every day at Andrew Fleming Hospital, so with my car gone I was had to hitch-hike on crutches every day to and from the hospital for three months – which did not please me. The police caught the thief, and he went to prison. I caught up with him one night after his release from prison and put him in hospital.

My mate Ron Rink, who was shot in the neck around same time I was blown up, used to drive me around because my leg was still a mess and I used to have a good time chatting the girls up on his behalf because he couldn't talk: it was wonderful, I was the only one getting lucky!

Ron and I and a few other mates then decided to relieve the Donnington Police of the meat they had in their freezer with the help of Bob Packer, who was a cop. We were caught, charged and prosecuted and I was the only one convicted, but Bob would have lost his police pension if convicted, so as the chief prosecution's main witness I knew I had to protect him. After a few minutes, the prosecutor, Danie Gous, realised what was happening and declared me a hostile witness. I was kicked out the witness box and with no evidence from me, Bob was acquitted. Ron had left for university after threatening the investigating officer that if he harassed Ron's mother any more to find out where Ron was then Ron would shoot him! Therein ended Ron's investigation. We had a braai every weekend for a few months per kind favour of the police, and my dogs had a roast every weekend.

While still recovering from my injuries I was transferred from the NEM office in Salisbury back to Bulawayo. I was at home before being moved to a mess in Northway in Bulawayo. One of the guys living there was Brian Foster. One night he was called out on a mobile fire-force to a local sawmill on the Vic Falls road where the sawmill manager had been murdered by the gooks. Brian came away with a brand-new chainsaw 'acquired' from the mill and he and I went into business cutting down problem trees. Two of the trees we took down went rogue, and one fell into the swimming pool and the other fell across a fence and part of a house doing quite a lot of damage; clearly, we had a little to learn about tree-felling.

Then, one Friday, we had a house party where a number of us were drinking alcohol in commercial quantities. One of the mess members by the name of Brian 'Carruthers' Peters was getting lucky with one of the young ladies in Brian Foster's bedroom. Foster had had more than enough to drink and wanted to go to bed and so knocked on his door telling Carruthers to get out, upon which Carruthers told him to fuck off and go and sleep in another bed. Fossie took offence, retrieved the chain saw from the garage and proceeded to cut a huge hole in the door. The poor girl came running out of the bedroom naked. That was the end of that little tryst.

In the same house was another friend of mine, named Tony Simpson, a hairdresser and was someone who was, if I can put it diplomatically, somewhat of a serious dope-smoker, who had also previously had it off with the petite, small, vivacious lady mentioned earlier. She gave Tony enough money so that when he left to go overseas, he managed to travel the world at no cost to himself. An eccentric fellow, he used to send me postcards from all over the world, writing phonetically, like 'HOW R U' and then sign it with a drawing of a pair of scissors! When he moved to Salisbury, he bought a house in Greendale, which he rented out and proceeded to live in a tree house he made for himself on the same property.

At this time, my workplace was in the same office as one Rozanne Trinder, a most lovely lady. On the 3rd September 1978, a civilian aircraft, an Air Rhodesia Viscount, was shot down by terrorists

1 – The Early Years

near Kariba. They used a heat seeking Strela 2 surface to air missile to bring down the aircraft. By some miracle the pilot managed to crash-land the plane, but both of the pilots were killed on impact. That is a day etched indelibly in my memory: it shocked the whole country, and seriously crushed our morale. A dark day in Rhodesia's chequered history indeed.

After the impact, two passengers, Tony Hill and Hans Hansen kicked a hole in the craft to make an exit. Then Tony, Hans and his wife Diana, started moving people out, including one of the hostesses, until the inferno made it impossible to continue. Within the fuselage, passengers fought the flames with their hands. One woman sat helpless, holding her baby tight while her clothes burned before a hand came through a hole and grabbed the child.

One of the passengers, Dr Maclaren, found himself hanging upside down looking at the flames closing in on him. He tried a window, but the handle snapped off in his hand. Struggling through the wreckage he reached Sharon and Tracy Cole, and along with young newlyweds Robert and Shannon Hargreaves, managed to exit the plane through a hole in the fuselage. Diana Hansen tried to comfort one of the hostesses who drifted in and out of consciousness.

A few sat silently trying to make sense of it all while terrified children clung to their parents. Some asked for water and bandages. Passenger Cynthia Tilley, who had just lost her 15-year-old brother when terrorists attacked the family home, was one of the first to go to the aid of the survivors. At this stage 38 were dead and eighteen survived. But stifling heat made water a priority, and Dr McLaren left the crash site leading a small party including Tracey and Sharon Cole along with the Hargreaves to look for water and seek help. Finding an African village they requested assistance but received an unfriendly response.

At the same time, 12 ZIPRA terrorists arrived at the scene. They ordered the survivors to a place some distance away from the wreckage saying water and assistance would be forthcoming. The crippled pleaded incapacity and asked to be left to lie where they were. Having struggled to the assembly-point, the children embraced their parents in terrified silence.

Those capable of standing were ordered into a row while the maimed lay on the ground. Satisfied all were in place, the commander unclipped his 'pig-sticker' bayonet and told the survivors; "You have stolen our land, you are white, now you must die."

With that the firing started and continued until the commander ordered it to cease. In order to conserve ammunition he led his men onto the bodies with their bayonets fixed. Brenda Pearson was struck five times by bullets, but lay there alive until she was bayonetted to death. One child, a girl of four had escaped the firing unscathed. She was stabbed to death hanging on to her dead father's leg.

Hiding nearby, listening to the unfolding tragedy, were Tony Hill and the Hansens. They lay dead still and went unseen. Also hiding a short distance away was Dr Maclaren's group. With the killers searching and shouting, McLaren kept little Tracey close to his chest. One noise from the child would have given their position away and meant death. The survivors made it through the night while help tried to reach them.

In the morning, an SAS contingent aboard a Dakota flew a grid-pattern but no one had any idea how far the captain had kept the aircraft aloft after losing his engines so there was a lot of guess-work going on. Eventually one of the SAS men spotted a metallic shine and shouted. The pilot went into an orbit and confirmed the wreckage below. The SAS guys then parachuted in.

1 – The Early Years

Of the 52 passengers and four crew, 38 died in the crash. The 10 survivors that remained at the plane were murdered. Tony Hill and the Hansens, along with the five that made up the group with Dr McLaren, survived.

The grandmother was Rozanne Trinder's mom, and the two grandchildren were her son and daughter. All were shot and then bayonetted to death. I was in the office when she received the phone call telling her about their murder. In the next office was my mate Graham Hancock whose brother-in-law and his wife, the Hansens, were still alive. A black day for all of us in Rhodesia, but the rest of the world looked the other way. All the casualties were white so that was seemingly okay for the international community.

Although not fully fit and still recovering from my injuries I was back in the army after six months and on various deployments in spite of my objections to being a liability to whoever I was with.

In April 1979 the first black majority government came to power under Bishop Abel Muzorewa, and I was called up with another 'lizard', as we who had been wounded and were not fully fighting fit were known. His name was Paul Schultz, a really good guy. During a contact, a spent bullet entered his kneecap and did a 'ring a ring a rosy' inside it. So two of us crippled warriors were left to our own devices in a mortar pit whilst protecting a voter point in Filabusi.

To entertain ourselves we used to hold daily boxing competitions amongst the *piccannins* (young Africans) where the first prize was a tin of bully-beef. We also taught all of them to salaam and chant. So when a group of foreign press arrived, we sent them running across to shout their chant! Colonel French, the Officer Commanding 2 RR, was also with them. The foreign press were very anti-white so they were not very impressed by this performance.

I decided during this time it was nonsense that, because of my physical condition, I should be a liability to everyone around me. I could hardly walk, never mind run, so I took my weapon and kit and went to the main road and proceeded to go AWOL and head back to Bulawayo. There I ended up in Jimmy Cromar's office at Brady where I totally lost my cool and ended up being sent to Detention Barracks (DB) to recover. An architect from town by the name of Rodney Cooper, who was a Captain in RIC (Rhodesia Intelligence Corps), arranged for me to be released and transferred to his command, which is where I was when the war ended.

After all we had been through it was a bitter disappointment watching Mugabe come to power, but he was the man Britain and the world wanted. I think, when you look at what has happened to the country, we were right to fight the war. Unfortunately, the world was against us, but we did our best. Looking back, those who proudly served Rhodesia in the war years realise that this little nation, with its tiny army of professional and conscripted soldiers, had produced, against all odds, with little or no support and in the face of global dissent, a massive and sustained effort to protect Rhodesia and its citizens that ANY nation in the history of the world would envy.

Dr John Pridgeon relates: "I don't even want to think about the pain and suffering Patrick endured from his many injuries but cannot ever remember him complaining even once. I looked after him for a few weeks in about 2007 when he was having his shattered ankle fused so that he could walk without the agony that he had already endured for almost 30 years."

Life after the War

The cease-fire imposed on us at the end of 1979 was not well received by Rhodesia's military, but we had to follow orders. Our worst fears were realised with the shock of Mugabe's electoral triumph. Australia's PM Malcolm Fraser was one of the first to congratulate Mugabe. We were very disappointed, but morale lifted when our new leader spoke about forgiveness and assured us whites that we were welcome to stay and be part of a better future. Despite this, about half the white population decided to leave the country. For those of us who stayed there were plenty of opportunities to fill gaps, and I wanted to take charge of my own future.

It was not very long before we were reminded that Mugabe was essentially a terrorist and that nothing had actually changed despite his conciliatory words. The Matabele, led by Joshua Nkomo, remained a threat. With his customary ruthlessness, he decided to teach them a harsh lesson.

Following a curfew imposed on the Matabele heartland in January 1983, Mugabe sent in the North Korean trained 5th Brigade under a murderous swine by the name of Perrance Shiri. Moving from village to village they spread a reign of utter terror, raping, murdering and pillaging. By the end of it, in the region of 20,000 innocents were dead. The so-called Gukurahundi was a series of massacres of Ndebele civilians carried out by the Zimbabwe National Army from early 1983 to late 1987. It derives from a Shona language term which loosely translates to "the early rain which washes away the chaff before the spring rains". Following the atrocities, there was a strange silence from the rest of the world and little or no criticism of Mugabe. The Conservative government under Mrs. Thatcher, who had put Mugabe in power, reacted to the news with understanding[7]. The Australian government offered no criticism: instead they sent tax collectors to assist the Mugabe regime. In so

---

7   Mugabe, they said, was responding to a 'legitimate national security concern'.

> **Zimbabwean farmer shot, axed to death**
>
> BULAWAYO. — A White farmer was shot and axed to death by six gunmen on his cattle ranch in northern Matabeleland, police reported yesterday.
>
> Mr Mark Sommer (31) was slain as he was trying to dig his Landrover out of a drift on his Kennilworth ranch at Nyathi, north of Bulawayo on Friday, police said.
>
> He was the first White to be slain in Matabeleland since October. More than 30 Whites have been killed in the province since 1982 forcing many others to flee their lucrative cattle ranches.
>
> The government blames followers of opposition leader, Dr Joshua Nkomo for the insurgency that has left at least 300 civilians dead, mainly in Matabeleland and neighbouring Midlands provinces since 1982. Dr Nkomo denies the charge.
>
> then axed in the head, police said.
>
> His body was found by one of his two brothers, Mr Geoffrey Sommer, after he failed to return home to the ranch-house for supper.
>
> Mr Mark Sommer married his widow, Celia Edwards, only four months before his death.
>
> Police said a shotgun and revolver which the rancher normally carried with him were stolen along with a briefcase and his watch.
>
> Some 20 fellow White ranchers and farmers from the area have joined troops and police in a

Speaks for itself, my best man Mark Sommer

doing, they focused virtually all their attentions on the whites who were mainly law-abiding and ignored Mugabe's cronies who were already stealing the country blind. If Ian Smith had done anything like Mugabe, I'm sure it would have triggered an invasion.

1 – The Early Years

Problems continued in Matabeleland after the 5th Brigade massacres with rogue former fighters that came to be known as 'dissidents' continuing to kill white farmers. The best man at my wedding was my good mate Mark Sommer, brother to Jeff and Henry Sommer. The terrorists murdered him on his farm at Kenilworth Estates outside Bulawayo. This act in itself made me want to kill more people, and I have never recovered from that news. Mark's brother Henry called me that day in Gwelo to tell me the sad news. I just hung up, I could not talk. I went from my house to a mate Basil Foster Jones whose best man at his wedding had also been murdered by the dissidents, and we proceeded to get rat-faced and cry.

As an entrepreneur in a rapidly changing country, I was available for pretty much anything and came to own several businesses and agencies. I initially started off with the Henselite Lawn Bowls agency, being granted sole rights to distribute in Zimbabwe. Then I acquired the agency for Abu Garcia, which was then taken over by Pure Fishing which then included Berkley, Fenwick, Mitchell Stren and Penn fishing products.

My mom and dad moved to Australia in 1985 soon after the birth of my son Sean and I went to visit them after my father had a stroke. They were living in a cottage my sister Sharon and brother-in-law Kevin had built on their property. During our stay, my sister introduced me to a Yugoslav by the name of Joe Ruzick, who had invented a one-man gold and precious stones panning machine which I saw an immediate use for in Zimbabwe. I talked him into giving me a machine to take back home and upon passing through customs I told the officers that I had made the machine in Zimbabwe and had taken it to Australia to see if I could sell it but was not successful in doing so. Sweet talking swine, the story worked, and I brought it in duty-free.

Another friend of mine Robin Dryburgh was employed by a gent by the name of Sam Bloor who owned a vermiculite mine. He saw the machine's potential and invested $1 000 000 in us manufacturing the product for distribution and sale in Zimbabwe and the SADC region.

Later, I became partners with an Australian, Tim Johansen, and we employed his brother Ben who I nicknamed 'Banjo 'who very successfully manufactured these machines from scratch, and we sold thousands over the next few years while paying Joe a royalty. We named the machine 'JR Ezi Panner' and the company we formed was Eezee Gold Pvt Ltd. Banjo became a partner.

Then I set up a group of music shops catering to the African market in a chain of clothing stores named Power Sales. The music shops were called 'Sounds Power'. Starting with one shop, my intention was to grow the business to accommodate all the Power Sales stores throughout Zimbabwe but after the 25th shop I was bored and sold the company to the group I was trading in and moved on.

From the initial agency on the Abu Garcia fishing products, we moved on to include PUMA sporting products. This all came about because the export manager for Abu Garcia was a Swede by the name of Lars Mansson, who became a very good friend and introduced us to Thore Ohlsson who happened to be the chairman of the board of the holding company Aritmos and they owned the German company PUMA. Thanks to Thore's introduction I acquired all the manufacturing, distribution and wholesale and retail sales rights in the country. I own these to this day.

During this time I also started a driving school in Kadoma called Elephant Driving School. My manager and partner in this enterprise was one Nelson (Cookie) Ndlovu and our vehicles of trade

1 – The Early Years

were four small vehicles and one Bedford truck. A good business but a very corrupt one as anyone could buy a driving licence for $500. We soon realised we couldn't beat the system, so we joined it. I purchased two licences for a friend of mine's wife who lived in Bulawayo and another for a friend who had lost his for ever for drink-driving offences. As he had given up the drink, I saw no reason not to assist him for which he was very grateful being at the tender age of 78 at the time.

Cookie was employed by National Parks when I first met him. Always looking for something exciting to do, I became involved in covert operations aimed at stopping the illegal trade in ivory and rhinoceros horn. Cookie pretended to be the man with the tusks acting on behalf of the poachers and I was the bad white guy with the money to purchase the contraband. This way we spread the word through the local criminal underworld and set up sting operations.

Once he phoned me after midnight to tell me he was about to meet some buyers at Birchenough Bridge on the Save River near the eastern border which was the other side of the country. I leaped out of bed, borrowed a mate's car (mine was in the garage), and drove eight hours to get to the agreed meeting point. With Cookie hiding in the trunk of the car, I drove with his contact man to meet with a group of poachers to arrange where to purchase the ivory. After this I dropped off Cookie's contact man and proceeded another five minutes to a secluded spot where I let Cookie out of the car. Together we had travelled hundreds of kilometres on dirt well into Mozambique but the sting operation was set up for the next day. Cookie climbed out of the boot covered in dust and pulled out his 'John Thomas' and must have stood there pissing for ten minutes – I thought he was going to die. The trap was sprung the next day when six poachers and the middleman were arrested together with

Cookie to make it appear more legitimate. A total of three Rhinoceros horn and eleven tusks were recovered.

On another occasion Cookie came to me to help him set up a classic trap and capture. My brother-in-law, Bill Taylor, an orthodontist in Bulawayo, was acting with me on a number of these covert operations and in this case, he was the supposed buyer who was transporting the 'middleman' – a big fat black momma was the contact dealer. She was then taken to a collection point to pick up the ivory and we were then proceeding to another address where payment was to be made. Bill was using a Mini Minor to transport the fat-lady and the tusks and when they drove around a corner into our planned roadblock with a number of armed National Parks people and police, she promptly evacuated her bowels on the front seat of the little Mini. I don't need to tell you how pissed off Bill was! And his mood did not improve when he was arrested and flung into the back of a police car so as to maintain his cover. In this instance, we recovered four tusks.

Cookie and I also began mining near the town of Gokwe in the north-west of the country. We purchased a three-stamp mill for processing gold ore which on its own was a good business if one managed to keep more of the gold than what was being stolen by the workers. But the mining operation was really a front operation for buying and selling gold, which was a very profitable business in its own right.

In Zimbabwe the government had a regulated monopoly on the trade in gold so there were rich pickings in the 'illegal' trade. There were also strict currency controls and all foreign currencies had to be traded through designated institutions at an artificially high value, so there were also opportunities in the 'illegal' buying and selling of hard currencies. I became involved in dealing in both of these com-

1 – The Early Years

modities. Import tariffs were also high, so I started smuggling spare parts for cars. For smuggling purposes I used a 21 ft boat known as the 'Eliminator' which had a false bottom and a VW Kombi with false back section. Henry, my partner in this enterprise, on occasion also used a Ford three-litre truck.

On one of these jaunts, Henry and I were returning to Johannesburg from Bulawayo after a successful trading trip when we gave a lift to a chap hitching to Pretoria standing on the outskirts of Messina. We were in the Ford truck towing the boat. As it was late in the day and as we had the usual delay crossing the border post in the heat, we were somewhat thirsty by the time we arrived in Messina, so we pulled into the first bottle store and loaded our cooler box with ice, Captain Morgan Rum and Coke. The rum we opened immediately, and I poured Henry and I a commercial quantity of Rum and Coke before collecting the hitchhiker and we left town heading towards Johannesburg.

On joining us I immediately poured our passenger an equally generous amount of Rum, Coke and ice without having asked him whether he would like one or not. I need not have worried, as it turned out, it was his regular drink and so he gladly joined in the festivities. He, we heard, had been standing in the heat at the border for several hours so he too was thirsty. By the time we reached Pietersburg, two hours later, our new friend was, shall we say, 'cooking with gas' and I carried on pouring him what we called, 'duma' tots.

By this time, Henry and I were jokingly discussing running the toll-gate at Warmbaths and not paying the toll just for entertainment value. It was only then that our friend disclosed that he was actually an off-duty policeman and that he did not think this was such a good idea.

This new development tickled both of us, making the whole idea even more enticing, so we ventured the idea that it might be a lot of fun if he was driving when we ran the barrier. Enjoying the moment, we drove on merrily towards the toll gate. The closer we got, the more serious Henry and I became about doing the dastardly deed and we got down to the details regarding what speed we should run it at to avoid the metal post that would spring up when dodging the tollgate. By this time the policeman was begging us not to do it and to please drop him off on the side of the road prior to us reaching the point of no return which just had us even more entertained. Suffice to say we did not drop him off and neither did we stop, speeding through the toll point with boat in tow at around 140 km per hour! All we heard from the toll booth cubicle was a lady screaming HEEEEEEYYYYY!!!

On the other side, now some kilometres down the road we stopped the vehicle to 'shake hands with the unemployed' still some 100 km from where the policeman said he wanted to be dropped off. He left the vehicle with his kit, shaking his head and refused to get back in so we bade him farewell and continued on our way. I can still see the lady's face in the cubicle as we shot through without stopping.

We also used to fly gold bullion to Geneva in form-fitting webbing for the aeroplane, sell the gold there and then with the resultant income purchase gold Kruger rands which for some reason were 20% cheaper there than in South Africa. We brought the Kruger Rands back and resold at anything up to a 20% profit so we were getting a double hit on monies earned.

All was going well when Ed Mavengere, the Chief Investigating Officer for Customs, did a raid on a friend of mine where he

1 – The Early Years

discovered documentation that implied I was dealing in so-called 'black imports' of Scotch and wine.

I was picked up as a result, under the so-called Emergency Powers, which allowed detention without trial, because they had no evidence. I was flung into the filthy cells at Donnington police station, where I was stuck for four days, but the case was dismissed and struck off the register as I had drunk all the evidence! My partner in this endeavour was the wife of an ex-Springbok rugby player.

Mavengere warned me at the time that he would place my wife in jail for six months if I did not tell him all I knew. I told him his threat was completely unacceptable: if he promised to keep her for at least a year then I would tell him everything. Neither Mavengere nor my wife were impressed with this proposal.

Meanwhile, bad governance was starting to show. As a result, the economy slowed, joblessness increased and the disparity between rich and poor grew exponentially. Millions of acres of land acquired for resettlement lay fallow as government paid scant attention to the needs of the poor. Within 10 years of independence, much of the national wealth was concentrated in the hands of an obscenely wealthy political elite while the overwhelming majority were worse off than ever under European rule. Despite this, we whites were always busy 'making a plan' by dodging stupid rules and regulations, so while our numbers continued to dwindle, many who stayed continued to live a good life. This appeared to irritate Mugabe, who fumed repeatedly and publicly about 'recalcitrant white racists' who ignore the blacks from the confines of their 'white clubs'. He became obsessed with the fact that we whites were plotting something in our clubs, and this may have been something to do with my punch-up that followed.

I was drinking at my second home, the pub at the Old Miltonians Sports Club. I was having a good time with mates and had had a few 'Captain Morgans' too many when my son and his friend entered the pub, passing by the Ladies' Rest Room where the door was open with a bed on display. I don't know what the boys said, but a group of black gentlemen and their entourage were seated around a table having their usual Friday night refreshments. One of them had a few words with my son Luke and then the rest of them began abusing him. I sidled up to them and just went from zero to ballistic, downing I don't know how many in a flurry of punches. One of those I was attending to was a club committee member and very full of himself until I stuck a fist so far into his ribs that he collapsed in a heap.

Now when all of this was happening, everyone was taking cover, and amongst other things were hiding under the tables and behind the bar counter. Leaning against the bar counter at the time was the long frame of Howie Gardiner, ex Rhodesian wicket-keeper and renowned 'six or nix' batsman, and his friend Ray Varkevisser, the former Rhodesian rugby player. All I heard coming from Howie was 'let's get the fuck outa here'.

The situation deteriorated when one of the fellas that I had flattened pulled out a gun and fired a few rounds into the roof – his first big mistake. He really should have shot me because I proceeded to make sure he would never use the gun again.

By this time, someone had called the police, and no sooner had I disarmed the one idiot than Nathan Conradie, my son's pal, also pulled out his weapon which I quickly removed from him and then handed both weapons over to, of all people, Kevin 'Fats' Vanner, a certified loose cannon in his own right. As I did this, in stormed the police with their AK's, who then arrested me and my sons Neil

1 – The Early Years

and Luke and took us in three separate vehicles to the main police station. We left leaving bodies strewn all over the inside and outside of the club. Both sons had come to my aid, but it was all over in no time at all and I didn't need any help. On the way to the police station I was seated in the back seat of a Nissan Sunny between two rather small and young policemen, and it really would not have been an issue to deal with them but as my sons were also in transit in other vehicles I let sleeping dogs lie.

Neil, Luke and I were sitting quietly in a room in the main Charge Office while outside the Minister for Immigration, who was part of the crowd I had just assaulted, was busy ranting and raving. He loudly demanded that we should go to jail, but as there had been the incident with them using weapons, he wound his neck in as the matter would have been taken a great deal further.

Now during this process I peeked around the doorway and saw my wife standing on the other side of the charge office counter with a most disapproving look on her face. She left when she established we were not going to jail. We ended up being fined tens of thousands of dollars (as the currency had started to run due to the self-inflicted inflation) and were then let go. Of course my sons and I went back to the club for a few more refreshments.

Despite all that Mugabe had done wrong, scum that he was, and all the people he had murdered, in 1994, Mugabe was made a Knight Commander of the Order of the Bath by The Queen at a ceremony in Buckingham Palace.

In 1996 I became seriously ill with double bronchopneumonia which put me into I.C.U for a few days where I nearly went to the happy hunting grounds. My sister Kathleen (Pie) was living in Australia at the time, and she phoned my doctor who told her there was a good chance I would soon be pushing up daisies. If she wanted to see me she better get on a flight fast. She did exactly that. My G.P at the time was Dr Geoff Pridgeon who was also a really close mate of mine. She and Geoff hit it off, and after she returned to Australia, she decided to sell her house and move back to Zimbabwe as she was missing the hell out of the place anyway and there was now a love interest in her life! Bugger brother Patrick who was busy trying to die at the time!

Kathleen was a computer expert and very adept at accounting, so she had no problem finding work in and around Bulawayo. She also found work in the Gwaai area near Hwange National Park where there were some big, privately owned game ranches. She was loving it, but then the cowards who called themselves 'war-vets' started stirring the pot and it was getting dangerous. I insisted she left the area, and she moved onto Charleswood Estates being Roy and Heather Bennett's farm in the Chimanimani Mountains to do Roy's accounts.

At about the same time the 'war-vets', marched on State House, demanding a huge increase in their pensions. This caused instant alarm and fear at the highest level which triggered an instruction to the Reserve Bank to immediately print mountains of money to satisfy the former terrorists.

The move sparked a collapse in the value of the Zimbabwe dollar and a shockwave ran through the markets. Having repeatedly assured white farmers their future was secure; Mugabe summarily designated over 1,500 farms for parcelling out to the war-veterans in November 1997. This caused further economic distress but, ever willing to help, the European Union, World Bank and International Monetary Fund hastened to his side and delivered financial assistance.

1 – The Early Years

By 1999 the country was on its knees and the MDC (Movement for Democratic Change) led by former trade union leader, Morgan Tsvangirai, became a serious political threat despite the lack of democratic space.

In the face of the political pressure and because he believed whites were behind the opposition, Mugabe played his political trump-card and seized over 4,000 commercial farms owned by whites that still provided what was left of a sustainable economy. Tens of thousands of workers now had no source of income. Outside of wars, the Zimbabwe economy became the fastest collapsing in history. This would cause millions of people to abandon the country and flee: most of them to South Africa. As Tsvangirai's popularity grew, Roy Bennett was at his side and so both Kathleen and I were drawn into the political fray.

Self at Chobe. Got really pissed there with my mate Joe Aylward so smashed that we took it in turns towing each other on a surfboard behind the boat teasing the crocodiles - seriously!

Heather Bennett's dad, 'Buck' Rogers, was a former Battle of Britain fighter-pilot and a massive personality in the central farming town of Enkeldoorn. When Smith declared UDI (Unilateral Declaration of Independence) from Britain, Buck decided he would do the same and declare Enkeldoorn independent of Rhodesia! This got him famous and the whole of Rhodesia had a good laugh! The farmers built a jail in the bar, and if you went into the bar without an Enkeldoorn passport you were locked up until you bought the locals a beer each.

Roy's dad came to Rhodesia from Ireland as a miner but then went farming and, like his dad, farming was all Roy wanted to do. He started in Karoi but then moved to the Eastern Highlands where he bought Charleswood Estates in the shadow of the Chimanimani Mountains.

When the land invasions started, Roy was asked by African community leaders in the Chimanimani area on the Mozambique border where he farmed to represent them in the 2000 parliamentary elections. This period was marked by widespread violence sponsored by the state against supporters of the opposition MDC (Movement for Democratic Change). A particularly nasty individual by the name of Joseph Mwale, a senior officer in the CIO (Central Intelligence Organisation), was tasked with organising a violent campaign to force Roy, his family and his staff, off the farm. Mwale was feared: he had recently been responsible for the burning to death of two MDC supporters who were pulled off the road, doused in petrol and set alight. After this incident, his sights fell on Roy. My sister, who was residing on the property, was now in the firing line.

Soon after Roy announced his candidacy in May 2000, hired thugs invaded the property. When the thugs arrived, I was notified in Bulawayo and straight away attempted to get hold of my sister

1 – The Early Years

but with no success. I was living six hour's drive away in Bulawayo, so I called my pal there, an artist by the name of Ducks Donaldson, to see if he could call at the farm and see what was going on. In the interim I managed to get the telephone answered by my sister in her office where, although I did not know it at the time, she and Heather were being confronted by these bastards with machetes, sticks and iron bars. She tried to tell me there was no problem, but I knew she was lying and started shouting at her, telling her to get the hell out of there. When she had put the phone down, I called Roy who informed me that he was aware of the situation and was dealing with it. After Kathleen ended her conversation with me, my mate Ducks rocked up at the gates to see what was going on and was immediately called upon to sing and dance and chant ZANU PF slogans. To this day we blame him for inciting the mob because he did not sing loud enough! Anyway, they let Ducks go, or at least he took the gap at the first opportunity where he returned home and filled me in on what was happening. They held Roy's wife Heather hostage in the rain with a machete to her throat when she tried to stop them beating her staff. Heather was pregnant at the time; she lost the baby.

The campaign went on for three weeks during which beatings continued, the property was looted, and livestock slaughtered. They fought on, and Roy won the election handsomely, and a seat in parliament.

In July 2001 the farm was occupied by the police and army while being divided up into plots and parcelled out to settlers without the following of any due legal process. Anyone caught working for the Bennetts was threatened with death. One worker was shot dead, another wounded and two young girls were raped. In October, police details arrived to confiscate Roy's maize crop and he was beaten up at the same time. He was told by Mwale again to abandon the farm and politics or face death. Roy carried on and in August 2002 Mwale arrived with the police, ordered work to stop and hauled the labour off to the police station where they were beaten and soaked in cold water for several days. On the 9th October 2002 Roy, along with two of his staff, was again arrested by Mwale with a pistol at his head. Once Roy was in custody, Mwale and two others set about beating him up on a cell floor before ordering him to leave for Britain immediately. His two staff were beaten through the night, their screams heard by all, but there was no intervention. Despite all this, Roy and Heather battled on at Charleswood, but eventually financial constraints forced him to do little other than try to maintain a presence in the hope there would be some future appeasement.

Moving to a smallholding in Ruwa not far from Harare brought no relief. They were soon visited by members of the Presidential Guard who claimed to be looking for stolen weapons. The beatings resumed and one of Roy's workers died as a result of a thrashing.

Kathleen had by this time been referred to another local farmer. His name was Arthur Harley and he owned Mara farms. Not impressed by this, I had a slight altercation with Roy because he had referred her to Arthur when he should have told her to get out and to a place of safety. His response? Has she ever listened to you? he asked. End of that conversation!

Adding to the pressure was President Mugabe, who explained to ZANU PF cadres that working for Roy was 'illegal' and that 'Bennett must go from here'. Three days after this speech, hundreds of ZANU PF Youth Brigade members arrived on the smallholding with an armed CIO detail and threatened to kill anyone still working for Roy.

1 – The Early Years

On the 9th April 2004, Army and Police arrived on Charleswood and forced everyone off, warning that anyone returning would be shot. Roy's great pal and supporter, Wally Johnson, who had been trying to keep nearby Mawenji Lodge going, was given 30 minutes to get himself and his staff off the premises.

In May 2004, during a parliamentary debate, the Minister of Justice, Patrick Chinamasa, referred to Roy's forefathers as 'thieves' and accused him of having stolen land. This was too much for Roy and he barged across the chamber and pushed Chinamasa to the floor. In an unprecedented procedure he was tried by a parliamentary committee, found guilty of contempt of parliament and sentenced to 12 months in prison.

I had contacts in the police at the time who were ex BSAP and one of them whose name I will not reveal, arranged for me to see Roy in custody. It was only for a short while, but we achieved a great deal and as a result we started making arrangements to get him out the country as soon as he was released.

He was initially taken to Mtoko Prison in a remote area, where the conditions were hellish. Heather was only allowed 10 minutes with him every fortnight and she had to talk slowly enough for the guards to be able to write down what was said. He was dressed in prison khakis that stank of excrement. The front and back of his shorts were torn to humiliate him. Denied a hat and thinning on top he had been blistered by the sun and covered in lice which was driving him mad. The cell was packed to the point he had trouble breathing and many of the prisoners had TB and Meningitis. The food was inedible, and Heather was worried he would starve to death until he was finally allowed food to be brought to him. He shared what he could with the other inmates.

Not long after being released from prison he was accused of caching arms of war and finally fled Zimbabwe, getting refugee status in South Africa.

It was because of Roy I became a Life Member of the MDC and an activist in my own right. Thousands of MDC supporters were murdered. My little sister suffered irreparable psychological and emotional damage as a result of the turmoil.

Apart from all the political trouble, one of the reasons we decided to emigrate to Australia was I wanted to get my son Sean out of Zimbabwe as he was getting into a bad crowd and going nowhere. I also had an opportunity to join my brother-in-law in business. Buying 30% of 'Opat', a commercial painting business which satisfied the Australian immigration requirements, and so we acquired residence status. My wife, Christine, who was originally born in Malaysia, had come to Zimbabwe via Australia and the UK. Her

My son Neil, self, Christine and son Luke

1 – The Early Years

father was a mining engineer who has plied his trade all over the world. My widowed mother, as mentioned, was already there, living on the Bremer River in Karalee, Ipswich in Queensland with sister Sharon and her husband Kevin.

In November 2008 I sold my shares in Opat. Having tried to purchase and get involved in a few other businesses in the general area, all the deals fell by the wayside and as a result I was none the richer having spent most of what monies I had trying to get set up. I looked further afield to Grafton (New South Wales, halfway between Sydney and the Queensland Gold Coast along the sea shore), as the money I had left after a year of no income was not enough to purchase anything substantial. Russell Pridgeon, who I knew from Bulawayo, was living there. It was actually Geoff and John, who passed me onto him such that he could act like an older brother, sort of like pass the parcel in an Irish pub. All the brothers were at Milton School and lived close to where I went to school at Christian Brothers College in Bulawayo.

There I purchased an ongoing sports business in the form of an indoor cricket centre where all and sundry came to play as well as participate in other sports like netball and mini soccer. Having bought this business, I then set up a PUMA retail sports store to entice my daughter Taryn to come and work and own a business of her own. The retail shop made money but not enough to give her the income I wanted her to have, so I relocated the store to the main street in Grafton where we traded for another year. Although the shop made more money, it was not making the profits I wanted it to make for my daughter, so I closed it down.

It was after the move to Grafton that I came to know about the problems Russell was having with his stepson, and the stepson's alleged abuse by his biological father, Dave Plankton. When I heard the story, I was furious and quickly agreed to help Russell and the youngster. Initially I was conscripted to drop the boy off for meetings with his father and then I set up surveillance on Plankton and set about trying to attempt to get to the truth. Little did I know where this would all lead.

William Russell Massingdon Pridgeon – My Early Life

I grew up at 14 Holdengarde Avenue, Hillside, Bulawayo, born into a new suburb, in a road full of young kids. My father's family were miners from England, who settled initially in New Zealand, before moving to South Africa and the Goldfields of the Witwatersrand, on the East Rand, around Daggafontein in the town of Springs.

My dad, Bill Pridgeon, was brought up on the mines near Johannesburg, in the 1930's. At that time there was still intense ill feeling between English and Afrikaans as a result of the Boer War: he had his nose broken four times in fights, and grew up the hard way. Essentially he was just an English-speaking schoolboy caught up in the bad blood that existed then between English and Afrikaans people. This was unfortunate because he held the Afrikaners in high regard and liked them; two of his best pals were Afrikaans.

He completed his senior school at Benoni Boys High and immediately enlisted in the South African Air Force as soon as he turned 17. He was selected for pilot training and flew in Egypt, Libya and Italy. My Grandfather fought in WW1: so successive generations were brutalised by war. After the end of hostilities my father went to the University of the Witwatersrand in Johannesburg as a returned serviceman and qualified as a quantity surveyor. He then and moved to what was then Southern Rhodesia in the early 1950's where he met my mother Kallah.

She had left South Africa because she was distressed by the

1 – The Early Years

Afrikaans-English antagonism, and in Rhodesia she found the harmony she was looking for – it was then a vibrant young country full of hope and opportunity where Afrikaners and English people got along well together: they were Rhodesians first, and Afrikaner or English second.

Once a year we travelled by train with my Mum to Matatiele in East Griqualand to visit her family. My maternal grandmother's family had arrived in the area as 1820 Settlers. Great-great grandfather, Trooper Thomas Green, rode with the Cape Mounted Rifles, and my great grandfather, Reverend Green, was the first Anglican priest ordained in the Grahamstown seminary. He then built 10 churches in East Griqualand parish, and I was baptised in the Matatiele one.

There is a family legend that he was at one of his outlying churches when the family heard of a marauding Pondo Impi coming their way, pillaging and murdering as they approached. The family, which included my grandmother Lizzie and her sister Freda, fled in their ox cart over the rolling hills but soon they saw the Impi in hot pursuit. They could not match the speed of their pursuers and were forced to look on helplessly as the marauders closed in. Much to their relief, the raiders passed them by but not before the Induna in command halted. Looking at my grandfather he shouted '*Umfundise*' – 'Learned One' – in respectful tone, and then set off about his bloody business.

My grandfather Wilfred and his brother Escort were articled to the legal firm of Coghlan and Welsh, who dealt with the Boer War reparations in the Cape. Wilfred spent much time in the concentration camps where the Boer families were incarcerated and wrote of what he saw. He moved to the warm dry air of Matatiele, East Griqualand for his health and there codified Native Law, writing

Seymour's 'Native Law in South Africa', which has been studied by every law student in South Africa since the 1930's. His Son, Seymour Massingham Seymour revised the book after his death.

My grandfather's brother married my grandmother's sister, which triggered the arrival of a huge tribe of Seymour cousins and second cousins. They were brash, argumentative, sometimes downright odd, but they were also fiercely loyal, and demanded high standards from all their family members. As a toddler, I remember walking the few hundred yards from my uncle's house to my grandparents' house with my mother. When I arrived at my grandparents' house I was admonished to walk road side of my mother – so to protect her – because this is what men were supposed to do. My uncle reinforced this by standing outside his house, watching us until we walked into the grandparents' house, to make sure my mum was safe.

Once, when I was very young, maybe five years old, I punched my cousin Pippa on the arm. It was not meant to hurt her, and she laughed when I did it, but after that, each one of my uncles spoke sternly to me, one after another, saying that this is not what we do: men do not hit women. Only cowards do that. My cousins also spoke to me about it. It had a lifelong effect on me.

Rhodesia was blessed with sunny skies and a temperate climate. There was no television in those days and the cinema was a rare treat. We spent much of our time outdoors and there was plenty of space. I had girls in all the nearby houses, so I played with girls as playmates, simply because they were there. The neighbourhood was very stable and safe. I started school on the same day as most of them, we went through school together, and I am still in contact with a few today.

Rhodesia was big-game hunting country, and my father was a keen outdoorsman. As a result I grew up wanting to follow in his

1 – The Early Years

footsteps and was desperate for a rifle. However, my parents were adamant that they were not going to raise any spoiled kids, so my pleas for a gun went unanswered for too long.

They eventually relented when I fell ill with measles and was unwell for a long time. My dad came home with a pellet gun, a Gecado 25 .177 calibre. I was in heaven. I used to hunt with my friend Dave Darwin, who was an equally keen lover of the outdoors, and we hunted every day in the bush, on Crown Land outside the city. Dave had a kindly uncle who passed on an ancient BSA .22-Long rifle. I was desperate to also have a .22 rifle in my hand and realised my only chance of this happening was to use my initiative: I read "Bevis" by Richard Jefferies, which gave excellent instructions on how to make a matchlock muzzle-loading gun out of steel pipe. I duly purchased a piece of steam pipe and set about making it. My friend Dave also made one and managed to buy saltpetre and sulphur to make the gunpowder. We burnt our own charcoal from firewood.

I had mine almost complete and was trying to fabricate the mechanism for the lock, when my mother became aware of my efforts and asked me if I intended to fire it. I answered that I certainly did. She then extracted a promise from me that if I never ever fired it, she would buy me a .22. I agreed immediately and so off we went to Mr. TJ. Otte's gun shop, and bought a Remington .22, which was astonishingly accurate. Dave's and my hunting adventures became more interesting. Pursuing our love of the outdoors and wanting to go up a level, we went on a survival camp in mid-October in the Matabeleland bush, which was witheringly hot, bone dry and devoid of game. We did not last long and went home with our tails between our legs.

Dave then left Bulawayo to live in Goromonzi, near the capital of Rhodesia Salisbury, as his headmaster father had been relocated, but he and I met up every school holiday. On one occasion his family invited me to Inyanga, in the Eastern Highlands. We heard there were trout there, and our imaginations were fired by the thought of catching one. We spent $2.50 each on a fishing license, and another $2.50 on a trout fly. This exhausted our very limited funds. We were dumbfounded when the trout failed to thrash the water to foam in an effort to eat our fly. After days of diligent fishing we hadn't had a bite. We felt we had been duped and were determined to obtain restitution. We collected grasshoppers all day and at dusk climbed over the high fence surrounding the trout hatcheries. Dave used a handline to haul in a good bag of trout from the well-stocked pond, which the family ate for breakfast.

Back home, my father was old school: he felt strongly that children should be seen and not heard and should entertain themselves away from the adults. As a result, my pleas to be included on one of his hunting outings were ignored until my mother intervened on my behalf and my dad begrudgingly agreed to take me along. In the field, my father shot a small antelope, a Duiker, disembowelling it in the process. He said I must gut it but did not give me a knife. I pulled the burst intestines out with my hands and cleaned the abdominal cavity out as best I could. I think this was some sort of test to see if I had the stomach for hunting – he might have been disappointed that I did not vomit or make a fuss. Eventually he sent one of the African guides to complete the task.

Later efforts with my dad were more successful. We went on another trip and were told to hunt along the riverbanks. We put up a Steenbok in a thicket, but Dave could not see it. The man who had been assigned to guide us, grabbed Dave's rifle with the intention of shooting it himself. Dave resisted, and a wrestling match ensued. I stepped out from behind them and shot the animal in the head.

1 – The Early Years

It was my first kill.

The wild remoteness of the bush was my refuge from the unpleasantness of daily life. I was a small, slight boy, and did not excel academically or at sport. In Rhodesia rugby and cricket were played and watched with religious fervour and I was useless, so I was on the margins. The bullying was relentless, and the floggings were frequent. I hated school and I remember spending the day before school term started in a sweat of fear. I saw boys punished for every possible infraction of the rules, but never for bullying, which went on under the teachers' noses.

On my first day in Latin class I witnessed the caning of a boy for the heinous crime of not doing homework. The extreme brutality shocked me, and I went to school after that in multiple pairs of underpants. Other teachers had their special instruments to inflict pain: one woman had a baseball bat, split down the middle to create a flat surface which she wielded with two hands to apply maximum force. The science teacher used a Bunsen Burner tube, reinforced by wire, the pain made me want to vomit. The PE teacher used his tennis shoes or 'takkies', with a five-yard run up: he would knock the boys off their feet each time. This brute was the Rhodesian weight-lifting champion. At times he would use hockey sticks, wielded two handed with a run up, knocking the boy down each time. He was known to give 14 strokes at a time. These experiences left me with a violent dislike of people who hurt children; I saw too many teachers enjoying inflicting pain, and it revolted me.

I couldn't see the point of school and only did enough to stay out of trouble. Still, I seemed to be in trouble constantly, and my parents were pretty tired of me. In an effort to improve my attitude they sent me to Outward Bound School to sort me out. It didn't work: when I came back I was still a right little arsehole, but a very fit little arsehole.

Brother John Pridgeon remembers: "My brother Russell was not my friend when we were boys. He meted out swift, and probably quite just and well-deserved corrective measures with his bare fists. It must be said that I can be very irritating! I soon learned not to do anything that might incur his wrath, as he took his parental/big brother role very seriously. And warnings? There were none. This often-punitive relationship sadly necessitated that (being allergic to pain) I avoided him and kept my distance."

On the way home from Outward Bound the train stopped overnight in Salisbury. I stayed with John and Joyce du Toit, John was an old air force buddy of my dad's. His wife Joyce fed me and talked about many things. While I was with her, an Alsatian dog walked up and put its head in my lap. I stroked it automatically and did not notice that Joyce had gone completely quiet. The dog left and she started to talk again, she said that the dog was notoriously vicious and would only let her son touch it, nobody else, ever. I mentioned that I had a way with animals. She said I should think about being a vet. This intriguing thought fired my imagination. It was of course far too late in my lackadaisical school career to start working, and there was no way I could gain admission to veterinary school with my mediocre school marks. I had to do a B.Sc. to gain admission.

After I had left school and was marking time before my National Service intake (123), an old friend of mine, Dave S, appeared for Sunday lunch. It was a common thing for soldiers to visit friends on Sundays in the hope of a meal. He was welcomed and fed with the very best we had. I had known him in school, and we had hunted together. His mother was a sadist, and Dave S would flee from the beatings with a sjambok and seek refuge with us. He was always given shelter, although my mum would always phone his family to

1 – The Early Years

let them know where he was. Dave S left school at 16 and joined the army, succeeding in joining the SAS. He suggested that I join the Army Medical Corps, and so I did, as did my brothers after me.

I was the only lad in my friendship group who volunteered to do military service before university. In those days, if you were accepted for university you were allowed to defer your National Service until after you had completed your course. At the time I was watching the political situation carefully and had noted how the duration of the National Service had increased from 4.5 months to 9 months as the war escalated.

On the designated day, my father drove me to Llewellyn Barracks outside Bulawayo and watched with unconcealed amusement as we were marched off in our 'civvies' holding our suitcases while trying to keep time.

As it turned out, I found the army training far preferable to school. While the training was uncompromisingly brutal it was a fair situation, the rules were clear, and everyone was in the same boat. Our Colour-Sergeant was a tough but fair man, and not without humour. While teaching us skirmishing to contact he told us: 'don't get shot, otherwise we will all have to learn to slow march.' A soldier who was discovered to have a dead fly in his locker was charged with keeping pets. Colour Riley was his name and I remember him as a good man. Looking back, I think us young Rhodesians were blessed in a way, as a result of having gone through that experience. It certainly helped me; it trained me to make the best of unpleasant situations and to endure adversity.

After basic training I did the MA3 (Medical Assistant Class III) training for the Rhodesian Army Medical Corps (1967 – 1980), gaining the exalted rank of corporal, where our responsibilities included:

- Command and control of all medical aspects in the Army and Air Force including advice on these matters.
- Conduct of training and upgrading of all medics in Rhodesian Army Medical Corps.
- Collection, treatment and, where necessary, evacuation of the sick and wounded.
- And our roles were:
- Treatment of the sick and wounded.
- Supply and replenishment of medical and dental stores and equipment.
- Promote health and. hygiene and to prevent disease by advice and inspection.
- Provide rehabilitation and convalescent facilities to members of the Security Forces.

I was sent off to the northeast border, with the Engineers, a very decent unit, who were remarkably kind to me. They were Territorials or Reservists, much older than me. I learned later that some of these men were among the many friends and people I knew who were killed in the Bush War.

I was kept on hand while they built a road in the Shamva district. One day, after some serious beer drinking, they told me to come along with them as they were going fishing. I was slightly bemused because there was not a rod to be seen. On the banks of the Shamva River I was surprised when the captain told me to strip off: I was to fetch the fish, he explained. This was not music to my ears because I could hear the hippo snorting just upriver and the banks were clearly marked with crocodile slides. As the last charge was thrown, the captain told me to jump in.

1 – The Early Years

"But Sir! What about the crocs?" I pleaded. With that he cocked his FN rifle and fired a magazine into the water on automatic. He was not too steady on his feet. I then stopped worrying about crocs and worried about getting shot. In I went with alacrity, scooped up all the stunned fish including a massive Tiger fish and back to camp we went for a delicious fish-supper. That was a day's fishing in the Rhodesian Army.

The latrines were just trenches dug into the ground, with a beam to sit on, and the flies were terrible. In an effort to discourage the flies, the engineers dumped a large amount of swimming pool chlorine on the piles of excrement. I learned in first year chemistry that this releases sodium hypochlorite which is highly reactive. This corrosive exhalation rose from the trench in concentrated form. The soldiers who used the latrine developed highly irritated florid rashes on the two moist areas of their dependent anatomy.

After time spent in the bush I was looking forward to some R&R in Salisbury but I was always turned around on the spot and told to put my kit on a truck and replenish my medical supplies for another deployment. My forwarding address became a number plate. My next billet wasn't so good, in a camp called Gutse, northeast of Sipililo, with an infantry company. The bush around there had been burnt, it was desolate, and boiling hot. I remember I drank 15 litres of water the first day and peed just the once. The flies were everywhere, small highly active flies, sitting on everything, crawling into everything. I would cut up my food with a fork while I waved the flies away with my other hand. When I stopped waving long enough to move the food into my mouth, there would be a fly on the food and I would eat it. As a medic I wasn't allowed to patrol, so the C.O. sat me in a large tree in the middle of camp as a lookout. I spent six weeks in the tree.

One chap came to me with sandworm; the only thing I had to treat it with was a freezing spray called ethyl chloride. I treated it gently, he came back and complained after a few days, I treated it a little more thoroughly; he came back and complained again, I gave it a very strong freeze. After that I could see him, from my perch in the tree, hobbling around the camp and showing everyone his blisters from my treatment. He is believed to be the only man ever to get frostbite in the Zambezi Valley in midsummer. He was not a happy man.

In all the months I was in the Valley I wasn't paid, my pay book never caught up with me, so my money was accumulating. My Corporals pay was $1.75 a day. When I was paid, I received over $200; it was a bonanza of unimagined wealth. In a way, the army showed me what I would be doing if I didn't work hard at university: It was a great motivator and lesson in life.

After discharge from my national service I made ready to go to university. I applied for a Bachelor of Science degree at the University of Natal in South Africa, with the intention of gaining entrance to veterinary school.

We left Bulawayo by train for the journey to Pietermaritzburg. On the platform I was introduced to Gordon and so developed a friendship that has lasted to the present day. He is a Christian Scientist and that interested me. After sitting in a tree for six weeks in the summer heat of the Zambezi Valley I had thought a lot about many things, including the spiritual questions that seem to beset the human race. My Mum had dragged us to church every Sunday, but Anglicanism just didn't seem to reach me on any level. I had absorbed the teachings of Christ, which I accepted on a very deep level, but the church as an institution and the rituals were lost on me. A major formative influence on my development was the Uncle

1 – The Early Years

Arthur books, which laid out a practical morality in a way a child could understand and accept. While I enjoyed the intellectual stimulation of Christian Science, it didn't engage me either. However I enjoyed talking to Gordon, he was a very moral man, seeing things in a very different way to me. He tried to live his life in an ethical way, and I admired that.

As it turned out, there was a very active and militant fundamentalist Christian presence at university. It troubled me that I did not see the fundamentalists living a moral life. It seemed to me that they were most interested in getting themselves to heaven, and their religious observances were based on self-interest. Later I learned about Buddhism, which attracted me because it taught respect for all life.

I had been at university for about six weeks, and I had a profoundly disturbed feeling. I did not know what caused it. Eventually I worked it out: for the first time in my life, there was no-one going out of their way to make my life unpleasant.

The academic work in the science faculty was quite gruelling. The truth is that my brain had never had to work at this level before, and I didn't have a clue what to do. I thought that if I could just work hard that would be enough. So I did. It wasn't satisfactory, and my mid-year results were atrocious. Chemistry 33%, Physics 22%, Zoology 36%, Botany 18%. Rocked by this reality, I worked even harder.

Slowly, I got into the swing of university: I grew my hair and bought Levi jeans, while becoming very left-wing and socially conscious. There was a formal programme of education during the first weeks of university to educate the students about the reality of apartheid.

That first year saw students at the University of Cape Town challenge the apartheid authorities on the steps of St Georges Cathedral where they were demonstrating for free education for blacks. People of colour were required to pay for their education including books and stationery, whereas white students got their books (and fees) for free in many cases. This demonstration turned violent when the police, for the first time, charged at white students after being continuously baited by a first-year student, Dirk Kemp. The following day the police lined up with dogs on campus at the bottom of the Jameson Hall stairs, and students were roughly carried off these steps in a confrontation with police.

A call went out to arrest the left-wing National Union of South African Students (NUSAS) president, Neville Curtis, who immediately skipped the country over the mountains into the independent enclave, Lesotho, and from there onto New Zealand. At the same

1 – The Early Years

time, the Students Representative Council (SRC) President, Geoff Budlender, a law student (who had changed degrees from medicine), was insulted in parliament by then Prime Minister John Vorster, who accused him of being a failed academic having switched degrees *because he couldn't cope with his medicine studies*. Budlender responded strongly, rejecting the insinuations with contempt. His sister Debbie was served with a banning order and placed under house arrest for five years. Today Budlender is one of the most senior legal experts in the country and the recipient of the International Bar Association (IBA) Pro Bono Award for 2021.

The St Georges Cathedral incident attracted worldwide attention and universities around the country joined in with demonstrations, including the University of Pietermaritzburg. It was an exciting time to try and rectify some of the ills and understand what the apartheid system was really about. We had no formal system of apartheid in Rhodesia, but it was not a fair and equitable society.

The Nationalist government responded by clamping down on dissent, using Banning Orders and embarking upon House Arrests. In solid opposition to the government was the Black Sash organisation which was very active. We admired those brave, silent women.

After examining the South African system closely, it was obvious to me that the Rhodesian system also had structural inequalities which were the cause of reasonable grievances by the Rhodesian blacks. I had to try and work out where the rights and wrongs were, in the context of the increasing polarisation of the black and white populations, the escalation of the war, and in confronting ethical and moral issues. I was obviously mindful of the fact that I had recently been a soldier acting in defence of the Rhodesian regime.

I don't remember much about the second half of my first year, apart from a tough and, I thought, hopeless struggle to pass exams. Astonishingly, I passed. We received the results in the post. Two out of the twelve students on the results paper passed all four subjects and I was one of them. I started to believe in miracles.

During the July 1973 vacation dad allowed me to take his old Land Rover on a trip to Gona re Zhou National Park, in south-east Rhodesia. Known as The Place of the Elephants, it is a beautiful wilderness area on the Mozambique border, and my time there was therapeutic.

Second and Third years at University of Natal Pietermaritzburg were easier. My brain became more functional. I learned how single-minded I could become. Passing became everything. Somehow, I lost sight of Vet school and refocused on medical school instead. I still had to pass with high marks and not fail anything. In the Pridgeon family you fail your varsity exams; you leave varsity, no debate.

Every vacation I was drawn back to the bush where I found so much peace of mind, but as the war in Rhodesia spread, trips into remote areas became more dangerous. Crossing the border into Botswana became a better option. The Nxai Pans were particularly beautiful with the arrival of the summer rainstorms. Most of my trips there were enjoyable, but the last trip was very unpleasant. The conflict in Rhodesia had spilled over into Botswana where, unbeknown to us, Joshua Nkomo's ZIPRA had several training bases, and we were harassed by Botswana Police from town to town, interrogated at length, searched at gunpoint repeatedly, locked up briefly and eventually fled into the bush. We were told by the station commander at Rakops that if we proceeded north we would come across a training base, and being white and in a Rhodesian number plated Land Rover, we *would* be killed!

1 – The Early Years

To my relief, I gained entrance into University of Cape Town Medical School. Second year medicine was extremely difficult; I passed, again by a miracle. As I became accustomed to the work, I started to enjoy Cape Town, diving for crayfish, walking Table Mountain and every other notable walk in the Cape. I bought a paddle-ski and spent every possible minute in the surf. Later I bought a windsurfer, just as they were becoming popular. I also spent a lot of time sailing dinghies and keelboats off the Cape. I determined that one day I was going to build a yacht of my own and sail around the world. This is still firmly on my bucket list.

Final year medicine was another highly demanding experience. During the year I read a book by Colin Fletcher: 'The Complete Walker', which extolled the virtues of solo hiking. I saved up and bought a decent rucksack, a down sleeping bag, and prepared to walk up the east coast.

To finally pass medicine in 1980 after so many years of intense struggle, against unlikely odds was exhilarating. I celebrated by buying a kayak and canoeing down the Orange River, from Augrabies Falls to Buitepos.

"Because we were not very close growing up in Bulawayo, I only really got to know Russ in my third-last year at the University of Cape Town," remembers his brother, John Pridgeon. "I was also studying medicine and he was in his second last year. I was 22, and he was 25 years old. I remember clearly bumping into him one day in a dark and dingy cafe on Main Street in Observatory, just below the UCT Medical School, where he lived in a fairly squalid digs with two other students. Russell was having his staple lunch: a pie, a cream bun and a Coke with zero nutritional value. He was painfully pale and thin, so I took it upon myself to ensure that every Saturday lunch time from then on, I cooked him his favourite meal – steak, egg and chips, something that we Pridgeon boys ate every night of our young Bulawayo lives – great Rhodesian fare! Actually, at that time Russ only lived about five minutes' walk from where I did, and I did not even know it. Prior to me adopting him on Saturdays, I think if I saw Russell half a dozen times in the previous five years we both lived in Cape Town, that was a lot. I remember he was a cheap date, two beers and I had to drive him home!"

After this, I made ready for the walk. I got a rescue-dog from the local pound: a small terrier type pooch, with a curly tail, and an undershot jaw. I named him Joey. My brother John dropped Joey, myself and my new girlfriend Pippa, with her dog Hilda, at Sir Lowry's Pass, and we walked into the forestry area and then along the coast, walking on pristine beaches, with the dogs running ahead.

Pippa had never hiked before, or even spent a night in a tent, so I took all the heavy gear to make sure she would cope. I used to think about that as I watched her strong ballerina's legs twinkling a mile ahead of me, while I trudged behind.

The beaches and the bush were beautiful, and I so enjoyed the solitude and the scenery. I was living on out-of-date dehydrated vegetables which I bought cheaply and in bulk from a company that was going out of business. It was light, and barely palatable, the dog ate the same as I did. It had an unfortunate effect on both of us, but happily we were in the open air. During the few times I was in a confined space with other people it created problems. I have a strong sense of social continence, but Joey did not. Nobody could believe that such a small dog could produce such terrible smells, so I received peculiar glances from everyone within half a kilometre of us.

I walked without a shirt, or a hat. I had two pairs of shorts and one shirt. My food was collected at post offices every three weeks;

1 – The Early Years

my rucksack weighed 80 lbs until I had eaten my way through the food. Unfortunately, I stepped off a sand dune and hyper-extended my right knee, which I had injured parachuting, and again in an incident involving a girl and a cockroach – another story for another time. As a result, I struggled with knee pain for most of the walk, and this was essentially the reason I finally called my Cape to Cairo stroll a day.

At one point, I was blown off the beaches by a violent cold front that created gale force winds for much longer than a week. I found a path off the beach after struggling for days and walked into a caravan park I had not expected to be there. The caravan rent was more than I could afford, but the owner came around with a thermos full of delicious soup with a lamb chop at the bottom of it. The taste of that soup has not left me after 40 years.

The Transkei coast was a lovely walk, with rolling hills and many river crossings. I had obtained a very old blow up lilo on which I lay, with my rucksack on my back, paddling with my arms, to cross the rivers. I had forgotten Joey. He disagreed with my plan that he should swim across unaided, and tried to climb on the lilo, puncturing it with his claws. It sank and we bobbed across the river together. The next river was known for its sharks. I gathered a collection of logs together and tied them together with all the twine I was carrying. As the collection of logs got to deeper water they rolled into their comfortable floating positions. My knots did not keep them together, and I ended up bobbing across the river again. Joey was swept into the surf at the river mouth; I rescued him in difficult circumstances. He was never going to become a surfer. There was a hotel on the riverbank; all I could think about was drinking a beer. I bought one, which tasted terrible, and listened to two chaps at the bar talking excitedly about the shark circling a collection of logs which was floating in the surf at the river mouth.

I kept walking: this journey was over 1,000 kms by road but many more by foot, eventually reaching Coffee Bay, at which stage I fell ill, with fever, headaches and profound malaise. I then hitch hiked to my Uncle Gordon Seymour in Matatiele. I noticed I had enlarged painful glands under my left arm, and a dark scab on the left shoulder, an eschar: I had rickettsiosis, or African Tick Fever. Uncle Gordon gave me antibiotics and I was fit to leave in a few days. I needed to rest my knee and so I visited my grandmother in Springs, Eastern Transvaal. She gave me an air ticket to visit my Mum in Bulawayo.

I arrived just in time to be present when Joshua Nkomo's ZIPRA Army tried to take over Bulawayo. This was during the time of an uneasy cease-fire called by the warring parties at the end of the Rhodesian war. By this time Robert Mugabe was in power, but the Matabele people were very unsettled. A powerful supporter of Robert Mugabe was then Australian PM Malcom Fraser. Many Rhodesians over the years questioned the self-righteous posturing of Australian politicians, pointing out that the African indigenous population increased dramatically under white rule, while the opposite happened in Australia, where not so long ago aborigines had been cruelly assaulted, their children raped and abused, and even had a bounty on their heads until the early 1900's.

Nkomo's troop carriers were ambushed by white-led, disciplined troops of the Rhodesian African Rifles (RAR) just down the road from our house and destroyed by Napalm Rifle Propelled Grenades. The combatants then adjourned to the Entumbane Township north of Bulawayo. I stood on the kopje on our property and watched the tracer bullets arcing through the sky for several nights.

1 – The Early Years

Fully recovered, I returned to the walk at Coffee Bay, and made my way north. I had decided not to walk in populous areas, so I hitch-hiked to Pietermaritzburg and stayed with my Uncle Jim and Aunt Doreen Seymour while I waited for a friend to join me for a traverse of the Drakensberg Range. He was late, we ascended at Bushman's Nek and as we walked I learned that his wife was very unhappy to see him go, and that he felt terrible being there. The trip was abandoned, and I returned to Pietermaritzburg and managed to get myself an unpaid berth on a zoological expedition to Kosi Bay. That was a lot of fun.

When it was over it was time to return to Bulawayo and start my medical internship. My walk had allowed me time to collect myself and reassess my commitment to medicine. I started my medical career free of the complete exhaustion that follows medical students from final exams into a punishing internship. I was determined to be the best doctor possible, and managed to keep that goal in mind through 40 years of medical practice, where I chose the hardest path time and time again.

Mpilo Hospital in Bulawayo was far friendlier and more relaxed than Groote Schuur, and I enjoyed it far more. I met an Englishman there, Stephen Jennison, who was an exercise nut. He challenged me to a run up a small hill. I gave him a run for his money, being fairly fit from the walk, so he adopted me as his exercise buddy, starting gym at 6 am, doing lunch time exercises in the physics gym and then a run in the evening.

Three of us went on a canoe trip up the Okavango Swamps. It was an eight-day trip, Steve and Edward did the catering, we ran out of food on day three. We ate once a day after that. Steve and Edward went fishing; caught about 40 fish each night, broiled them on a frame of sticks over the fire, and ate them to the bones. We awoke early each morning with raging hunger pangs. It was a great trip, with three lunatics paddling frantically all day. Steve and Edward were good companions. They sang English university drinking songs. I remember feeling rather provincial in their presence. I had three T shirts made, with "OKAVANGO WEIGHT WATCHERS SOCIETY" on the front.

Back in Bulawayo the political changes had brought little joy and the atmosphere was not friendly. The Police were antagonistic, and the foreign exchange allowance was pitiful. I decided I did not want to make my life in Zimbabwe, and left Bulawayo for South Africa with $40 in my pocket. I had a single suitcase. Refugees have left with more.

My overwhelming ambition was to build a yacht and sail the world. I would invest seven years of my life in this foolish endeavour, during a time of high inflation, where I was being paid a very modest sum for 120 hours of work a week. I abandoned the boat and the dream when I left for New Zealand.

After graduating I committed myself to practicing medicine in black communities where I could be of best use to the poor and worked in the most violent townships during a time of tumult in the country. The hours and conditions of work were extreme, and I would work 100-140 hours a week: unsustainable

The conditions were poor and the work was very demanding. Most of these hospitals worked at 20% of their proper staffing levels, and the after-hours duties were very tough; 100 hour weeks were considered quiet, 140 hours a week was a bad week.

A normal day might start working in outpatients, seeing all comers, and either treating them, or admitting them to the various wards, or sometimes sending them straight to surgery. Very ill patients were

1 – The Early Years

sent to the Resuscitation Unit before surgery. At other times we might be sent to the Obstetric Unit or the Operating Theatres, to do surgery or anaesthetics. It was very possible to rotate through all of these areas in a single day, the work was extremely varied.

The clinical teaching was almost non-existent; the rule was: 'see one, do one, teach one'. The pressure of work was enormous, and everyone was working at their extreme limit of competence. It was not uncommon to do 15 Caesarean Sections a day, often alone, doing the spinal anaesthetic and then the Caesar, resuscitating the baby if required. I could do a Caesar in 12 minutes, with good assistance. Despite the harsh environment, I enjoyed the feeling of universal competence; It was excellent training, but a very poor option as a long-term career. It is for this "thrown in at the deep end" reason that African Doctors are so sought after elsewhere in the world. If you do not figure out how to help them, they will die. You are their last hope.

I would drive past roadblocks, burning cars and the scenes of bombings, on my way to and from the hospital. At times I saw 250 patients a day. It seemed that every patient I saw was bleeding.

The apartheid laws said that doctors were legally obliged to report gunshot wounds to Police. We knew that the SA Police would shoot peaceful law-abiding people indiscriminately as they drove past in their trucks. Victims of these senseless illegal shootings were then prosecuted for being shot. Every doctor had to decide whether to participate in the evil of apartheid or whether to describe these injuries as something other than gunshot wounds. Apartheid was the law, but it was morally wrong: it was an appalling evil, and I had to come to terms with the fact that the law is not necessarily always in the right. This applies as much in Australia today as it did in South Africa in the 1970s.

I met my wife Hilda while I was working in Port Elizabeth. She was a teacher, an anti-Apartheid activist, and involved in black literacy and many other anti-apartheid activities. The communal house we lived in, with other activists, was frequently raided by the security police. Our phones were tapped (like mine is in Australia today), and the people in the house were arrested frequently and interrogated. My wife and I fled a day ahead of mass arrests and became fugitives. Our friends were arrested and spent a year or more in jail, often in solitary confinement. We managed eventually to leave South Africa for a long period of time.

When we returned, we lived in the Transkei, an autonomous apartheid homeland, where security police could not find us. We stayed in Port St Johns, where I worked as a GP, in private practice. I worked in two small rooms, without water or electricity. It was a salutary experience for any left-wing liberal to be confronted by the greed and brutality of black community leaders towards illiterate tribesmen. I realised that Africa's problems were not only across the racial divide.

After two years we left, on the day of the election results when the left wing Progressive Federal Party was replaced by the far-right wing Conservative Party as the official parliamentary opposition.

I determined that I would not stay in South Africa to witness another war and made plans to leave. My wife was deeply opposed to leaving as she regarded South Africa as her home. But I could not see myself surviving hospital practice working 100-140 hours a week, so we packed our bags for "Down Under".

My perspective was always coloured by the terrible bloodshed that I was forced into contact with every working day. So we left when things looked very dark I did not foresee that an enlightened

1 – The Early Years

man like FW de Klerk would release Mandela and that Mandela would be the enlightened leader he proved to be.

I was not committed to RSA in the same way Hilda was, I was already a refugee from Zimbabwe. Why go from the frying pan into the fire?

CHAPTER 2 – THE ARRIVAL

Russell arrives in New Zealand

We left for New Zealand in 1988, which was a bad choice, with my wife in a state of anger and grief, from which our marriage never recovered.

We arrived in Riverton, 30 kilometres west of Invercargill. A small fishing town, it is one of the oldest settlements on South Island. Nearby, Taramea Bay provided safe swimming, excellent surf spots and we often saw dolphins swimming up the estuary for feeding. This made life better, and we looked forward to those summer days.

Hilda hated NZ and was extremely unhappy there, blaming me (reasonably) for being there, and I was working too hard to provide her with any support. We both suffered from SADS: seasonal affective disorder.

Of course it was a bit of a shock coming from hot, tropical Zululand, to the wet, damp, cold winters and short summers, but also to the green rolling hills. It took time to adjust, especially for Hilda, but the folk were just like back home; genuine people who would do a deal with a handshake and welcome you into their homes. We felt safe and secure from the memories of the Rhodesian war and South Africa in turmoil, to a land of peace, tranquillity, and the rule of law. The immigration requirements meant that I had to practice in a rural area for 10 years, but I enjoyed being in the country, so that was no issue for me.

2 - The Arrival

Rural general practice was less gruelling than African hospital medicine, but relentless, and with hindsight I realise that I swapped one ideology; that of being Dr Albert Schweitzer 'Mark II' in rural Africa, to become a Traditional Rural GP in southern NZ. How we become entrapped by our ideas of ourselves.

Seeking an ethical investment, I was struck by the phenomenal growth of trees in the volcanic earth, high rainfall and high UV radiation of New Zealand. I bought a 240-acre farm and planted 100,000 trees, doing my own forestry maintenance, thinning, pruning, and pest control.

I faced an intense spiritual and moral dilemma when every bird and animal in the area damaged or killed the seedling trees I had planted. As a devout Buddhist I had to decide on abandoning the enterprise or modifying my beliefs. Eventually I came to terms with the reality of culling the introduced possums, rabbits, hares and deer, and returned to my hunting life, which I had abandoned during my year in the army. After over 20 years the trees were huge, and to walk beneath them was an intense spiritual experience, like being in a cathedral.

My work life was all-consuming, with the demands of medical practice occupying my life from sunrise to late at night. Every woman and child in Riverton had a better call on my time than my wife and child. By the end of my time in NZ my son was a stranger, and my wife was lost to me. Nothing lasts forever, except regret. There were many difficult experiences; I found the deaths of children hardest to cope with. When I returned to Riverton after leaving, I always visited the graveyard to stand before these little graves, seeing their faces, reliving their deaths.

So much sadness, but there were also good memories: meeting Rebecca at age 18 months, with her Mum desperately trying to care for her. I learned to admire, then respect this great person, and then her husband, who became one of my closest friends, as we worked together to keep Rebecca alive: she had a life expectancy of 2-3 years, she died aged 18, having never spoken a word, yet drawing many dozens of people towards her to be present in the atmosphere of love that surrounded her. I had emigrated to Australia by then. I drove from Grafton to Brisbane meaning to attend her funeral but didn't have the courage to board the plane.

One day, while still in New Zealand, we received the clinical notes of a patient moving to the area, which spoke of an extremely angry and abusive man. I was the first to see him, after someone had knocked him off his motorbike. He was incandescent with rage, I did my best to mollify him, spending an inordinate amount of time listening to his rages. A known miscreant and drug user, he rattled around Riverton, abusing and threatening everyone he encountered. Eventually he came to police attention, they wrote to me asking whether he was fit to own or possess a firearm. Without divulging any clinical detail, I said he was not. He then made a complaint to the medical authorities, asking that I be severely punished. I was the subject of a medical disciplinary process that took much longer than a year, at the end of which I was found guilty of professional misconduct.

"When Russell, was found guilty of patient-doctor confidentiality breech by the New Zealand Medical Council in 2000, I think it was one of the lowest points of his life," writes brother John Pridgeon. "This was a betrayal that really hurt him."

The whole process was catastrophic to me; I could not comprehend the prosecution and became profoundly depressed. After reading the dishonest and slanderous account of the findings against me I wrote to every single doctor in New Zealand, laying out the

2 - The Arrival

situation. I received 8-12 phone calls an hour from doctors all around New Zealand, as well as hundreds of supportive letters. It was an odd experience to feel the depression that had entombed me, falling away, hour by hour, until, by the end of the day I was completely well. I returned the many cheques sent to me to help pay my legal bills.

It was one of many evil and distressing experiences that I have had in my life that I regard as gifts, sent to me to give me insight and understanding into the circumstances of others, so that I might learn empathy and pity. But it destroyed my enjoyment of medicine for years, and finally made me determined to leave general practice and New Zealand. I studied Acupuncture and Musculoskeletal Medicine as a way of doing so.

I had become active in medical politics in New Zealand, opposing the ideological moves by the government to privatise the public health system and gut the resources allotted to rural GP's. To do this, the government had to discourage use of the public health system and force people to get private health insurance and use the private sector. The waiting lists became interminable, the suffering and neglect of the patients on the waiting list was horrible. My patients were dying while they waited for surgery. One of them, Colin Morrison, was a young man in his 40's, a hard-working farmer, who developed angina, and had to wait for 11 months before he could even be evaluated by a specialist. After 18 months he was found to have a 98% blockage of his main coronary artery: he booked for coronary bypass surgery, but his surgery was years away (in Australia he would not have been allowed to leave the hospital and would have been given emergency surgery).

I went on local radio to plead with Bill English MP, Minister for Health. I was ignored. Colin died and I went on TV calling for Mr. English's resignation. This was a poor career move for me, and when

I sought to practice Acupuncture and Musculoskeletal medicine, I was denied ACC and General Medical Subsidy; as a result I could not earn a living and was forced to emigrate.

Russell arrives in Australia

It was a relief to emigrate to Australia in 2001, the light was healing. Australia had similar immigration requirements for doctors which meant I was again expected to work in a rural area for ten years.

I worked first in Merriwa (upper Hunter Shire, New South Wales), re-entering General Practice reluctantly. My life there was just more of the same rural General Practice that I had done for decades: working all day and on call all night, and weekends.

The doctor who was employing me was exhausted after doing the same for 10 years. As soon as he realised that I could *speaka da eengleesh*, he went on long holidays, leaving me in charge of the general practice and the hospital. Again, although I was sole parenting my son, I hardly saw him. Hilda arrived in Australia months later. I fetched her at Sydney airport on 9/11: the airport TVs were showing looped videos of the planes crashing into the twin towers. We tried to start again, but our relationship was too damaged. After nine months of this I looked for other employment and landed up in Grafton.

One of the other doctors left, and within a few months I became the practice principal. The work was much easier and I refused any work that gave me after-hours obligations. I worked hard to re-establish my relationship with my son and was rewarded by a renewed closeness. My recreation included gardening, fixing up old Series-One Land Rovers, bushwalking and hunting.

I was feeling much happier about life in this pretty town, of 20,000 people, on the Clarence River with blazing jacaranda trees, hot summers and plenty of rain. Behind the town, green rolling hills, waterfalls, and not too far from the beautiful beaches of Byron Bay.

Debbie and Christopher

My life was set to change in many ways when, in 2008 Debbie and I were married, and her five-year old son Christopher came into our home. She had fallen in love with Dave Plankton, who lived in the Byron Shire, and owned a 40-acre property. After a four-month affair she found herself pregnant, after which Plankton became abusive, such that Debbie fled to her parents' farm in Grafton, whereupon she brought Christopher to see me. I had previously treated her parents. She went back to Plankton a few times; eventually she left him and ended up marrying me in 2008.

A court decision in 2008 gave the father unsupervised contact time (a week of shared care initially, and later every second weekend and half of the school holidays). After this contact began, Christopher changed from a happy thriving child to one who was anxious and distressed, particularly around contact times. Initially we thought this was due to Christopher missing his mother, and possibly due to some unpleasantness from his father. Christopher also developed a disordered bowel habit, and abdominal pain, which was we thought must be due to unsanitary living conditions in his father's dwelling.

After an extended school holiday stay with his father in January 2010, Christopher's behaviour became grossly abnormal: He developed markedly distressed behaviours with frequent nightmares, crying in his sleep, tooth grinding, bedwetting (at age six: after he had been dry for years), marked insomnia, usually still awake at 11pm, afraid to go to bed, afraid to go to sleep because of the nightmares, night terrors, he would throw himself out of bed during his nightmares, we would hear the bump, and go and put him back to bed.

He became unable to leave his mother's side, following her around the house as she did the housework. He developed marked school aversion; getting him into his school uniform each day and off to school was an absolute trial. He refused to go to school by bus as he had previously and every day. Debbie would have to drive him into town, and push him into the classroom, to get him into year one. We then discovered he had learning difficulties; his school performance dropped off markedly and his school reports reflected his distress. This was despite him being a highly intelligent and articulate child, with an excellent grasp of complex concepts and an advanced vocabulary. He became suicidal, telling us he did not want to live. Although we did not understand it at the time, these symptoms are universally accepted as classical presenting signs of child abuse.

Debbie asked him what happened to him, Christopher said he couldn't remember, we were beside ourselves with anxiety. To address the problem we took him to psychologists (Chris Collyer from Grafton, and Sacha Rombouts from Pathways in Brisbane), who dealt with his school aversion, and this helped with this problem, but many of his trauma symptoms remained.

In July 2010 Christopher returned from time spent with his father and complained to Debbie that he had a bleeding bottom. He would spend extended periods in the toilet, using reams of toilet paper. Only later did he tell us that it was because his bottom was so sore that it was impossible to clean it normally. As the long Christmas holidays of 2010/11 loomed Christopher's anxiety worsened again. He began to disclose, little by little, his abuse; being punched in the solar plexus with a closed fist, being smothered in a blanket, being urinated on, having his anus washed 'in a yukky way', with his father laughing while he did it. Christopher said that his father had told him that this was their 'big secret'. In December 2010 he drew graphic pictures, depicting his father's abuse. Children, even with their vivid imaginations, simply do not know enough to make this stuff up.

We could not understand why anyone would urinate on a child, but after Googling 'urination on victims' we learnt about 'urolagnia', a 'paraphilia' or sexual deviancy in which a person obtains sexual arousal or gratification from the sight or smell of urine, or the sight or action of urination on another person. Later we would learn that this is relatively common perversion and that children commonly mistake urine for semen.

In light of all this, we contravened the court orders and did not send Christopher to his father for the impending holidays in December 2010. A Recovery Order was then taken out by the father's solicitor. This was highly irregular, taken out in the local Magistrates Court instead of the Family Court, with no imminent threat to the child's safety, issued *ex parte*, where Debbie had no opportunity to explain her actions. All this during the Christmas vacation, when legal advice was unobtainable. As a result, Debbie was obliged to leave our home with Christopher, pursued by the Federal and NSW Police. Subsequently our house was searched repeatedly, daily or twice daily, while she was a fugitive for several weeks.

Debbie reported Christopher's disclosures to the Department of Child Services, and on 24 December 2010 we went together to the Grafton Police station where the Domestic Violence Liaison Officer (DVLO) took our statement and advised us that the case would be referred to the Juvenile Investigation Response Team. Much to our dismay, we were advised that the level of offending was not serious enough to fall within their purview.

Christopher was eventually interviewed by a detective, who determined that 'there was no criminality involved' in the urination and anal 'washing' and that punching a child to the ground fell within the limits of normal parental discipline. He told us that the father would be spoken to about the bottom washing and the 'peeing' in the shower and told by NSW Police that this behaviour would have to stop. He said that if it continued that this would show 'criminal intent', and that Police would then prosecute. The abusive behaviour continued; no prosecution has ever happened.

We discovered later that the DVLO had sabotaged the entire brief: they determined that Debbie was presenting with 'Munchausen's Syndrome by Proxy'[8]. This was a bizarre diagnosis that originated from a policeman without any formal psychological training! As a medical practitioner I have never seen or heard of a patient with this diagnosis, and even though I have been a GP for 25+ years, a Fellow of the Royal Australian College of General Practitioners, with particular training in mental health, I would never consider myself competent to make a diagnosis of a mental illness as rare, as controversial and as pejorative as this. At the Interim Hearing the father's solicitor also alleged that Debbie was presenting a case of Munchausen's Syndrome by Proxy, and that Christopher's behaviour was due solely to the mother's mental illness affecting him.

The Police then defied our subpoena (and the subpoena of the Independent Children's Lawyer) and withheld the tape of the Police Interview with Christopher for the interim hearing, thus depriving us of our only direct evidence.

The Federal Magistrate said it was good for children to have clean bottoms, that people commonly urinated in the shower, that it was unlikely that Christopher could have been punched in a public place.

---

8   Munchausen syndrome by proxy is a mental illness and a form of child abuse. The caretaker of a child, most often a mother, either makes up fake symptoms or causes real symptoms to make it look like the child is sick.

2 - The Arrival

She then ordered ongoing unsupervised contact with the father, who continued his abusive behaviours.

Christopher became extremely averse to going with his father for weekends; he absolutely refused to get into the car to go to school on contact days. We were forced by The Family Court order to send him back to his father, under threat of losing him to Plankton full time if we did not comply. In that event we would have had no way to protect or support him. I was between a rock and a hard place, but I felt I was complicit in following an order that would result in further harm being done to a child I was responsible for. I have never recovered from this or forgiven myself. I have never been able to forget or forgive my part in Christopher's abuse. The experience of transporting this terrified child, crying, screaming, sweating and shivering with fear, to his father for unsupervised contact, was one of the worst experiences of my life.

Christopher made further disclosures in July 2011 that his father had in fact inserted his finger into his anus, and that his bottom bled afterwards. Later in 2011 he also explained that sometimes his father's penis was erect, and that the urine was sometimes yellow and sometimes white. He also revealed that his father's breathing changed to 'faster and deeper'.

After Christopher's disclosure about the digital penetration there was a formal JIRT interview. They advised that they did believe him, but that he was too young to testify in open court due to the adversarial nature of the cross-examination. They were concerned that his evidence was 'contaminated' because he had spoken of his abuse to family and friends, and because Debbie and I had spoken to him about his abuse. As we have seen so often before and since, the authorities will use any excuse not to prosecute. We explained that after Christopher's initial disclosures in late 2010 we expected support and protection from further abuse, this did not happen, and we were forced by the courts to facilitate further contact with his abuser and send this child for further abuse. So we had no choice but to help Christopher help himself: we used Prof Brigg's book: "Teaching Children to Protect Themselves" as a way of helping Christopher to understand that no-one has a right to abuse him, and that it is absolutely wrong for anyone to do what his father had done to him. We also made it plain to Christopher that he should tell as many people as possible, because the more people who believed him, *the safer he would be*.

The father was interviewed and denied any abuse, he denied urinating on Christopher at any time, denying even showering with him since infancy, saying only that Christopher had urinated on him. The investigation was terminated directly after this. (Interestingly the father later changed this testimony several times, eventually admitting in court to showering with him, and some urination.) Debbie was described by the JIRT team in their report as 'emotionally and psychologically abusive'. We were advised by the attending Police Officer that it is 'not a crime under the Crimes Act to urinate on a child'. Despite Christopher's direct disclosures to these Police Officers, he was given no protection. They said they were unable to interfere with the proceedings of the Family Court.

This is actually not true, but despite this they refused to make any recommendations; they refused our request to take out an AVO and left Christopher completely at the mercy of his abuser. An AVO or Apprehended Domestic/Personal Violence Order is an order from Police and/or the court prohibiting certain behaviour with the aim of to protecting the Person in Need of Protection. The father's solicitor has represented this as proof of the father's innocence and has sought to have Christopher removed from his

2 - The Arrival

mother, with sole custody given to his father.

As our nightmare continued, it became absolutely clear to us that to all intents and purposes it was practically impossible to prosecute a family member who is a child sexual abuser in Australia. We began to understand why the appalling statistics about child sexual abuse are a reality in Australia today. From the best research available here and overseas we know that:

Only 30 abused children per 1,000 will disclose to anyone in their lifetimes. Of those who disclose, 10% will get a prosecution, 10% of those will get a conviction. It is also reported that 98% of child sexual abusers are known to the victim and only 2% of cases involve strangers. One girl in three will undergo contact sexual abuse before the age of 18, as will one boy in six. The real question one asks oneself after considering the above is: why is there this culture of complete disbelief about something that is so dreadfully common?

We sought help from Child Protection organisations and became involved with them, eventually using our experiences to assist and support others. We quickly learnt that our experiences, as traumatic as they were, represented the mild end of the scale. Many protective parents had lost their children altogether with no contact, or with supervised contact orders.

We learnt of the 'Bravehearts dossier cases' where the Family Courts had removed abused children from their protective parents and given custody to the abusive parent. We realised that what we had undergone was part of huge problem, where there was a systematic process of trafficking children to their abusers, perfectly hidden by the secrecy of the Family Court. As the Chief Justice, Diana Bryant, has repeatedly pointed out: the Family Court of Australia does not have the expertise or the resources to investigate child sexual abuse, so when the Police and Child Protection Authorities refuse to act, they create the perfect crime: Child sexual abuse cannot be prosecuted, the child is effectively trafficked by the authorities who are tasked with protecting him, for sexual abuse.

Bravehearts founder Hetty Johnson was regarded as one of Australia's foremost child protection advocates fighting for the rights of victims of childhood sexual assault. She called them the 'New Stolen Generation'.

This case was 'Case 1' of Abbeys Project which was a Discussion Paper written by Bravehearts that highlights the failings of the Family Law System. Published in June 2016, the Paper puts forward 30 recommendations, the first being that a Royal Commission is established to scrutinise the failed Family Law System. In the report, Christopher was called John, Debbie was called Sarah, Plankton was called Rob. This case was withdrawn from Abbeys Project after reference to it was made by the Australian Anti-paedophile Party on the AAPP Facebook page and Plankton made a complaint.

Christopher was again forced into continuing unsupervised contact with his father in 2011. When Debbie or I were present at the handovers we were blamed for Christopher's extreme reluctance to go with his father. The father's solicitor demanded that we should stay away from handovers. On one occasion in June 2011 Christopher was being collected from Westlawn Public School on Friday afternoon by his father and his father's male friend. As they were taking him to their car, Christopher wrenched his hands out of their grasp, tore his school bag off his father's back, and ran to the school library.

He disclosed his abuse to the principal, who sought advice from the Education Department. Directly after this, she attempted to

2 - The Arrival

hand Christopher over to his father. Christopher absolutely refused to go with his father, nor his father's friend, despite intense coercion. He stayed in Grafton and avoided abuse that weekend.

The father's solicitor and the Independent Children's Lawyer (ICL) together applied to the court, without Debbie being advised or being allowed to make a submission, to bring the trial forward from April/May 2012 to 1 February 2012. They also transferred the subpoena documents relating to the hearing from Brisbane to Lismore, where they both worked. Debbie was then prevented by the Lismore court staff from having any access to these documents. As a self-representing mother, how was she supposed to prepare her case? While the documents were in Brisbane she was allowed free access to them.

Debbie became ill in the weeks before the hearing, with a suspicious tumour on her left ovary that required urgent surgery to treat what appeared to be a malignancy. Her application for adjournment of the hearing was opposed by both solicitors, who applied to the Family Court Judge to hold the hearing without Debbie, who was in hospital recovering from the surgery of the previous day. Fortunately this was denied. The two solicitors then assured the judge that they would only need two days for the hearing which was set down for 28 March 2012.

At the hearing the father's solicitor argued that Christopher had been coached by his mother to say untrue things about his father. As before, not one shred of evidence or proof was offered to support this assertion – and none was requested by the Judge. This is because it never happened, and they all knew it.

Despite all the corroborative evidence about Christopher's traumatised behaviours that all indicated the child sexual abuse stated in my affidavit, Debbie's affidavit, and Debbie's daughter's affidavit (who was staying with us in 2011, and directly witnessed Christopher's distress and trauma), Plankton's solicitor and the ICL joined forces to seek orders that Christopher would live solely with his father, and that he should not have any contact with his mother for 12 months, thereafter Debbie should only be allowed supervised contact. It is easy to realise that if the mother's contact is supervised, then the child cannot disclose further abuse. This is a common practice of the Family Court and is highly protective of abusive parents.

At the hearing Debbie was cross-examined for two and a half days, I was cross-examined for one day; the father was cross-examined for less than half a day. Who was the criminal here? The audio and audio-visual evidence of Christopher's interview with the Police/*JIRT/DOCS* was withheld by the NSW Police in defiance of our subpoena for the third time; only by the direct intervention of the judge was it couriered up in time for the final day of the hearing. This was the first time we had been allowed to see it. The experience of seeing Christopher clearly and consistently disclosing his abuse was a harrowing time for me.

While we waited for the verdict and directives from the judge, Christopher was again ordered into contact with his father. He was ordered to have four hours supervised contact at See Park in Grafton each Sunday. We made a decision to have a private investigator witness and record the contact, because the judge had ordered a disabled female girlfriend of his as the supervisor (I had watched her laugh while we were viewing Christopher's videotaped disclosures in the JIRT interview).

For the first time we were able to have recorded direct evidence of Plankton's abusive behaviour towards his son. This man has always convincingly portrayed himself as a loving and caring father, whose son loved him, and loved to be with him. His friends and supporters wrote glowing affidavits supporting this.

The video evidence clearly showed Christopher's constant aversion to his father's presence. He was observed running away repeatedly and being hunted down by his father and friends, at every contact. It shows Christopher move away every time his father approaches him, it shows the father's violence to his son, throwing him into the back of a car, leaving finger bruises from the force of his grip. It also shows the supervisor, who, despite advising the judge that it was not the case, appearing to be in an affectionate relationship with Plankton. Also shown was another friend, Lindy Waterman: a vocal supporter of Plankton's, who I had seen laugh while watching Christopher explain his torment.

Despite our best efforts, much of the violence against Christopher was not recorded because it occurred out of sight of the investigator's video camera, but the videos exposed their vile falsehoods for what they are. As a result, the judge was persuaded to accept Christopher's version of events, and henceforth Dave Plankton was only allowed supervised access to Christopher and Debbie was awarded Sole Parental Responsibility. My stepson was at last safe from ongoing abuse.

This was a huge relief, and it should be stated that it is exceptional for a protective parent to gain custody of an abused child. Far more commonly, the Family Court of Australia gives custody to the abusive parent and the protective parent is only allowed supervised contact.

Despite the ruling, Christopher remained very distressed by ongoing contact with his abuser, and eventually the courts recognised this and a 'No Contact Order' was brought against David Plankton. Christopher was finally free of fear and able to live a normal life.

It is important to remember, intra-familial child sexual abuse is a crime of secrecy; the crimes are committed in the privacy of the family home, behind closed doors, and if the child's disclosures are disbelieved then it creates the perfect crime. No thanks to the police, we were indeed fortunate to obtain this evidence.

Incidentally 'coaching' or 'training'[9] as it is called in Queensland, has been studied repeatedly, in Australia and overseas. The results are remarkably similar, from country to country, and within the Family Court and outside of it, between 2-5% with females, and a higher rate with males where 'coaching' is actually in play. So when the courts or the child protection services accept coaching as a defence against accusations of child sexual abuse, by simple arithmetic, they traffic 95%+ of children back to their abuser.

As a divorced man with a son, I am well aware what it is like to miss out on a son's childhood. I am strongly of the opinion that all children, boys and girls too, need contact with their fathers, and other good men, to assist with their normal childhood development. I am a strong proponent of the men's movement; I am proud of men's achievements and their contribution to the world. But this is not a gender issue, it is a child safety issue, no good man or woman can choose to ignore child sexual abuse.

I have been an unwilling witness and sometime participant in this unpleasantness, having been obliged to protect my ex-wife Debbie and Christopher from Plankton's abusiveness many times.

---

9   When a parent deliberately coaches the child to tell lies about the other parent, in an effort to alienate the other parent and influence the court outcome.

2 - The Arrival

As I was drawn deeper into this developing situation, I had excellent reason to examine the issue from all sides: it has cost me dearly – I have spent in the region of $250,000 in legal fees, and much more through lost days at work, in court, doing affidavits, and taking Christopher to and from contacts. It would be fair to say that my involvement in Christopher's ghastly ordeal devastated my life for years. I have examined the situation minutely, seeking any indication of the alleged coaching, so that I would have reasonable grounds to honourably withdraw from this awful obligation. I have found none.

What I have personally witnessed is Christopher's extreme distress, and I have heard his disclosures first hand. I am absolutely convinced, owing to my direct personal experience of living with this child, drawing on my experience as a parent, as a mature man, and as a doctor of 36 years, that this child has undergone multiple abuses at the hands of his father, including penetrative sexual abuse.

I have exhausted myself and been in a state of constant distress trying to counteract the bizarre decisions of persons who have been trusted to protect Australia's children, who appear, at best, completely ignorant of the strategies of psychopaths and paedophiles, whose actions are informed by urban myth, rather than scientific research. At worst, they are highly sympathetic to paedophiles themselves.

I have been repeatedly baffled by these officials' pre-occupation with the 'emotional abuse' of the protective parent, and their complete disregard for the well-documented lifelong consequences for the child, of contact with the abuser and the inevitable sexual abuse arising from that.

Any accused paedophile father understands that as an abused child like Christopher grows older, his testimony becomes more credible in the eyes of the law, and the likelihood of successful prosecution improves exponentially. Christopher's videotaped testimony to the police was courageous, articulate, consistent and graphic, well validated by his descriptions of his sensory and psychological experiences.

Presently Plankton has a case in Family Court against Debbie, who is again forced to protect her child, despite his disclosures and documented abuse. Meanwhile, Christopher has been awarded $10,000 compensation by the Victims Services NSW, who assisted Debbie and Christopher to move to their present place of hiding. How is this horrific persecution even allowed by the authorities?

Their whereabouts has been discovered, and the house has been repeatedly buzzed by a light plane. I believe they are in grave danger, as there is a significant mortality for women and children in Australia in these situations. Debbie tried repeatedly to initiate a prosecution against Plankton although the Grafton Police consistently refused to do this. Eventually, after representations to many people, she managed to involve the NSW Child Sexual Abuse Squad, who conducted a thorough investigation and produced a brief of evidence which was forwarded to the DPP. The DPP refused to prosecute saying, 'there was insufficient evidence'. Again: any excuse not to prosecute, as in so many other cases.

CHAPTER 3 – PROTECTING MY CHILDREN

Desperation

Lizzie had started looking for other options. The girls had been living with their father fulltime for two years, spending time with their mother each week at a supervised contact centre. By this stage, she had been mulling over the idea of protecting her children by abducting them.

She was in touch with Russell prior to the event; she was distraught and desperate to get her children to safety. He knew she needed his help and he felt he really had no choice. Russell could not live with myself knowing these children were where they were, with nobody in authority prepared to do the right thing.

A review of the situation at this stage which is excerpted from the Freda Briggs Report:

- Police had failed to investigate allegations of child sexual abuse after the CMC CCC upheld Freda's complaint, and operated at the outset from the premise that the mother had trained the children to make false reports.

- The children sought help from 13 people -- none of them were interviewed.

- These children made over 30 disclosures to 13 different adults when they were between the ages of four to five over a period of 18 months and only one of these adults was interviewed by the police.

- The mother only had supervised contact with her children and yet police accused her of 'training' them to make the reports.
- Detective Sgt David Miles and Officer Michelle Faint bullied the mother, told her that the father had never abused the children and never would (an assurance that no responsible professional would ever give).
- They acted as quasi-psychologists and threatened to charge the mother (who was director of a paediatric health centre), with an undisclosed offence if she examined her daughter's genitals.
- Miles said that police would never investigate any further disclosures of abuse, as a result of which the father would know that that he could do whatever he liked, and police would not intervene.
- Detective Miles ordered the mother to respond to future allegations of abuse by telling the children that it was 'just a dream'.
- It was later revealed that the idea of the 'dream' came from police, not the child and, furthermore, both of the twins disclosed sexual abuse.
- Professor Freda Briggs (RIP) lodged a formal complaint with Queensland Crime and Misconduct Commission. The complaint was accepted. Professor Freda Briggs was concerned that a Brisbane Police Inspector Craig Weatherly was appointed to investigate the complaint against fellow police. The concern expressed was that the inspector was unlikely to have the expertise to judge the developmentally inappropriate language that was used when interviewing children of this age.

3 - Protecting My Children

- Lizzie Morris contacted Professor Freda Briggs with the news that one of her children had a sexually transmitted infection, which the father had previously passed onto her. She also found that one of the girls had a damaged and bleeding anus, which was reported to Brisbane Inspector Weatherly

While the CMC/CCC acted against the junior officers, S/Sgt David Miles escaped censure because they asserted he was not involved. This was untrue, and moreover he was the Officer in charge of the Townsville Child Protection Investigation Unit, and therefore legally and administratively responsible for everything that occurred.

In the later case of Christopher Gordon, Miles submitted reports to two courts wherein he stated that the boy had been interviewed on three occasions and made no disclosures of sexual abuse. This was in direct contradiction of what appeared in the TCPIU report which indicated that Christopher made clear disclosures to the contrary.

In a final attempt to get some help Lizzie sent an email to Inspector Weatherly:

Thursday, April 3, 2014 10:13 AM

This is a photo of Charlotte BEFORE she started bleeding from her rectum and contracting another vaginal infection.

Painfully thin, eyes sunken in her head, and apparently absolutely no need for concern in regards to how well she is being 'cared' for '

Can you imagine what state she is in now?

They say a picture says a thousand words. This is the reality of her life right now.

Lizzie

Weatherly did not respond to this e mail but informed Freda Briggs that he was trying to arrange mediation for the mother and

Detective Miles, whilst admitting that this was unlikely to be successful.

Lizzie takes the Twins

At 8am on the 4th April 2014 David Morris dropped off his children at their school, Hermit Park State School in Townsville. "I dropped them off and was watching them walk up to the school gates, together with other kids all around them," he recalls.

Waiting behind the hedge leading to a path into the school grounds, Lizzie was watching. Once he left, she approached the girls, and said something like 'would you like to come with me and see if we can get away'. She managed to collect the twins from outside their school and fled with them in breach of the court order, with hope but no real plan. After she had rescued the children, Lizzie sheltered with people in Northern Queensland.

"That was the last I heard or saw of them," remembers Morris. "About 3pm, I walked through into the school grounds and one of their little friends said: 'Where was Charlotte today? She wasn't at school'? I was puzzled by that. I walked up towards the classroom and the teacher came out on the balcony and saw me. She had this look on her face, like she was pretty shocked to see me there."

David then contacted the Queensland Police Service (QPS) who subsequently located Lizzie's vehicle promptly (because there was a GPS tracker on the car) later that day, unlocked, abandoned at a local park with the keys still in the ignition, and with the children's schoolbags and uniforms in the back seat. Lizzie had fled with the children. She drove to Anderson Park in Pimlico. Things were very intense, because there were thorough efforts to locate them. After 13 days Lizzie contacted Russell to ask for help.

By April 7, the Family Court had issued a Recovery Notice for the girls. Lizzie's parents were threatened by the judge to tell Lizzie to come home and hand the children back, whilst the police appealed for information from the public. On the 11th of April, the grandparents of the two missing girls appealed to their fugitive daughter to come home. They denied helping them disappear and explained they had no idea of their whereabouts. "It's tragic ... we can't do anything," Mr Weber said. "She's committed a pretty serious offence."

Meanwhile, police were appealing for any information to help track the trio down, and by April 17 there were reports of the missing twins 'seen' across Australia. Detectives trying to find the twin sisters taken by their 'fugitive' mother released images of twins stating that they had received reports of sightings across the country.

Townsville Child Protection Investigation Unit, Detective Senior Sergeant Dave Miles, said unconfirmed sightings had been reported in Western Australia, Southeast Queensland and New South Wales.

"We don't believe they're in any physical danger whilst in the custody of their mother, however they're not lawfully entitled to be in her custody and that's what gives us the most concern," he said. "We would only be making guesses as to why she's done it. Everyone we have spoken to, by and large, is saying they had no information this was going to occur, and they've had no contact with Lizzie since she's disappeared."

Russell and Patrick enter the fray
Russell: "The rescue was entirely opportunistic. She ditched the car, which she knew had been fitted with a GPS Tracker, and fled. She was sheltered by friends in northern Queensland for a while, but it was very dangerous. There was an intense effort made to find her. She phoned me at work and begged me to transport her to a safer place. She asked me to pick her up from Charters Towers and gave

me very little time to get there. I had no idea of the distances and agreed before I worked out the logistics. I hired a car and drove flat out for 22 hours through the back roads of Queensland to get her. I didn't sleep. Just stopped for a 10-minute eye close when I had to. I drove right through the night with the cruise control set at 120km per hour, at times weaving my way through herds of kangaroos. I touched a few but didn't hit any hard enough to hurt them. I arrived 20 minutes before the deadline.

"I never knew the people who brought Lizzie to that place. We were never introduced. We never used our names. We barely talked. The only person who knew everything was Lizzie. There was never any child-stealing ring. This was a fabrication by the Australian Federal Police. I took Lizzie where she asked to go and left her on the Northern Territory border with people she knew. I don't know who they were to this day."

The official report of the investigation into the actions of Russell and Patrick is as follows:

- On 17 April 2014, Russell hired and paid for a rental vehicle from Hertz at Grafton, NSW.

- The vehicle was returned to Hertz at Grafton on 25 April 2014 having travelled a total 4,190km. Pridgeon was charged a total of $2,138.21 for this rental.

- Between 18 April 2014 and 20 April 2014, Patrick and Russell conveyed Lizzie, Charlotte and Jane Morris in the Hertz hire vehicle to the vicinity of Camooweal, QLD where Lizzie, Charlotte and Jane were then conveyed to Kununurra, WA by Neil Robinson and/or Freda Plaisted (the daughter of Patricia Ann Plaisted who was good friends with the Weber family).

3 - Protecting My Children

- On 21 May, Lizzie and the children departed Kununurra, WA and travelled to Guilderton, WA, arriving on or about 25 June 2014.

- Then, 20 June, using the vehicle owned by Russell, Patrick drove from Grafton, NSW to Guilderton, WA, arriving on or about 26 June. Patrick then drove Lizzie, Charlotte and Jane from Guilderton, WA, arriving in Grafton, NSW on or about 29 June. At times during the drive, Charlotte and Jane were made to hide in the back seat of the vehicle covered by a blanket.

- Lizzie and the twins then lived under the care of Russell for about the next twelve (12) months. Meanwhile, there was great interest in this story in the media as the public came out in support of both David and Lizzie.

In June that year, bank and social media records led detectives to the Strathpine and Everton Park areas, and David flew south to look for his daughters.

Meanwhile, Freda Briggs wrote a letter to Premier: 10 November 2014

To: Recipient: Rosamund Thorpe; Arthur Weber; Amanda Gearing; Dalton, Trent

Dear Premier

It is some time since I wrote to you about the Morris twins who, for about eight months, have been in hiding with their mother. Can I remind you that I lodged very serious complaints against Townsville Police Det Sgt David Miles, Michelle Faint and the child safety officer who ignored the children's disclosures of sexual abuse by their father, bullied them and their mother and left the 5 year old children alone in a room for an hour... all of this captured on CCTV. The mother fled with them because police (illegally) banned her from making further reports of abuse (ignoring my reports) threatened to arrest the mother for examining her daughter's genitals and ignored a sexually transmitted infection and torn anus, reporting abuse by the father and his influential friends to 12 witnesses who were never interviewed. Lawyers asked me to critique the DVDs of interviews. The bullying of the mother was so serious (46 pages of transcript) that I had the language analysed and an article was published by Cambridge University Press in the recent edition of *Children Australia*. It will also appear in a law journal. We are about to analyse and publish the language used with the children. It is now 18 months since my complaint went to CCC who sent it to another police officer (who is not an expert in child development) to investigate themselves. The relationship between police and the father is such that the father received a copy of my complaint (which was not about him), put it on the internet and wrote offensive emails to me. I met the police officer responsible for the inquiry 3 weeks ago and he said that his report was completed at the end of last year. It has disappeared. The Commissioner of CCC said that he would trace it and contact me 3 weeks ago. He didn't. With Hetty Johnson (Bravehearts) I met the advisor to the Attorney General. We would like an inquiry into the handling of this case. You suggested some time ago that I should meet your Minister responsible for children. She refused to see me on the grounds of 'privacy'. I have been told by a reliable source that she proclaims that 'the father is innocent' and the mother is mentally ill. I said I wished to discuss my complaint, not the case in question. She refused. In the meantime Det Sgt Miles has appeared on TV as the officer still responsible for child protection in Townsville and he was said to have been working in Brisbane advising on handling family violence, which, given his history, is ludicrous. Given the time that has elapsed, I am left with the conclusion that state authorities are ignoring the serious allegations in the hope that the children will be traced. The Family Court Judge has already said the mother will be jailed and no doubt she will be banned from seeing the children until they are 18, which has happened in similar cases . You can then all blame the Family Court when the real problem lies within state services.

3 - Protecting My Children

I hope that you can take some action in this case because right now Queensland's reputation for protecting children is in jeopardy.

Yours sincerely
Professor Freda Briggs AO
Emeritus Professor in Child Development
University of South Australia

Which was followed by Freda Briggs follow-up letter.

10 November 2014, Freda Briggs was so disturbed by what she had seen concerning the twins, she wrote the Premier a follow-up letter given that she had not received a response to her first letter.

Lawyers asked me to critique the DVDs of interviews. The bullying of the mother was so serious (46 pages of transcript) that I had the language analysed and an article was published by Cambridge University Press in the recent edition of Children Australia. It will also appear in a law journal.

It is now 18 months since my complaint went to CCC who sent it to another police officer (who is not an expert in child development) to investigate themselves. The relationship between police and the father is such that the father received a copy of my complaint (which was not about him), put it on the internet and wrote offensive emails to me.

I met the police officer responsible for the inquiry 3 weeks ago and he said that his report was completed at the end of last year. It has disappeared. The Commissioner of CCC said that he would trace it and contact me 3 weeks ago. He didn't.

With Hetty Johnson (Bravehearts) I met the advisor to the Attorney General. We would like an inquiry into the handling of this case. You suggested some time ago that I should meet your Minister responsible for children. She refused to see me on the grounds of 'privacy'.

I have been told by a reliable source that she proclaims that 'the father is innocent' and the mother is mentally ill. I said I wished to discuss my complaint, not the case in question. She refused.

The main concern for the meeting – is that the Morris twins, if found, will be returned to their father DAVID Morris' care without any new and thorough investigation being carried out, taking into account and recognising the inadequacy of the previous investigations.

Once again, she received no reply!

The Search for Lizzie and the Twins

Meanwhile, the Family Law Court made the rare decision to release details of the custodial case after the reported disappearance, and called for people to come forward if they saw Lizzie with the children:

A Townsville Paper reported: 'Fugitive mother of two, Lizzie Morris, remains on the run more than a week after she is believed to have abducted her twin daughters from their Townsville primary school,' the statement read. 'By now, she could quite literally be anywhere in Australia. The suspected abduction is unlawful and in breach of Family Court orders which Ms Morris consented to and asked the Court to make less than a year ago,' a court spokesman said. (Lizzie is adamant that she never consented to Family Court orders) "It is inevitable that someone has seen the trio in their travels and may even know their present whereabouts. Any assistance knowingly provided to a criminal avoiding punishment is in and of itself a serious crime.

Lizzie's parents, the Webers, reached out publicly to their grand-daughters and daughter. 'Charlotte and Jane, we're looking forward to you coming home to look after your chooks and dogs and budgerigars,' Mr Weber said. 'Lizzie: problems can be solved.'

David Morris, now based in Townsville, having completed a graduate program for the Department of Health, said he believed his wife had been helped by various organisations and people. 'There's various organisations who do help people in certain situations where they believe them to be at risk ... and the mother's been involved with some of these organisations for some time,' he said, 'and that somebody, somewhere, must know where they are.'

Morris said he thought it would be a while before the girls were located and was concerned that the time away would upset them. 'It's going to hit home for the girls that they're not at home. They're not with their friends and their regular routine is going to be right out the window,' he said. 'They're going to be really upset about that. They love school, they love their teacher, they love their friends.'

He then set up a Facebook page called **'Help find Charlotte and Jane Morris'** and a website 'findthetwins.com'. At the same time, he launched a fundraising effort 'FundRazr' with the by-line; 'Help get my twin daughters back to a normal life'. He started off the fundraiser with $2,500 of his own money. "Let's get these girls back to a normal life where they can be little princesses, rather than made to live as little criminals." He stated that Jane and Charlotte had a stable home, were doing very well at school, had lots of friends, were very well behaved, and loved singing and dancing. "My seven year-old girls are living on the run from the law, not going to school, not playing with friends, not seeing their families – their lives have been taken away."

On the Run

"I later learned that after taking the children from school, Lizzie had subsequently done a big circuit of Australia, landing up in Perth where she stayed for a while until she was recognised and had to move on," said Russell. "During this time Patrick and I were under constant surveillance. Our phones were bugged, and my house was entered and searched frequently. My car was tracked by a GPS tracker.

"Lizzie then phoned me and asked me to shelter her in Grafton. I then asked Patrick to help, and he drove to WA and brought them back to Grafton. Patrick arrived to collect them, bearded and unkempt after a long journey which gave the kids a bit of a fright. I managed to find her a safe-house and moved her in when she arrived.

"The house I found was isolated but not invisible from the road and there were occasional unwanted and uninvited people who pitched up and had to be dealt with. The previous tenants were disgusting, and I worked very hard to unblock toilets and clean the house and the yard before they arrived. I moved many trailer-loads of rubbish to clean the yard up.

"When Lizzie arrived, she invited two women friends to stay. They were very helpful and supportive when the moving in work was being done. However they had both had bad experiences with male abusers and were suspicious of me. One remarked to Lizzie that I was going to expect favours in return for my support. This was concerning, and I made an agreement with Lizzie that she was never to touch me and I was never to touch her. And I was never to touch the girls. In this way we could never misconstrue each other's intentions. We were doing this for the children. Lizzie remained very protective of her girls all the time she was with me. At no time was I allowed to be alone with them. I approved of her attitude: lionesses make the best mums!

"From time to time I would stay overnight at the house, particularly if there had been a scare or an inquisitive passer-by. I slept on

3 - Protecting My Children

the couch with my dog. I would hear Lizzie getting up for the girls when they were having nightmares. This occurred multiple times a night for the time she was in Grafton.

"The girls told Lizzie that they were bleeding from their bottoms and had sores on their genital areas. I never attempted to examine the girls. They were terrified of men and would never have consented. I did see Jazzie leaving the toilet in tears. The toilet bowl bore traces of the blood she had passed. I still wonder what a man has to do to a seven-year old girl to make her bottom bleed for eight weeks. The father had genital herpes. I hope the scientists create a vaccine against genital herpes before these children grow up.

"Unfortunately, the first winter there was very cold and Lizzie suffered from the low temperatures because her SLE was more symptomatic in cold weather. To make life a little more comfortable I put a wood-burning stove in for her second winter. The mobile phone reception was poor so I erected a high aerial to improve it. Lizzie was a good tenant and worked hard to repaint the house while she lived in it. I dug a garden for them and once it was fertilised and mulched it produced a steady amount of fresh vegetables and flowers. It was an excellent way to get the girls involved, and they enjoyed the garden and the food. We also planted fruit trees which gave the house a permanent feel to it. Later they got chooks, a goat and a sheep named Baroo which they loved. At one stage they had around 100 chickens; and all were rescued from cage-egg farms. The very timid Isa Brown ladies were loved and rehabilitated, and the girls sold the eggs as their own business which they ran with spreadsheets showing income vs expenditure! Entrepreneurs in the making! Sometimes the girls would hold a chook each and swing gently on the hammock under the macadamia tree .... and the chooks would fall asleep. Beautiful memories!

This is Marshmallow the duck

Here are 'Missy' and 'Elmo', two wild king parrots

"Also adding joy to their lives were 'Missy' and 'Elmo', two wild King Parrots we befriended. Missy was so named because she was judged a real 'little miss' and Elmo because he is red and had an awful singing voice! They would perch on the girls' arms and feed out of their hands. Missy would bring her new babies to meet us as soon as they learnt to fly. Beautiful! In charge of the goats, sheep, dogs,

3 - Protecting My Children

Baby Baroo, the sheep (not goat remember) with his jumper on... Chook giving you the eye!

chickens, horses and guinea fowl was Marshmallow the duck. She took nonsense from nobody and used to lead the walks when all the birds and animals set off in the afternoons with the twins. Baroo and Marshmallow used to snuggle up with the girls at night to and soon they would be happily asleep.

"It was heart-warming watching the little girls improve in body and mind. When they came to Grafton, they were very small for their age and looked unhealthy. I regret that I did not measure their height and weight and subsequent growth over time. I believe their father had purposely underfed the children to stunt their growth and make them more attractive.

"I bought them bicycles and scooters when they arrived to give them exercise and occupy them in the hope that the mental strain and loneliness did not become a problem. With all the riding, running and walking and the improved nutrition they were soon putting on weight and looking better. After a year under my wing they were unrecognisable. It filled me with happiness.

"Charlotte had taken the name of 'Jasmine' or 'Jazzie'. She was the smaller twin, with dark hair, very quiet and shy with me, even after a year. Jane had called herself 'Kelly' or 'Kel'. She was more outgoing and athletic. She dyed her hair blonde.

'The girls were very fussy eaters. My shopping was a time-consuming process. I bought every fruit I could. They ate the very best food I could find and with vitamin supplements. Yet it was a joyous thing to do. I sought out anything I thought they would enjoy and loved watching them eat. I used to visit a gift shop that sold semi-precious stones. I bought new ones every week. Soon they had a collection to be proud of. When I arrived with shopping bags full of food and treats and gifts, the girls would descend on the shopping bags as soon as I put them down with little cries of delight. I would sit quietly and enjoy their pleasure. I thought of them as little birds, chattering with excitement. It was the time I enjoyed the most. I also visited book shops and bought them piles of books. They were voracious readers and read everything I bought by the next week I also bought school books and equipment.

"Lizzie home-schooled them every day. She obtained schoolwork from other friends and then tested the girls against national standards. They were a couple of years ahead of their age group and still at the top of the class. They were astonishingly intelligent, and it was a revelation to see them work diligently together. At one time they were interviewing a guest about his occupation for a school project. Their engagement with each other was absolutely

3 - Protecting My Children

serious and intense. It was touching and yet delightful. I smiled with a melting heart.

'Lizzie was always terrified of being caught and having the girls taken back to their father. Like most abusers he enjoyed the excitement and sense of power and impunity and invulnerability he gained from abusing the girls when under scrutiny. He never stopped. The danger Lizzie feared the most was being discovered by Morris alone. She was quite certain he would murder them all without mercy. He was too well protected to worry about consequences. The police were feared too. But not nearly as much.

"It was a very intense existence. Morris had engaged a private investigator who probed us regularly. The police and probably others were silent intruders in my home. My house was entered weekly or more often. I could smell the intruders frequently. Leather, body-odour, clothing and their sweat. I never tried to improve the house security. As long as they thought they were undetected they would not redouble their efforts. I would see fresh car tyre tracks on my driveway and know I had had visitors. It required steady nerves. All my cars were tracked by paedophiles and their helpers using GPS trackers. Paedophiles love doing this. It gives them a sense of power and control. And a God-like sense of entitlement and authority. The hallmark of cowardly child rapists and wife-beaters. I purchased a device that detects radio transmission and used it to keep track of which car was being tracked. Before I headed off to visit the little family I would drive the vehicle in the opposite direction for 20-30 minutes. If the device detected a signal I would swap cars or even drive into town and borrow a car to deliver the groceries.

"I would often share a meal with them and enjoy the quiet and happy interactions between mother and children. Lizzie was an outstanding mother. She dealt with her children with love, kindness and humour. I watched her like a hawk, as one would when involved in a situation like this. I could not fault her. In all situations, even the very difficult ones we faced together, she was exceptional. The girls quietly stole my heart while I wasn't looking. At first they were terrified of me. They would tolerate my presence at the meal table but moved away as soon as they could.

"Later on they engaged with me happily but there was always a reserve. Kel was more relaxed and on occasion took my hand when we were on walks. I felt as though I had gained the trust of a wild animal. I bought them musical instruments to play as part of their education. The recorders were replaced by ukuleles and then a discussion followed about playing a proper instrument. When I bought the ukuleles Jazzie appeared upset. I did not understand why until Lizzie told me gently that what Jazzie really wanted was a violin. Jazzie was afraid that she would anger me if she appeared ungrateful. I assured her that I would love to buy her a violin. I asked what colour she preferred. Fortunately I was able to find a purple violin. I was rewarded by their concerts as the girls showed their progress. Kel wanted a keyboard and found it easier to play than a violin.

"Like so many abused children, Jazzie and Kel were gifted and exceptional beings. They would be talking quietly between themselves and then suddenly start singing together in perfect harmony. After a brief while they would stop and quietly go back to their schoolwork. It was like being passed by a flight of angels.

"At times there was unpleasant and unwanted attention from outsiders, and we closed the house up and drove long distances to other friends. I would return and place hunting cameras under the house to monitor intruders. I would walk in each night and check the cameras. If there were no intruders over several nights, I would drive and fetch Lizzie back home.

"Sometimes Lizzie would not respond to texts or phone calls. I would drive out to the house hoping that Morris hadn't found her. I would park the car a distance away and walk in pitch darkness without a torch to check the little family was safe. I used to carry a weapon while doing this. I am glad I never had to use it.

"It was important to give them breaks from the house. We went on bush walks and found swimming holes. The Land Rover took us along impassable roads to wild places where we were safe from prying eyes. Going to town was never an option. We taught the girls to hide using bush as camouflage and cover. They were remarkably proficient after a while.

"The girls thrived. They grew daily in body and mind. The memories and the fear moved into the background. Kel revealed real athleticism and ran with the dogs on long walks. I used to leave Lizzie alone for periods of time. She was extremely self-reliant and resourceful. Her courage was outstanding. She paid an enormous price to protect these children. And is still paying it."

"I delivered the odd set of groceries and toys when they needed my help," remembers Patrick. "I was concerned about Lizzie's frequent trips to town and the risk of her running into a police roadblock, but she made it clear she would do as she decided. After she had been in Grafton for a year, she moved on to a safer place because they were becoming too well known in Grafton. It was probably the right decision as there was a $50,000 reward for her arrest and people were getting to know her."

While Lizzie was on the run, Freda Briggs complained about an unsatisfactory police investigation, and a complaint was lodged with the Crime and Misconduct Commission.

This eventually resulted in a finding in March 2016 that the investigation had been 'inadequate' and 'unprofessional'. The Commission concluded that the Townsville Police dealt with the children incompetently and unprofessionally. In 2016, these police were supposedly retrained and one resigned, and yet David Miles, who led the team, came out of the inquiry virtually unscathed. He remained free to feed the media a very distorted version of events.

"After she left Grafton I had minimal communication with her, just Christmas cards, until she contacted me in 2017. I met her again and gave the children some presents. A new violin for Jazzy and a recurve archery bow for Kelly. She had changed. The fierce fire had gone. She was a woman who was just hanging on. The paedophile meme is that women try to prevent good fathers from seeing their children out of spite and malice. This does happen, but rarely. The actions of these vile women sabotage the efforts of loving parents to protect abused children.

"Let it be said that Australians are decent people as a whole. They abhor sexual violence against children and women. When I needed help, I asked people I trusted. They responded positively without fail. I was able to shelter the little family during difficult times with good people.

"The actions of the Australian government authorities is completely opposite to this. They disbelieved and ignored the abuse and did everything possible to hide it. They then behaved as if the children's disclosures were malicious acts done by Lizzie and took the children off her in line with the Parental Alienation Syndrome theory that dominates the courts."

Townsville Community Cabinet Meeting 29/03/2015 - **Review of the Minutes re Jane and Charlotte Morris**

In attendance:

Yvette DÁth MP

Jo-Anne Miller MP

Shannon Fentiman MP and a Deputation with Ministers for Child Safety and the Police amongst others, as well as the missing children's grandparents and Professor Rosamund Thorpe (Family Inclusion Network).

Main concern for the meeting – is that the Morris twins, if found, will be returned to their father DAVID Morris's care without any new and thorough investigation being carried out , taking into account and recognising the inadequacy of the previous investigations.

Major concerns

1. Inadequacy of investigations to date by Police and Child Safety,
2. Failure of the Independent Lawyer for the children (Joanne Meade, employed by Legal Aid in Townsville) to place a prime focus on the needs and interests of the children,
3. Biased, negative mindset of all the government employees – Police, Child Safety , Independent Lawyer for the children, against the mother and ALL witnesses to disclosures made by the girls.
4. Failure of the government employees to consider that they may have been charmed (groomed/conned) by the father. This is a serious omission, given that "grooming "is well-documented in research on child sexual abuse.

Elaboration of these concerns

Inadequacy of investigations by Police and Child Safety

1. Failure to consider all the evidence re Child Sexual Abuse (CSA) and, in particular

    a). Reports submitted by contact supervisors

    b). Statements submitted by all other people who heard the girls make disclosures

    c). A notification that one of the girls had reportedly been diagnosed with an STI and a torn anus

2. Disbelief accorded to disclosures made by the two 5 year old girls in interviews with Police and Child Safety. This was particularly marked after:

    a). Charlotte retracted her disclosures after 3 nights in a foster home, saying "it was a dream". This is consistent with **research on young children's pattern of reporting disclosures** but the government professionals appear to not have this knowledge and appear to have been predisposed to accept the retraction at face value, possibly on account of the bias they held in favour of the father.

    b). Charlotte tells the police interviewer that mummy told her to tell the police about what Daddy does to her and her sister. This was misinterpreted by the police as mummy having coached Charlotte in what to say whereas, from the contact supervisor's reports, it is clear that mummy simply encouraged the girls to tell other people what they had told her. There is NO evidence of coaching in the contact supervisor's reports, it is clear that mummy simply encouraged the girls to tell other people what they had told her. There is NO evidence of coaching in the in the contact supervisor's reports and, indeed, the complex detail in the disclosures made to the police by the girls could not possibly have been coached at all – let alone by a mother whose contact with the girls was supervised.

3. Failure of the Child Safety staff present in the interviews with police to act on the *balance of probabilities* that the children had experienced harm and were at risk of future harm if left in the care of their father. The Child Safety staff appeared to have deferred to the Police who need to assemble evidence *beyond all reasonable doubt* in order to lay criminal charges. In this way the civil principle of the *best interests of the child* was subordinated to the interests of police re criminal charges. This indicates failure on the part of Child Safety staff to:

a). Believe what young children say about abuse, **against all advice of child sexual abuse literature.**

b). Prioritise concern for the protection of young children, especially in a "Family Court case". In such cases research **has demonstrated** how professionals continue to give precedence to a 'scepticism paradigm 'rather than to child protection.

c). Consider the possibility that they, the professionals, may be being groomed by a perpetrator of child abuse – **grooming by perpetrators is well documented in research on child sexual abuse.**

d). Value the efforts of a protective mother, rather than misinterpreting her behaviour and deeming it to have caused "emotional abuse to the children without double-checking their assumptions against the contact supervisors'" reports. This is a key failure in the investigations by police and child safety and **contrary to all recommendations emanating from CSA research.**

4. Restricting the mother

a). From making any further reports of possible abuse, asserting that: they would not be investigated; charges would be laid against her, and they, the professionals, would recommend to the Family Court that she lose all contact with the girls.

b). From reading a child protection book with the girls, despite the girls enjoying both the verse and the little black cat. Astonishingly, using this book was perceived by police as tantamount to 'coaching 'even though it's use is recommended by police and Child Safety.

c). From looking at the girls genitalia, even when, on supervised contact visits, they complained about being sore in that region of their anatomy. If she did, she faced arrest.

Failure of the Independent Lawyer for the children (Joanne Meade, employed by Legal Aid in Townsville) to place a prime focus on the needs and interests of the children.

1. Failure to forward all supervisor reports which contained disclosures of CSA to the Police and Child Safety.
2. Failure to submit all the supervisor's reports to the Family Court.
3. Attempted – at the father's request – to influence a psychiatrist to revise his assessment of the mother's mental health.

Biased, negative mindset of all the government employees, Police, Child Safety, Independent Lawyer for the children – against the mother and all witnesses to disclosures made by the girls.

1. Statements by the police and child safety staff that the mother is mentally ill have been made with no evidential foundation and **contrary to the assessments made by two psychiatrists and four psychologists.**
2. Claims by the police and child safety staff that the mother has fabricated allegations of child sexual abuse, seemingly based on a glib assumption that "this happens in Family

Court Cases". Such scepticism on the part of professionals is based on the **now discredited** theory of *parental alienation*. This outdated knowledge base is a serious concern, since it can lead to failure to protect children from harm.

3. Claims by the Police, Child Safety staff, and the independent lawyer for the children, to take seriously the statements of all persons (contact supervisors and others) who heard the girls make disclosures of CSA, despite the complete lack of evidence in the contact supervisor's reports that this happened.

4. Failure by the Police, Child Safety, and the independent lawyer for the children, to take seriously the statements of all persons (contact supervisors and others) who heard the girls make disclosures, on the grounds that the girls had been coached by their mother. This is despite the complete lack of evidence of *'behaviour that is of a sustained and repetitive nature during contact with the girls'* as claimed in a notification to Child Safety dated 17/07/12. How this could have been substantiated by child safety without considering the contact supervisors' reports and interviewing the supervisors is simply incredible.

Failure of the government employees to contemplate that they may have been charmed (groomed/conned) by the father. This is a serious omission on their part, given that 'grooming 'is well documented in research on child sexual abuse.

1. The bias of police, child safety staff, and the independent lawyer for children in favour of the father and against the mother (and against all witnesses to the girls disclosures) has been palpable throughout this case and, once entrenched, has not been exposed to critically reflective scrutiny. Or, if it has, there has been a built-in inclination to not revise their professional judgements and admit to having been wrong.

2. In this regard there appears to be an implicit assumption that while the girls and their mother are missing, this critical scrutiny is not necessary and that, when they are found, it will continue to be not necessary, as the mother will be incarcerated and the girls will be returned to their father's care .

Conclusions and Recommendation

This latter outcome – return of the girls to their father's care – is our greatest concern. It is our belief that if this happens the girls would be at risk of serious harm in their father's care and the authorities would be guilty of failing to act to protect young children from harm.

In our view, it is essential that if, or when, the children are located that they be placed in the care of loving family members, or close family friends, rather than strangers such as foster carers!

Due to the fact that the paternal grandmother, Mrs Patricia Morris, lives with a serious mental illness and also suffers with many physical health issues. In our view it would be in the best interests of the children to be placed with the maternal grandparents, Heather and Arthur Weber Heather and Arthur are Blue Card holders, and they still have the children's bedroom as it was when they lived at their home in 2011, with some of their animals also there for them to play with. It would be very familiar to them and would afford a sense of security.

Response from the meeting

From: Weber to Freda Briggs
Cc: Hetty Johnson; Rosamund Thorpe; jawheadx@bigpond.com; Amanda Gearing; Dalton, Trent

3 - Protecting My Children

Dear Freda,

On the afternoon of Sunday 29th March 2015, we organised a deputation to meet with some ministers in the new Queensland Labour Government:-

Attorney General etc. Hon Yvette Dáth MP

Minister for Police etc. Hon Jo-Anne Miller MP

Minister for Communities etc. Hon Shannon Fentiman MP

We were allotted a time slot of 2.45 pm with the Hon Jo-Anne Miller MP the Minister for Police etc.

Our deputation included Heather and I, Emeritus Professor Rosamund Thorpe, specializing in Social Work and Community Welfare, with over 45 years' experience, Ms Virginia Hall, Adjunct Senior Lecturer Community Welfare, Mrs Rae Greaves, Dip. Community Welfare, worker for many years at Sera Women's Shelter and volunteer at Domestic Violence Service Centre Townsville and Mrs Rhonda Lane. The last three ladies were registered supervisors of Lizzie while with her daughters Charlotte and Jane Morris. These supervisors were approved by the family court, Independent children's lawyer, Ms Joanne Meade and Mr David Morris. These supervisors and ourselves had been told by Jane and Charlotte, allegations of sexual, physical and psychological abuse perpetrated against them by their father Mr David Morris.

The Minister for Police was assisted by the Queensland Police Commissioner, Ian Stewart and another high ranking police officer whose name escapes us.

From the outset, the Commissioner 'took the floor', was not interested in any evidence we presented, as he stated it was only 'hearsay 'or anything we had to say. He kept repeating that we should let Mrs. Morris, Lizzie, know that she should be brave enough to come forward and state her case and allow the children to be further interrogated, as it was the only way that the case could be solved. He also stated that the police had been away from their father too long.

The Commissioner admitted that he had not viewed the tapes of the Police interview between Det Sgt David Miles, Constable Michelle Faint, Child Safety and the children. He also admitted that he had not viewed that interview of Lizzie with David Miles and Child Safety and refused to accept the analysis of that interview by Dr Pamela Schultz, that he had not read any of the supervisors' reports of abuse by the father against the girls or viewed any of the other police interviews of the girls with Police and Child Safety.

The Commissioner continued to 'shut us down' every time we attempted to speak, repeating his line that nothing could be done until Lizzie returned with the children. He inferred often that we knew where she was and would be able to contact her, even saying that her brothers and sister would surely be in contact with her on social media.

The Hon Jo-Anne Miller MP sat throughout all of the dialogue, saying very little and often with her mouth agape as she appeared quite horrified. She did say, on at least three occasions, that we should be speaking with the Minister for Child Safety.

Bear in mind that if Lizzie and the girls were 'brave enough' to come forward and be interviewed by Police and Child Safety to only be told, yet again, by Det Snr Sgt David Miles that she was a liar and he did not believe her or the children, she is not likely to come forward.

A short meeting was arranged with the Minister for Child Safety Hon Shannon Fentiman MP and even though we had to sit and wait for some time, we feel that it was worth the wait. This delegation included, Michael Hogan, Director General of Communities (including child safety), the new North Queensland Regional Director for Communities, Sandra (?) and the Regional Director of Child Safety Nicola Jeffers.

We had been informed that the Review being conducted by Child Safety for some 10 months had been finalised and all other relevant material. This was

3 - Protecting My Children

encouraging. He informed Heather and I that he would be arranging for us to be interviewed, in the near future and that we should present all evidence.

I let the 'dust' settle before writing this as we were all breathless by the ignorance shown to us by the Commissioner.

We will keep you up to date.

Heather and Arthur Weber

CHAPTER 4 – RUSSELL TAKES ACTION

The Australian Anti-Paedophile Party is formed

Russell: "By 2016, frustrated by inaction, it seemed all I could do was write letters as far and wide to anyone with influence. Two letters went to the Honourable Dianne Farmer, Minister of Child Safety, and copied to all and sundry, to anyone who might listen, but the silence was deafening.

"It had also been brought to my attention that Morris had an uncle: Mick McArdle, who was the Deputy Leader of the Opposition Liberal Party in Queensland during this time.

"The inspiration to pursue a political course of action came about in a strange way while I was in contact with Lizzie. She reported that Morris used his mobile phone to photograph and film his actions. The Police knew this but did not investigate. I reasoned that if we could hack into his computer, we could obtain photographic proof of the abuse, and force the Police into action.

"Intrigued, I found a book, co-written by Julian Assange and Suelette Dreyfuss, about hacking. I contacted Suelette in Melbourne and flew to meet her. She was very kind but could not help me with hacking. However she did introduce me to a retired Australian Federal Policeman, who left the force in disgust. He was blunt: he told me I was wasting my time trying to save these children, he said if I wanted to make a difference I must go where the power is: become an MP and enter parliament.

4 - Russell Takes Action

"I also learned that Australian law prevents anyone who is NOT a politician from releasing evidence regarding cases that are currently being dealt with by The Family Court. The penalty for divulging ANY information pertaining to an active court case was serious jail time, and/or, a heavy fine. I tumbled to the fact that if the Anti-Paedophile Party won a seat in the senate, it would also enable our representative to name and shame perpetrators under parliamentary privilege. We hoped to build a balance of power party in the Senate and in the Australian Federal Parliament. As such, we aimed to force legislation through parliament that has been too hard, too contentious and too controversial to gain traction with the major political parties.

"The intention of this legislation was to protect children from child abuse in all its forms, especially child sexual abuse. We intended to become the parliamentary voice for all organisations with similar aims, to more effectively advocate for child safety We wanted the party to use parliamentary privilege to override court gag orders and to call for a Royal Commission into processes of the court given that to all practical purposes it's almost impossible to prosecute a child sexual abuser in an inter-familial situation".

"I was not an Australian, so I could not enter parliament, others would have to stand for elections, but I thought I would run and fund the party.

"It was 2016 and the national senate elections were approaching so I contacted all those people who had previously been in touch with us around the country concerning child abuse and informed them the party would contest for four senate-seats: three in New South Wales, and one in Victoria.

"Our Facebook page was run by Patrick and other helpers, mostly women who had been abused in childhood, who were passionate about preventing abuse of today's children. Our website and social media pages became magnets for people who had been abused, or who had lost their children to abuse. The stories we received were unimaginably horrible and traumatised everyone involved. More than once I visited and found Patrick sitting at his computer crying uncontrollably after hearing about the loss of someone's child to abuse.

"The sickening reality was that most of the child trafficking in Australia is taking place THROUGH government agencies; the very institutions who are entrusted with the welfare of the nation's children, or the associated private sector institutions they send the children to.

"We came to understand that in the Children's Court, the process is remarkably simple: When a parent has difficulties with a child, perhaps a special needs child, or one that needs extra care, the parent will approach the government organisation for assistance. They are assisted very attentively, and told, that, yes, certainly, there is much help that may be given. The parent is given a lot of paperwork to sign, which they do, as we all do, without paying it too much attention. The paperwork is then taken away, and never seen again. However this sets in train an inexorable process: the parent has just signed their parental rights away, and the child is now a ward of the state.

"The parents receive the assistance, often in their own home, the child is apparently well cared for and for the while all seems easier. However after every visit a report is written up, with each report becoming less satisfactory. After two years the child protection workers approach the parent and advise that unfortunately it been observed that the child is being badly cared for and for the child's own protection it must be taken out of the care of the parent and sent into foster care. The child is seized, often using numbers of armed police, and is lost to the parent, who is so traumatised and bereft, that their lives are destroyed. Each worker appears to receive a large financial bonus for seizing a child. The institutions that receive the child are also able to gain payment of huge sums of money from Government, for this service.

"This system often takes children from caring, competent, loving parents and funnels them into a system where people and organisations gain huge payments for fostering them out where there is no accountability, and where they are subjected to frequent abuse. Paedophiles seek these children out and exploit them.

"None of this will ever reach the notice of the Australian public because the secrecy laws are so wide and so draconian, that nobody can publish anything, even on social media. To mention the child's name, even in connection with a birthday is likely to result in a two-year prison sentence.

"In the Family Court the views of Dr Richard Gardner are unfortunately frequently relied upon. His theory of Parental Alienation Syndrome argues that child sexual abuse seldom occurs and when it does, little harm is done to the child. Gardner wrote uncritically of adult-child sexual relations. Following this line of thought, if the child or the protective parent accuses the abuser of sexual abuse, it must be because the protective parent is malicious and has coached or trained the child to make false allegations.

"This being the case, the Family Court finds that the protective parent is 'emotionally abusing' the child by alienating the child and the child needs to be protected from this by giving the abuser sole custody. The protective parent is not allowed to see the child for an extended period of time to 'sanitise' the child from the pernicious effects of the emotional abuse.

"It is difficult to imagine a more effective way of silencing and isolating the abused child and protecting the abuser from prosecution. The child loses hope, the protective parent is destroyed, becoming so traumatised that she becomes incoherent, easily dismissed as a demented person. Stockholm Syndrome and Trauma Bonding does the rest.

"This is happening many times a day in every Family or Federal Circuit Court in Australia, carefully hidden by the gagging legislation, Section 121, and the cowardice and indifference of Australian mainstream media.

"We sought to remind the electorate the Government accepts that one in three girls will experience contact sexual abuse before the age of 18 years. The statistics suggest that one in four to six boys will be subjected to abuse, but Australian research suggested that boys are abused earlier, more often and by more offenders than girls, and this is not recognised in statistics because they don't report it.

"We were seeking to network with all of the organisations and individuals who oppose CSA and wished to work with them to apply pressure on the government of the day to pass legislation to make Australia a safe place for our children. It was not intended that we become an official opposition to the government of the day.

"Officially, as a single-issue party, we did not offer an opinion on those areas of government that did not impinge on the policies of our party. In this way we would have been better able to trade our votes with the government of the day for the child protection legislation that we sought. Nor did we propose to interfere in any way with the workings of any non-government child-protection organisations. We only wished to support them, listen to their knowledge and ideas, and work with them to make many changes to the ways things are done in Australia, so that child sexual abuse becomes extinct. We hoped we could work with them.

"Our ideas were based on the situation at that time, and it was to be hoped that the individuals and organisations who joined the executive would bring their own ideas, experience and knowledge to bear, and that these strategies would evolve and develop with democratic input from everyone.

"We needed to form working parties of groups of individuals with special skills to create a strategic policy framework and make plans for our parliamentary demands, so we could present a coherent and considered plan to the government of the day as we negotiated our demands.

"We did not intend to publicise this party until several months before the elections, at which time we aimed to create a publicity campaign. The reason for this was we were taking on organised crime, a multinational multi-billion dollar industry. We needed to be able to progress quietly, without distraction, until we were ready. In so doing we could rather direct our efforts to creating effective policies and strategies so that we could hit the ground running.

"In contesting the election, an informal alliance was sought with Derryn Hinch's Justice Party which he formed in October 2016 with a view to winning a senate seat in Victoria. The approach was declined. The former radio shock-jock turned anti-paedophile campaigner, warned that campaigning against sexual abusers could be a minefield. He spoke from experience, having been jailed twice for naming paedophiles in contravention of court suppression orders. But he did say, 'Dr Pridgeon's heart was in the right place,' and his party was 'trying to do some good stuff.' He warned, 'In this business, you've got to be very careful. I'm very cognisant of making sure information is accurate. The people I've been to jail over have been convicted sex offenders.'

"So the Australian Anti-paedophile Party (AAPP) was registered as an Australian political party with the Australian Electoral Commission during 2016. It was known as the 'Australians Against Paedophiles Party'. By this time, On the 7 September 2016, an arrest warrant was issued by the Magistrate's Court of Queensland against Lizzie for the offence of child stealing.

"We eventually nominated a total of four senate candidates (one each in New South Wales, Northern Territory, South Australia and Tasmania), and one House of Representatives candidate (for the Division of Robertson) in the 2016 Federal election.

"Then, without realising it, the party was sabotaged by the changes in the electoral laws that Labour and the Coalition forced through that destroyed the chances of the minor parties gaining seats.

"Our names were in bizarre places on the huge ballot sheet. We had not understood that if we had one candidate for each state, you couldn't find the name on the ballot sheet, as they placed it in an obscure position, such that even our most experienced and ardent supporters took hours to find us, or not find us. But if we had two or more candidates, then it would have been placed in a more prominent position. It is difficult to think of these difficulties placed in our way as coincidental.

Sadly, Australia declined to support us. The AAPP did not succeed in gaining a seat, but unknown and underfunded, this was always going to be a very long shot anyway. The Turnbull government was returned at the election with a reduced and very narrow majority.

The party was disbanded and voluntarily deregistered shortly after the elections on 25 November 2016.

Plankton Sues

In the lead up to the election, Russell's problems mounted when John Plankton launched defamation proceedings against him in the Supreme Court of New South Wales. Plankton claimed he had been falsely branded a paedophile. He also sued a Grafton newspaper over an interview they published with Russell that mentioned his personal experience of dealing with child sexual abuse.

"Plankton argued that our website defamed him by implying that he is a 'sinister and very effective paedophile.' In a Statement of Claim filed in the Supreme Court, he argued that anyone who knew he was the father of my wife's son and knew that the three adults had been involved in disputes over the boy, would have known that the website material was about him. He pointed out he had not been charged with sexual abuse offences, and consequently, the accusations were false.

"On the website, I said I was left feeling powerless and traumatised after navigating the system and felt that parliamentarians lacked the will or the courage to act on child abuse. 'Each story that I hear of is as horrific as all the others,' I posted.

"I well knew that Christopher and Debbie lived in hiding from this man, and that Christopher was devastated by the apparent refusal to believe his brave testimony and that reference to his father such as a birthday card, caused a recurrence of his terrible nightmares. David Plankton had taken advantage of the DPPs failure to prosecute by proclaiming his innocence to anyone who will listen by claiming to have been exonerated by the Police, the DPP, and the Family Court. I pointed out that he had convinced

Debbie's family that Christopher had been coached by his mother to make false allegations against him, and that this had led to her totally estranged from her extended family. I also made it clear that she was living in hiding, in isolation, under constant legal attack and fearing for her safety.

"The reason he was able to sue me was because the DPP had not acted against him. The man who made that decision was Patrick Power.

"Power was admitted as a barrister and worked for 16 years as a prosecutor in serious criminal cases (including sex cases). He was also the chairperson of the New South Wales Youth Justice Advisory Committee. He was instrumental in promoting and helping draft the Young Offenders Act 1997 (NSW) which instituted restorative justice conferencing for young offenders. He was a consultant to the New South Wales Government on the implementation of restorative justice processes for adults.

"On 4 July 2006, Power required repairs to his personal computer which had been experiencing technical problems. During this process, the technician examining the computer discovered evidence of files associated with child pornography including 31 video files and links to additional material on a removable hard drive. The technician notified his superiors and Power was subsequently arrested on 6 July 2006. He was then also suspended from his duties but remained on full pay until his formal resignation in January 2007.

"Power pleaded guilty to possessing child pornography during his court appearance at Sydney. Chief Crown prosecutor Jeremy Rapke said Power had collected in excess of 29,000 pornographic images including 433 pictures and 31 videos depicting children. He said, they were of 'the worst and highest-grade pornography' involving 'humiliation and sadistic bestiality.'

4 - Russell Takes Action

"Fifty-nine members of the community, including former colleagues provided references of Power's good character to the court. This included a statement by the state's most senior Crown Prosecutor, <u>Mark Tedeschi QC</u>.

"On 9 May 2007, Power was sentenced to 15 months imprisonment, to serve a minimum of eight months, but was released on bail when his lawyers lodged an appeal against sentence. The appeal was dismissed on 14 June 2007 and Power was imprisoned for seven months. A case against the Daily Telegraph was withdrawn by the Law Society on 20 November 2007 because an apology had been printed by that newspaper. Power's practising certificate was removed from the Roll of Legal Practitioners by the NSW Bar Association. He was released from gaol on 18 January 2008. Is it any wonder they could not get him to prosecute Plankton?

* * *

7 September 2016, an arrest warrant was issued by the Magistrate's Court of Queensland against Lizzie for the offence of child stealing.

On the 11th of December 2017 police were listening when Patrick was heard on a call to Marney Macdonald (previously the AAPP candidate for the Northern Territory), where he sought the assistance of Macdonald to establish a Facebook page in order "to abuse the NSW Attorney General" and stated that he is 'having a full go at that paedophile David Morris.'

Macdonald did his bidding and titled the page: *'NSW Attorney General Mark Speakman protects Rock Spiders[10].'* Later in a call to John

---

10   Rock Spider, is a derogatory abusive English speaking South African term for an ignorant stupid Afrikaner.

Shipton, the father of Julian Assange, Patrick is heard saying he intends to 'fix' Morris, 'come hell or high water.' Pursuing this, he is heard asking for Nadine Frost's help in finding Morris, having discovered his membership of the Brisbane Golf Club and goes on to state that he wants to 'put Morris in hospital because he threatened my daughter'.

These transcripts raise legitimate questions about the mindset and motivation of the investigators. In law there is always reference to the thinking of the somewhat elusive, 'reasonable man' and one can only wonder what such a 'man' would have deduced from the thrust of what they were hearing. Did nobody conclude, from what they heard, that they were not eavesdropping on dangerous criminals seeking to sexually abuse children or traffic in their custodianship for nefarious purposes or monetary reward? Did nobody at any level, deduce that there was no real criminality at play? Rather they were listening in Patrick's case, to a hot-headed man outraged by what he believed was happening to children, seeking to protect them from further harm and a concerned doctor; that both were simply doing what they believed was their duty? Obviously not, because arrest was imminent.

***

The AFP in an announcement to the media: "It is now 4 April 2018, FOUR years in hiding without a hug from their dad, a lesson from a schoolteacher or a hint of normality, that's the reality for Charlotte and Jane according to their father. There are still no real leads on their whereabouts. Its just time for Lizzie to do the right thing by the girls; she's obviously thought this is the right thing for her but this can't go on forever."

Townsville Child Protection Investigation Unit officer-in-charge detective Senior Sergeant Dave Miles said. Further that Townsville detectives were working in partnership with the Australian Federal Police in an effort to track down the girls.

"The reality is no matter how long Lizzie waits she will have to confront the Family Law Court in relation to her actions," Sen-Sgt Miles said.

"We have no doubt at all that there are individuals out there assisting Lizzie in remaining at large with the children in contravention of the Family Law court order," Sen-Sgt Miles said.

"While whoever is supporting Lizzie believes that they are acting in the best interests of all parties, they fail to appreciate the long-term effects this will have on the girls and their ability to lead normal lives in the future. We continue to respond to all information regarding possible sightings and their location. The longer she continues to remain at large the situation does not improve and it's only going to serve to make things more difficult for her and the children into the future. They might be on a farm somewhere, on a homestead, in a remote area. They might be in an alternate community where they're hidden away," he said.

"But it could equally be they are in suburbia. They could be anywhere, we have really no leads at all. It's just time for Lizzie to do the right thing by the girls; she's obviously thought this is the right thing for her but this can't go on forever. The most important thing for me is that they get back to a normal life and not be made to live on the run from the law."

"I'm not worried that they don't know how much I love them, I'm concerned they'll think I'm disappointed with them or angry with them that they're gone," said Mr. Morris.

He said he feared his daughters were being robbed of a proper childhood and healthy development. "It's four years without these kids being at school or being in a normal home."

"They're definitely in danger in terms of developing as a normal adult or a normal childhood. It"s out of the question while they're still on the run," he told 'Australian Current Affairs' at the time.

"These people are likely to think they are doing the right thing by the children, but police are calling on them to come forward." He added the girls were registered as missing persons and a warrant had been issued for Lizzie's arrest if she was found. He also said that it was likely their mother had changed their appearance.

On the fourth anniversary of their disappearance the 'Help Find Charlotte and Jane Morris' Facebook page wrote: 'There is no excuse for keeping children hidden from society and their basic rights to education, healthcare and family. Children are not objects to be used to hurt someone.'

Clearly the fact that the AFP had not been able to locate Lizzie and the Twins was proving to be a huge embarrassment. They had their suspicions concerning Patrick's involvement with the website, and by implication, Russell's involvement, so they received a judge's permission to focus their attention on Russell and Patrick, and later on Lizzie, such that despite Russell's cautious strategy, they are no match for the experienced professional AFP.

In 4 April David Morris, spoke to Sam Bidey of the *Townsville Bulletin* and lamented the failure to the recover his children.

"It is now 4 April 2018, four years in hiding without a hug from their dad, a lesson from a schoolteacher or a hint of normality, that's the reality for Charlotte and Jane according to their father. There are still no real leads on their whereabouts. It's just time for Lizzie to do the right thing by the girls; she's obviously thought this is the right thing for her, but this can't go on forever."

"Townsville Child Protection Investigation Unit officer-in-charge detective Senior Sergeant Dave Miles said Townsville detectives were working in partnership with the Australian Federal Police in an effort to track down the girls.

"The reality is no matter how long Lizzie waits she will have to confront the Family Law Court in relation to her actions," Sen-Sgt Miles said. "We have no doubt at all that there are individuals out there assisting Lizzie in remaining at large with the children in contravention of the Family Law court order," Sen-Sgt Miles said.

The Bugging

During much of the investigation the Australian Federal Police (AFP) were listening in, having bugged the phones of Patrick and Russell and planted GPS devices on their cars in the hope of their revealing both their intentions and the whereabouts of Lizzie and the twins and possibly use against them in a court of law.

Although Russell and Patrick were taking precautions, and knew the AFP were 'sniffing' around, they were initially unaware that they had actually being bugged, such that this produced a trail of information which disclosed their movements and others involvement, future assistance to others, as well as their intentions.

Now the intercepts seemed to reveal that Russell may have had another plan, as on 13 September 2017, he paid $70,000 for the yacht "56 South", a Hans Christian 36 that sailed the Sydney to Hobart moored at the Fremantle Sailing Club.

He further discusses Patrick travelling to Perth and his intended trip back to Grafton, and that Patrick had undertaken the trip before "with the little girls on-board", being the children, Charlotte and Jane.

Following a call from John SHIPTON (Julian Assange's father), the Director of The Wikileaks Party on 26 January 2018, Patrick reveal that Lizzie Weber (name used today) is still in Australia, and what she did by running with the children was right given the alleged corruption in the Family Court, police and child safety, and alleged rape of the children by David Morris. Patrick goes on to say that he is going to "fix" David Morris "come hell or high water".

Then on 9 February, during a conversation with Patrick, Russell indicates that he is ignoring 'Signal' messages from "that little prick", HOLT and that "he expects me to be his free Doctor whilst he screws me for hundreds of thousands."

Ann and Christopher Gordon

"It was as a result of the Facebook page we put up on the AAPP website that we were contacted by Ann Gordon," recalls Patrick. "Ann was the grandmother of Christopher Gordon. We learned from Ann that both of Christopher's parents, Candis and Hayden Hussein, had drug problems and the boy was being badly abused. Hayden, we gathered, had led a life on the wrong side of the law and was prone to violence. I was also told that Hayden was under witness protection because his brother was accused of murdering someone. So in spite of the fact that abuse of the child had been reported to the FCAA, the alleged perpetrator was under police protection.

"Ann had sent a message explaining that she was in a similar situation to Lizzie and sought our guidance. She had been given custody of her grandson, Christopher Hussein by court order in March 2016, but was growing increasingly desperate as the court orders were amended over time to allow the father increased access to the child.

4 - Russell Takes Action

"We spoke frequently on the phone and these conversations were recorded by the police. They heard me loud and clear referring to 'paedophile judges' and my strong desire to knock the shit out of David Morris. At the same time, I was in touch with Pat Plaisted, a friend of the Webers. I told her I was trying to organise iPads for Lizzie and the twins, and that I had arranged for a journalist to talk to both Lizzie and Ann and others involved in helping the children.

As it turned out, the 'journalist' was an undercover AFP agent which I established when I checked his credentials at the reception of the motel he had booked me into. He was the one who offered the iPads. When I figured these would be tracked, I realised what he was up to. He gave me a voucher for $100 for them to spend at Woolworths so I used the vouchers to purchase underwear for my son in Townsville which snookered them. We were desperate to get the media involved but throughout this saga we have had little luck. As far as I'm concerned, the Australian press is gutless.

It now becomes interesting, as on 21 February 2018, Patrick is heard to say to an unknown person that "we were going to stick these kids on there". This was followed by a call to Ann Gordon, where Patrick and Ann have a conversation about the "paedophile" judges, their suspicions that their telephone calls are being intercepted, and Patrick's threat to kill David Morris.

That same day, there is a conversation between Patrick and Plaisted where Patrick offered to provide iPad's for Lizzie Weber and the children, admits to publishing more S93A interview videos online, and that he has arranged for a journalist to interview people associated with Lizzie and Gordon, including Lizzie, Thorpe, Arthur Weber, Beth Tinning and Clancy.

This is followed on 25 February, by a call from Ann Gordon,

where Patrick and Ann have a conversation that she is on "the verge" of "taking off" and Patrick admits to "personally" helping Lizzie "and the kids escape".

"When Ann told me she was planning on doing a 'runner' with Christopher. I cautioned her against this, explaining the problems and pitfalls that lay ahead. Having said that, I also assured her that if she ran, Russell and I would do our best to help her and the child. She had legal custody of Christopher so I did not see why she should not take him away if she felt so inclined."

27 February 2018 Ann Gordon wrote to Tony Tonkin of the Child Protection Party (redacted)

Subject: Child abuse of Christopher

Hi Tony

I am very concerned for my grandson Christopher. I believe he has been getting sexually abused for some time. He cannot remember when it started and he's now 7, he said it has been happening for a long time. He has stated it has also got worse since it started.

We are trapped in federal circuit courts in Townsville.

I am 56 and don't know what to do. I'm on the verge of trying to run away but even then don't know where to start.

I have told the courts what is happening and, when I do, the father finds out and the child gets bashed.

I am worried that the father will end up killing Christopher, and the damage from the sexual abuse must be a live death in itself.

He's 7 and last night has asked when he can die and go to heaven. I said I will miss you and he said it's OK, I will be waiting for you: I have subpoenaed the father's health records as he has mental health issues to which he has objected to the courts.

4 - Russell Takes Action

I am the Maternal Grandmother of Christopher and the current orders say that he lives with me and spends two out of three weekends with his father.

The trial is part heard. I am screaming for help as he is a prisoner of the courts and being bashed and molested by his father, Hayden Hussein.

I have been in Christopher's life since birth and helped my daughter, and Candis Gordon, raise Christopher, up until December 2015, when he came into my primary care full time.

The mother who was a good parent at first fell into drugs when trying to reconcile with the father in Early 2015, and progressed to crime until around January 2016. Then spent two and a half months in jail in mid-2016 and is now on parole.

The father had drug issues from the age of Ten and a long criminal history as well as mental health issues.

The father's brother was charged with a brutal murder of a man from Charters Towers in September 2015.

In January 2016 the child disclosed that the maternal grandfather had put his finger in his bum.

I reported this to the police and told them that only the father and grandfather had had access to the child previously.

The police questioned the grandfather and said they did not believe the grandfather had interference with the child but believed something probably happened by someone at some time.

I asked were they trying to say it was the father and would they interview him. They said we cannot, as the child said it was the grandfather and this was not on record.

The father had been sentenced around the 5/2/16 only days before taking the child on the 20/2/16 for drunk driving, explosives, weapons, ICE and cannabis which were a few of the charges from June/July 2015 and was put on probation to which there have been more police records after this date.

The mother and her friends went to try to retrieve the child and a DVO was placed on the mother and were not successful.

I put a recovery order into the federal circuit courts of Townsville.

An interim order on the 2/3/2016 was made that the child remain in my care and the father spends time with him two weekends out of three.

The child then returned on numerous occasions complaining of a sore penis. He was taken to the doctors on two or three occasions and urine tests and an ultra sound were done. Results came back with no explanation to why this was occurring.

In April 2016 a child inclusive interviews were held.

There had been numerous times the child had come home complaining of a sore anus to which I assumed that the child had chaff. The child would not let me have a look and I had not even contemplated that it may be from sexual abuse but thought it was probably due to poor hygiene when toileting.

In May 2016, the child made disclosures after school holidays with his father of needle use, violence and fire arms and the father giving money to men this was reported to child safety and was unsubstantiated. It was also reported to the police to which little was done and they only went to speak with him. There were many reports made to child Safety to which were all said to be unsubstantiated as there was not enough evidence.

On another occasion where the child was exposed to extreme violence from the father and girlfriend's domestic violence and the police had attended twice in one day on the 9/4/17 that they would not be continued action because they would need proof of psychological damage from a psychologist which the father refused for the child to see.

Police also interviewed the child around July 2017 after the child disclosed to the doctor that the father hit him across the back four times because of telling his father's secrets.

The child had said that he would hide under the bed and cry when the domestic

4 - Russell Takes Action

violence occurred between the father and his 17 year old girlfriend (who had a history of violence and drugs) at the time or go and put earphones on as I had suggested. He speaks of bloodshed, punching and so on.

On the 8/12/17 Xmas holidays, the child went for three-and-a-half weeks to his father's ordered by the court.

On Christmas day I collected the child for one night. He was to return the following day.

When I was at the transfer to return the child, the child said dad had touched him. I said rude? He said yes.

On the 2/1/18 he was playing when he said dad doesn't touch me every day, only every second day. I don't think he was talking to me but talking to his toys. I asked Christopher did he do it again he said yes.

On the 5/1/18 I took Christopher to a police interview to which I have not seen, but Kate, the officer, told me that Christopher had said that dad touches him and that he does not want to go there any longer.

The child then made numerous short disclosures over the next week of: dad put his penis in my mouth and finger in my bum. Said sometimes it really hurts and I cry but dad doesn't stop.

I asked did it bleed? He said no, to which the father's barrister stated that to ask the child that was not appropriate.

Dad touches my penis and bum all the time.

The trial was adjourned to 18/1/18 for another interim hearing.

The ICL had no present view but said I may be coaching the child. The father said I was coaching the child, and the judge agreed that there was a possibility of coaching to which he was very biased in his views and has been throughout the case.

The judge ordered a further family report and said that he would talk to the family report writer to tell her his views beforehand and that he was impressed by the father and how far he has come. Which seems to have disappeared from his reasons for his decision.

At trial the judge said he would like the child to live with the father. This same comment by Judge Coker has been made throughout this case several times. Coker then set down a three day trial for August 2018, and he put an injunction on me not allowing me to take the child to police, Child Safety, speak with a psychologist even though has been referred three times by paediatricians and Qld health campus. I am not to take the child to any allied health departments. I need written permission from the father and ICL which I do not believe the father will do to report him.

The child then came home on the 18/2/18 with a bruise on his nose and red with light bruise under his eye, red mark on the side of his face, red ear, and hair missing.

The child later said that dad bashed me, pulled my ear and twisted it, hit me in the face and pulled my hair, and said 'why did you tell Ann about the kangaroo'.

The child was distraught and could not go to sleep or school the next day, and I could not take him to the doctors in fear of being accused of coaching.

The last weekend on the 25/2/18 the child said he was so tired he couldn't wake up in the morning and dad woke him up and told him to roll over so he could play with his bum and told him not to tell anyone.

The father has put an application in to have the child for the whole school holidays for Easter and up until trial where he wants full parental responsibility as well as the child to live with him and I visit supervised in the contact centre.

I believe he will get this due to things the judge has already indicated.

The judge has been biased, verbally abusive, intimidating and belittling me.

My biggest concerns are abuse, sexual, physical and psychological.

Kind Regards,

Ann Gordon

22 March, Patrick sends an SMS informing Ann that he may "have somewhere" for her and that he "will explore the option and get back to" her. The inference is that he is referring to accommodation on board the yacht.

Meanwhile Arthur Weber was clearly involved, when he attempts to deposit two hundred and fifty dollars ($250) into Gordon's Bank account, and a day later two hundred and fifty dollars ($250) was deposited into a Bank account in the name of "Wiki Detectives Pty Ltd". The signatory to this account is Holt's.

"On 26th March Ann attended a hearing of the FCCA in Townsville where she and Hayden received new orders giving Hayden more custody rights regarding Christopher," recalls Patrick. "It was clear to her she was losing control of her grandchild.

29th March she contacted Christopher's school to tell them he was sick and would be absent. Then she prepared to get on the road. The Police were listening. From the phone recordings they worked out where she was and that it was Graham Jones who was helping her.

"When she called to ask me to help, I made immediate arrangements to meet her at the Bunnings Warehouse in Rothwell. Knowing the cops were listening, we switched to the 'Signal' App to discuss future plans. I set off from Grafton in Russell's car loaded up with food and supplies.

"On meeting them I was immediately struck by Christopher. He was an impressive, likeable youngster, articulate and very forthcoming in explaining what had been done to him. My blood boiled.

"I booked them into the Kallangur Motel for the night under a false name and used cash. The next day, I collected them, and we discussed how best to plan ahead and avoid detection by the authorities. We decided Ann would go by the name of 'Shell' and Christopher would be 'Ben'. I explained to Ann she must regularly delete text messages and call logs from her phone. I also suggested they pass themselves off as mother and son.

"The two of them then caught a train to Ballina where Russell had organised a friend to collect them and take them to their temporary accommodation. He then met them in Ballina and took them south to Taree to safety where they stayed until the end of April. Once there, Russell organised a video recording in which Christopher explained in detail the abuse he had endured. This was sent to the AFP Townsville police who ignored it."

The following day, April 02, as Patrick is preparing to travel from Grafton to Brisbane to collect Ann and Christopher, Patrick tells Russell that he is "going to sneak in a blanket as well. Just in case they need to cover up." It was believed that Patrick took a "blanket" with him for the purpose of concealing Christopher Gordon in the vehicle, as he had done with Charlotte and Jane in 2014.

This is followed by a conversation where Russell informs Patrick that he has packed food, fruit and water in the boot of the vehicle. Patrick then departed Grafton, driving north towards Brisbane in Russell's vehicle.

Then, during a call from John Leonard, Patrick says he is "coming on a clandestine trip" as he has "got to pick up some grandmother and her grandson because they're going into hiding, but that's between you and me". Patrick enquires about long-term accommodation, and says that he is not paying for the accommodation, that it is "someone else's money". It is believed that Patrick's reference to "someone else's money" is a reference to Russell.

A short time later Ann and Christopher arrive at Bunnings Redcliffe where they meet Patrick.

4 - Russell Takes Action

On their way, Patrick stops the vehicle in the vicinity of Anzac Avenue, Kallangur, a suburb in Moreton Bay Region, Queensland, where Gordon visits a Lifeline store and attempts to purchase hats for herself and Christopher. She also visits a pharmacy and purchases hair dye/bleach, finally they arrive at the Kallangur Motel, Kallangur.

The next day, Patrick collects Ann and Christopher from the Kallangur Motel. Ann has adopted the name of "Shell" and Christopher the name of "Ben". Patrick provides instruction to Ann about regularly deleting text message and call logs from her mobile telephone. He also suggests that Ann and Christopher pass themselves off as mother and son. They arrive at an address in Coes Creek, in beautiful rural highlands on the Sunshine Coast Region, Queensland, where Ann and Christopher remain until about 24 April 2018.

Now Patrick sets about further attempting to locate David Morris, as on 5 April Patrick informs Nadine Frost that he wishes to elicit Frost's support to locate David Morris that he has searched the internet "every which way" he can for his address but with no success; however he has found out David Morris's partner's occupation and membership of the Brisbane Golf Club; and that he is trying to "find people that are in the system that can find out (her) address" and David Morris's address "via the Brisbane Golf Club" because if he finds "a member there and he's confident enough with me, he'll be allowed to find out his address"; He also wants to "put Morris in hospital because he threatened my daughter", and "that will come in due course".

During a conversation between Patrick and Russell, they discuss seeking the assistance of Plaisted, "the person to go to", to assist with longer term accommodation for Ann and Christopher.

The next day they discuss their attempts to source a caravan for the longer-term accommodation of Ann and Christopher. Patrick says that he could not locate "any fucking reasonable priced caravans".

20 April, Patrick and Russell then drive 610 kms from Grafton to Sydney, with the intention of cashing gold bullion owned by Russell. On the way Russell says to Patrick, that "Nabiac. That's where they were."

Subsequent investigations revealed that Lizzie and the children were residing in Coolongolook, the neighbouring suburb of Nabiac (283 km north of Sydney via the Pacific Highway and 24 km northwest of Forster-Tuncurry).

Russell continues; "they have been supported by Ros (Thorpe) at FIN before they flew the coop? Patrick enquires, "do they have money and food?"

Then following a call from Ann to Jones, Patrick makes arrangements to transport Ann and Christopher Gordon to the accommodation sourced by Plaisted, including that this friend Russell will collect Ann and take her "where she needs to go", but he needs Ann to arrive in Grafton no later than "Tuesday night/Wednesday morning"; as "what we've got is someone south of Newcastle".

23 April, Ann tells Patrick that she and Christopher are on a train heading to Brisbane. They discuss arrangements for them to travel onto Ballina, NSW north coast by bus.

Adams conveys them to her residence in Alumy Creek, where they remain for the evening (Adams is the landlord of Russell, who resides in a studio apartment attached to her residence).

Now the Plaisteds and Lizzie get involved given that Plaisted and

4 - Russell Takes Action

her husband Ridley are family friends of Arthur and Heather Weber.

Lizzie tells Plaisted that: Pridgeon is "slagging me off and I've organised this."; she "knew it was going to happen", that "all the money that [Pridgeon] wasted buying the boat"; and that Pridgeon purchased the boat in spite of her opposition.

During the same call, Lizzie refers to Charlotte and Jane as "Kel" and "Jaz", respectively. They discuss the schooling and exam results of "Kel" and "Jaz"[11].

April 24, Lizzie calls Joyce Evelyn Fazldeen, where she tells Fazldeen that "that lady (Gordon) can be there at two (2) o'clock tomorrow (ANZAC Day)." Plaisted then informs her that "at this stage they are looking at 2.00 pm! The dr is the driver!". The "dr" is a reference to Pridgeon.

Lizzie then asks Rex "Jack" John Parsons, the brother-in-law of Fazldeen to collect Ann and Christopher from Taree and accommodate them for one night.

Russell, in the company of Ann and Christopher, arrive at the South Taree Service Centre. and shortly after is joined by Parsons. Russell introduces Ann to Parsons as "Shelly" and that "this is our Ben" (Christopher Gordon).

On 26 April, Fazldeen collects Ann and Christopher, and conveys them to her residence in Argenton, NSW, where they reside until about 7 May 2018.

Later Lizzie calls to Fazldeen, where she asks Fazldeen to find out if there is, or has been, any media surrounding Gordon; and how long Gordon has "been away?".

- Fazldeen says since March and adds, that "it hasn't been long";

---

11 At the time of Lizie's arrest, Charlotte and Jane used these names

- Lizzie then says that she doesn't understand all the "secrecy", and suspects that Pridgeon is "going to his extremes" and he "likes to be the savour"; and asks whether there are any "court orders or anything" whereupon Fazldeen says "not yet";

Lizzie says that she was told that Christopher Gordon "was being sexually abused by the father"; but that she is "suspicious of everything Doc does now"; and further that "if there's no Family Court orders, then there's no nothing, there's no police after her, there's you know. It all seems a bit extreme to me."

And the AFP were listening in…

April 27, Patrick and Ann have a conversation to the effect that Patrick knows that she is "out safe and sound". Ann mentions that she liked Patrick's friend, Russell; she has had her hair dyed and cut in Nambour; whilst "Ben" (Christopher Gordon) is good, but a little bored;

Ann confirms she has pulled the battery and SIM card out of her mobile phone; and Patrick says they won't call to "keep security that way" but they will use it to use the Signal; he goes on to say that "we will keep working on it to improve your situation"; to which she responds that Russell was explaining to her that 'if there's three towers, then your locations off" (being a reference to the triangulation of a mobile telephone handset) but where she is, there is only one tower surrounded by hills, so she "should be alright"

Then on 28 April, Lizzie calls Fazldeen, to the effect that Gordon has been "told all this stuff" from Pridgeon, which is "freaking her out"; that there has been no media surrounding Gordon; and that Pridgeon is "making out it's just like her and it's not". She says that Pridgeon "had us scared of our own shadow as well", and that

4 - Russell Takes Action

- Pridgeon advised Gordon to "have an encrypted phone, you gotta do this and they triangulate from the thing, I'm thinking 'God' he watches too many movies.";
- Lizzie agrees that if Gordon had a phone in her own name, she would need to be concerned;
- Pridgeon had "freaked her out" such that she's "gone and bought another' phone; and
- while Lizzie and the children were residing with Pridgeon, Pridgeon "rung us up and the girls had just gone to bed and he said you've got to go bush now it's an emergency. So I've got them out of bed and we're in the bush, in winter, in the night time and when he finally rings back, he said 'it's ok now'. I said what happened and he said 'I saw a police car driving down the road' and this road is, you know, fifty (50) or a hundred (100) mile long and he's at the front of it and a police car drove down. And it's like what?";

....she adds scornfully that both "Russell and Patrick are white Zimbabweans";

Fazldeen then confirms to Lizzie that Christopher Gordon's father (Hussein) is "trying to get custody" and that Ann "said something about a Court order she's breached because she hasn't allowed him visitation."

It's now **2 May**, and things are hotting up. The AFP are on the trail of Russell, Patrick, Lizzie and the others. Clearly they have built up a dossier as to how the boys are assisting both Lizzie, Gordon, and the children. They make their own interpretation and inferences concerning the yacht, whilst they have a rough idea where both Gordon and Lizzie are hiding. It is time to act!

Lizzie (Morris) Weber arrested

On 3 May 2018 an AFP member watched as Lizzie Morris *(also known as Lizzie Weber)* attended an appointment at the Albert Street Medical Centre, Taree. There, she was observed to register for an appointment, sit in the waiting room and then respond to the name 'Miriam', when called by the doctor. She stood and entered the consultation room. Following her appointment she drove to Coloongolook north of Sydney.

The following day, 4 May, 15 AFP officers arrived at her residence, arrested her, searched the house and took the children into custody. She was then conveyed to the Taree Police Station and charged with abducting her daughters, and held without bail. The twins were immediately returned by AFP officers, back to their father, David Morris, this despite the fact that the AFP were completely aware of the children disclosures of abuse when they returned the children to the man the twins had identified as their abuser.

She appeared in Taree Local Court on Saturday the 12th where her extradition to Queensland was approved. The general message from the media after the arrest was one of great relief. Finally the children were safe.

'Missing Townsville woman and twin girls found four years on ... like pealing church bells," shouted one newspaper.

Amanda Gearing, AAP wrote: "Twin girls from Townsville who went missing four years ago have been found safe and well. Charlotte and Jane Morris, now 11, who were taken into hiding by their mother Lizzie Morris on April 4, 2014 and not seen since they were found in Taree, NSW on Friday morning. The children's grandmother, Heather Weber, said she was relieved to hear from her daughter after four years of silence. 'We had a phone call from Lizzie saying she was in police custody in Taree. She was found with Jane and Charlotte.

Lizzie sounded very composed,' Mrs Weber said. *'It was a bit of a shock but it was just lovely to hear from her.'* Mrs Weber said she and her husband Arthur are preparing to seek custody of the children, now aged 11. The discovery of the children followed a four-year police search for the missing trio. The father of the children, David Morris, had mounted an ongoing media campaign to try to locate the children.

05 May, Gavin Butler for the Daily Mail wrote: She (Lizzie) has since been extradited to Queensland and charged with two counts of child stealing. She will face court in Brisbane on Tuesday 08 May.

Mr Morris said that after several years he was acutely concerned about the effect the situation might have on his young daughters' development. He had wondered whether this day would ever come, but always held on to the hope he would hold his daughters in his arms again. "You start wondering when it could happen after we tried so hard and the police tried so hard for such a long time," Mr Morris said.

"It was quite a shock because I had no idea what was happening this morning … the police were always reassuring me that they were working on it but it all came to fruition today. I was in a meeting at work when the call came through from the Federal Police. I jumped in the car and drove straight to Taree to be with my children."

He said he was thrilled to bring his girls home and provide them with the life they deserved. "My girls have obviously been through a lot over the last four years," he said. "A bit of excitement and a bit of nerves, I guess, but I'm just looking forward to my girls being able to get back to a normal life after years of insecurity and instability. It's going to take a lot to work through the damage that's been done. The number one I thing I think they need is a normal, stable life … a home and a school and friends and sport and everything kids do in order to have a normal and secure upbringing."

Lizzie had kept them off the grid for four years, with no formal schooling on a lonely property.

Authorities did not reveal how investigators tracked down the girls but had been calling for people to come forward with information. The long awaited breakthrough came just a month after the Bulletin reported on the fourth anniversary of the girls' disappearance.

But there were people who differed from the official view. They posted comments on social media.

- "So sorry these poor girls given straight back, how shocking this system is to allow it, criminal!"
- "Lizzie's parents are so overwhelmed with everyone's comments and support. It has given them hope that the truth will be told, no more cover up, no more lies. A big thank you on their behalf."
- "We all need to stand together and let the world know that the shame isn't being a victim of child sexual abuse... The shame is not standing up for survivors/victims.... These kids need a voice NOW."
- "This story gives me goosebumps...how dare they be handed back to him."
- "Absolutely true... And who knows what they're being subjected to as we speak! He's a stranger to them and a SCARY ONE AT THAT no matter how you look at it."
- "So many closed-minded people... It's frightening think how many people have their heads buried in the sand about this one..... children of four do not lie about being sexually abused. The person who has allegedly committed these heinous crime..."

4 - Russell Takes Action

- "The girls should never have been released to their father until there was a proper investigation done!"

Now it was the time for the AFP to find out what Tim Holt knew, as on 5 May: Holt was cautioned and provided his rights pursuant to Part 1C of the *Crimes Act 1914* (Cth). His home was searched, and amongst the evidence were the 5x compact discs marked "interview" being the Queensland Police interviewing David Morris, Lizzie Weber and the children; which Lizzie had stolen.

Under caution, HOLT stated:

- He is the Director of Wiki Detectives Pty Ltd;
- As Wiki Detectives, he hunts paedophiles online via social chat rooms, posing as a 13 or 14 year old child and is "known as Australia's best paedophile hunter";
- He established the "Free Missing Twins" Facebook page and website and did so at the request of the "Anti-Paedophile Party", being O'Dea and Pridgeon;
- Only he and O'Dea can administer and publish to the "Free Missing Twins" Facebook page and website;
- He was contacted by the "Anti-Paedophile Party" because they believed that David Morris was a paedophile;
- The discs were sent to him in the mail by the "Anti-Paedophile Party", whose Directors are "Patrick O'Dea" and "Russell" (Pridgeon), with instructions to publish the "interviews" on the internet;
- He published the interviews on YouTube and the Free Missing Twins website;
- He did not know the contents of the discs before he published them on the internet;

- He had never met Lizzie Weber, Charlotte, Jane or David Morris;
- He is aware of the prohibition of publishing Family Court proceedings;
- He could shut down the Free Missing Twins website "at any time";
- He had not received any benefit or compensation, directly or indirectly, from the "Anti-Paedophile Party" for his work.

6 May, Patrick confirms with Ann that he is aware of Lizzie's arrest and the recovery of Charlotte and Jane, whilst a day later Parsons informs Arthur Weber that Lizzie and the children had been with him for two (2) years. Further, Patrick says that he "just received a message saying you're going to hand yourself in. Remember, we have a contingency plan".

7 May, Ann calls Hetty Johnston (Bravehearts), where Johnston congratulates her for "taking the child and doing the runner". Johnston encourages Ann to make an official complaint to the Queensland Crime and Corruption Commission (CCC) "before the police find you because, once they do, it's too late".

Johnston offers to go to the CCC with Ann. She also tells Ann "to hang in there" and that she will work with Gearing in the meantime. Johnston says that she "worked with" Briggs in relation to Lizzie Weber. Johnston will "take it higher" and tells Ann "good on ya" and to "stay put for just a little bit longer and we'll see if we can sort this out another way. We've got to get this complaint in before you come out of hiding". Ann says that she "probably won't come out of hiding" and will "run for as long" as she can.

Later that day, there is a further conversation between Patrick and in which Russell says: "I told her to get rid of and hide anything

4 - Russell Takes Action

and tell them all to get stuffed if they come near you, it's as simple as that." They also discuss the AFP's execution of a search warrant upon Tim Holt's residence. Holt had been hired by the AAPP to handle their social media account.

17 May, Lizzie appears before the Supreme Court of Queensland in Brisbane for a bail application. Her solicitor Phil Rennick produces a signed letter to the Court from Russell as an attachment to his affidavit in support of the bail application. In this letter, Pridgeon states to the Court that:

"On or about mid-April 2014, I was asked to attend to a woman and her two daughters, who were in hiding from a particularly abusive and violent man, I was advised. I was given to understand that they were travelling under false names. I did not ask what their real names were. I have subsequently learnt that this woman was Lizzie Morris, and the daughters were Charlotte and Jane Morris."

18 May, Amanda Gearing, interviewing Lizzie for her publication, asks whether she knows Gordon, whereupon Lizzie replies "yes". Lizzie indicates to Gearing that she believes Gordon was used as part of a "set up" to find her.

This is followed by a call between Lizzie and Matthew Morrison where Lizzie says she believes that Gordon was a police "setup". That's why we got caught".

However it all comes to nothing when on the 22nd May 2018 Ann and Christopher were apprehended at Wauchope Train Station in NSW. Patrick says. "Her mistake was using her original phone to book a taxi to take her and the boy to catch the train back to Townsville.

After her arrest Ann was charged with Child Stealing under article s363 (1) A of the Queensland Criminal Code. Her bail conditions included a bar-tracker on her ankle, despite having no criminal record.

"Somewhat ironically", remarked Russell, "she was travelling as she planned to appear in court for her scheduled appearance. The arrest warrant was for the offense of child stealing. The following day she was extradited to Queensland by members of the Queensland Police Service. Seven days later, on the 29th May, the FCAA ordered that the boy should reside with his father who would have sole parental responsibility."

This enraged Patrick, and he set about involving the Outlaw Motorcycle Gang (OMCG). On 30 May Patrick references his attempts to contact the OMCG members and provides Hayden's name as the person who abused Christopher Gordon.

He tells Ann that he has made an attempt to involve the "Rebels" (OMCG). Later, in a conversation with Russell, he informs him that he "got hold of a biker gang in Townsville and because that Grandmother (Ann) previously testified in that murder case, they know all about it because it was one of their guys, and I told them the father's name, and told them to make sure the father doesn't touch that kid, and I gave him all the info and said to make sure he places that kid with the other lady." Russell replies, "When you can't go to the cops you need to go to the bikies."

"Although I was facing charges, my involvement with Ann was very peripheral," says Russell. "Patrick was the prime mover and the only reason I became involved was because Patrick was away when she passed through. I met Ann for the first time when she stayed the night and drove her to Taree the next morning. Since then I have had almost nothing to do with her. The point is that the child was forced into contact with the abuser despite his disclosures of abuse. The charge against Ann of child-stealing was vexatious because she had custody of the child at the time. There is video evidence in the Operation Noetic brief of the child disclosing sexual abuse. But

4 - Russell Takes Action

David Miles, the CO of the Townsville CPIU, issued a statement saying the child (Christopher) was interviewed three times and did not make disclosures of sexual abuse, especially by the father. The father is a career criminal, has a history of violence and has been using drugs. Christopher has been back with him for almost four years."

Russell's response to Lizzie's arrest: "I was overwhelmed with anxiety when I thought about them, and as a desperate act I wrote to the Minister of Child Safety (Hon Di Farmer) and the Minister of Police in Queensland, the Federal Attorney General, and the shadow ministers, on 31st May, identifying myself as a person who had sheltered Lizzie and the twins while they were on the run.

I described the children disclosures and the malfeasance that led to them being forced into the custody of the father, despite their clear and multiple disclosures of abuse by Morris. My e-mails were ignored and blocked. The AFP would have been notified about this correspondence. This is the letter I posted:

Letter to Dianne Farmer Minister of Child Safety 30 May 2018 (redacted)

Dear Ms Farmer,

My name is Dr William Russell Massingham Pridgeon. I write to you on the most desperately urgent matter.

I am deeply concerned about the immediate safety and wellbeing of the Morris twins, Jane and Charlotte, now 11 years old, who have been fugitives from Australian law after their mother, Lizzie Morris was unable to protect them from ongoing rape by their father, David Morris, and his friends, over years. Finally, in desperation, Lizzie uplifted the children from school and fled with them.

I am one of many people who sheltered and protected them in the four years that they were free of ongoing. At various times I drove vast distances to transport them between places of safety, and when I was able find safe accommodation for them I sheltered them in a safe house in my locality from about Easter 2014 for more than a year. This was one of the greatest privileges of my life to be able to help these children escape the horrific abuse inflicted upon them by fiends, and enabled by rogue judges, lawyers and policemen who actively hid the truth, ignored evidence, and facilitated child rape, effectively trafficking these children to paedophiles.

When the children came to me, they reported recurrent agonisingly painful genital ulcers, which could only have been genital herpes. I treated these with antiviral medications. Their father has genital herpes.

The children also reported that they bled from the rectum: Jane bled for about 2 weeks, Charlotte, the smaller twin, bled for more than 8 weeks. At no time did these children permit me to examine them, indeed it took almost a year for them to trust me, but I was able to observe Charlotte emerging in distress from the toilet, which I observed to show traces of the blood she had lost.

The father, David Morris, has a history of violence and abuse towards Lizzie and the girls. Unbelievably, Federal Magistrate John Coker, awarded sole custody to David Morris while there were AVO's in place against him for Lizzie and Charlotte. At no time were the people who had heard the children's disclosures of sexual abuse allowed to testify.

These children disclosed their physical and sexual abuse on numerous occasions: there were more than 40 disclosures to 14 different adults, including child psychologists, occupational therapists, general practitioners, other professionals, family and friends. These mandatory reports were ignored. Only ONE of these people was ever interviewed by the Police. The Police investigation, so called, was a farce.

There were also twelve court appointed supervisors who were witness to the twins ongoing disclosures of sexual abuse, during Lizzie's supervised contact with the children, yet they were never allowed to give evidence and were never interviewed by the Police.

When the supervisors reported the children's disclosures to the ICL, she passed

4 - Russell Takes Action

the information to David Morris immediately. The children reported being punished for each disclosure, yet they continued to disclose. Eventually the supervisors stopped reporting the disclosures because they feared for the children.

During the two years and four months after Lizzie lost custody of the children she listened to her children disclose their ongoing sexual and physical abuse each week, during her supervised contacts, powerless to help. Eventually she did what any mother would do: she rescued her daughters and fled. Child Safety completely betrayed these children, although they had the power and the means to rescue them at any time.

The Police accused the children during interviews of disclosing abuse only because their mother had told them to do so. The Police lied to Lizzie: telling her that the children had not disclosed abuse to them, when of course they had. The Police explained the children's disclosures as dreams.

I am absolutely begging you to act immediately, without warning, and retrieve these children to a place of safety, where they can once more be safe.

Yours sincerely,

Dr Russell Pridgeon

What was puzzling to Russell was why none of these journalists covering the story thought to ask why a highly educated woman like Lizzie, once a respected member of her community, who ran her own 'Early Learning Centre', should 'steal' her children, become a fugitive, living rough, in very uncertain situations, with the certain knowledge that she should eventually be found, arrested, and face extended jail time. What could have happened to make Lizzie do such a thing?

"And here was I telling everyone in authority who might be interested, exactly what I had done. Five months later, the police led the public to believe my arrest was the result of their excellence as investigators; what a lot of absolute rubbish."

"I got busy, immediately tweeting and sending messages as far and wide as possible," remembers Patrick. "I was trying to get the public and the press to understand what was happening; these poor girls were now back where they should not have been but no-one in the press was listening. There was a media blackout to protect the police and the judiciary; it's diabolical. The fact is Lizzie had listened to her children disclose sexual abuse by their father which had been occurring since the age of two years."

* * *

Meanwhile, on 31 May, Patrick tells Russell that solicitor Rennick will not tell him the location of Charlotte and Jane. Russell indicates it is probably because they are worried Patrick will go and "knock him off" (David Morris). Patrick responds that "I will for sure, that's why I want the address and nobody is giving me the address".

1 June, Russell calls Amanda Gearing, the reporter who records an interview with Russell wherein:

- He admits that he treated the children, "looked after them .. in hiding", "sheltered them", "fed them", "clothed them" and "provided them with the necessities of life";
- "Neither child would allow me to do any intimate examinations of their genital areas, nor did I attempt to do so against their wishes";
- The children never made any disclosures of sexual abuse to him and he never asked;
- He believed that "they were suffering from genital herpes" but that he had never undertaken any pathology;
- With respect to Lizzie Weber and the children, that he would "be deeply, deeply ashamed not to do everything that I had done";

4 - Russell Takes Action

- He "absolutely" knew that the children were in hiding at the time;
- He was motivated by his own experience in the Family Court;
- Briggs analysed drawings of his step-son which "in her opinion showed severe sexual abuse";
- Briggs put him in touch with Lizzie Weber "long before" she went into hiding;
- Lizzie Weber (Lizzie) said "that she would run with these children as soon as she possibly could, she had no choice";
- He "learned to disregard law that is obviously inhumane and completely and utterly wrong";
- He is aware that "there is no defence at law, especially if I am in front of a Judge who is trying to hide his own professions malfeasance";
- Second letter from Russell to Minister of Child Safety Dianne Farmer 3rd June *(redacted). See footnote*[12]

---

12 *Dear Ms Farmer,*
I have written to you previously about the Morris twins, who are in the custody of their father, David Morris, since they were apprehended with their mother after being fugitive for four years.
I have expressed my gravest fears for the safety and wellbeing of these twins and begged you to immediately rescue them and place them in a place of safety.
As I have explained before, these children have made disclosures about their father, David Morris physically and sexually abusing them, to professionals, family and friends, on more than 40 occasions. Twelve Court-appointed supervisors also heard the children disclose their abuse during supervised visits with Lizzie. These would have been mandatorily reported. There is more than enough prima face evidence to take these children away from David Morris.
Not to do so is an unspeakable act, and it places you in an absolutely untenable position.
Your Department keeps saying that their legal advice is that they cannot act, which is quite contrary to the advice I have received from a Queensland Barrister at Law, specialising in Family Law:
YET YOUR DEPARTMENT USES ANY EXCUSE NOT TO ACT!

Then on 11 June, Holt participated in a Record of Interview where he was cautioned and provided his rights pursuant to Part 1C of the Crimes Act 1914 (Cth). During that interview, he said:

- He "speaks cyber" and worked for ASIO, CIA, FBI and the AFP;
- He is aware of the prohibition of publishing Family Law proceedings and has knowledge of the section 121, Family Law Act 1975 (Cth) offence;
- He posted videos of the police interviews with the Morris children on 'You Tube' which he agreed was a public social media platform;
- He agreed that the videos identified the Morris children contrary to the section 121 offence;
- He received packages of evidence from Lizzie and anonymous others;
- He has not received any benefit or compensation, directly or indirectly, from O'Dea or Pridgeon for the Morris matter;
- The $27,000 deposited into the "Wiki Detectives" (by Pridgeon) was a "donation" and in response to assistance he provided Pridgeon with his civil defamation case; and
- "Wiki Detectives" is a 'not-for-profit' organisation.

14 July Patrick tells Russell about sitting outside Morris's residence, to the effect: "I sat outside our friend's place today. No sign of anything but the cars were all there. And I'm going to do it again in due course, you know?"

19 July Patrick tells Holt that he "staked out that pig's place (David Morris) where he stays in Brisbane" and that he "sat there for a couple of hours and nobody came or left but I checked under

the garage and there were kids bikes in there and whatever. So when I'm back up that way again I'm gonna go and sit and have another wait and see." Further, that "if I see him it's going to be difficult not to deal with it."

Patrick: "At this point I was still keen to get my hands on David Morris. Apart from what I knew about him, he had threatened my daughter and I wanted to let him know he was messing with the wrong guy.

David Morris had set up a Facebook page titled 'Taryn loves cock'. He then sent Patrick's daughter, Taryn, a Facebook message. "I know your father is behind the 'Find the Twins' website (which the AFP closed down). Let him know I've been in contact." The message was implicitly threatening.

CHAPTER 5 – THE LAW COMES CALLING

Arrest of Russell and Patrick

On 17 October 2018, Russell arrived at his surgery in Grafton, New South Wales, to be surprised by the sudden arrival of a convoy of police cars. He was quickly surrounded by around 20 armed officers who were immediately followed by dozens of reporters and photographers.

"To my huge embarrassment my surgery was then searched, and all my electronic equipment seized along with documents. My car was searched and something I had never seen before was retrieved from my trunk.

Darren Williamson and Dr. Russell Pridgeon

5 - The Law Comes Calling

"We then went to my place of residence which was a converted garage rented as a boarder from Dottie Adams, a kindly lady who was threatened by Sergeant Christopher McGregor and warned sternly not to cause any trouble. What they expected her to do remains unclear to me.

Dottie has been a rock. She treated me like family and has given me peppercorn rent. It can't have been easy. Many other people have been kind, no one more than Dottie.

Watching them search my house I was struck by the fact that they had been there before. They took my laptop, iPads and phone along with all my financial papers. None of these have ever been returned. As a result I have not been able to complete a tax-return or apply for a pension.

"From there I was shackled and transferred to Grafton Police Station where I saw Patrick. He had been arrested that morning at home under similar circumstances. We were denied police bail."

Patrick: "Bearing in mind I had been in the face of the politicians, police and judiciary for years asking – no begging – them to reinvestigate the case, it was ironic that these little darlings arrived at my door as they did; 28 armed Federal Police to arrest me and at the same time arrest Russell. Big brave mice they were! All they had to do was phone me and I've been down to the station, but they needed to prove a point. It became the biggest, most expensive police case in Australian history – and they were going after a couple of ex-Rhodesians who just wanted to help children.

"Jail was no big deal. The coppers were really good guys – I think they knew the story and Russell was a GP to a couple of them. They were kindly, gave us coffee whenever we asked for it and food was via McDonalds who they obviously had an arrangement with."

AFP arrest Patrick O'Dea in Grafton

"Russell and I were processed and jailed. In the holding cell there was just the two of us. We were still allowed to talk to each other at this stage and we were not at all worried about discussing the bullshit and how to respond to it. The local police allowed Russell's landlady to bring us fresh clothes whilst a local solicitor assisted us, pro bono.

"The next day the AFP drove us to Brisbane, Queensland, a journey of 380 kms. Russell and I in separate cars. Very comfortable drive in BMW's. I was alone with two of the AFP guys. Very decent and of course the whole way down I rabbited on. Before we left the station in Grafton they asked that I not discuss my case at all. Again the press were present at every stage of our move and we were filmed and featured prominently in the media. We didn't understand yet that we were being portrayed as 'Child Stealers', with all the imputations that we were paedophiles."

"Brisbane watch-house was different; altogether harder and more aggressive," remembers Russell. "I watched Patrick as we were being grilled; he was standing at ease, hands behind his back, expressionless gaze into the middle distance, in his mind he was back on the parade square at Llewelyn barracks. But the officers dealing with us here were bullies, unworthy of any respect. We had been shat on by the best from the SAS and RLI; but they were real tough guys, they had been through the fire, and worthy of respect. The irony was here we were in jail having left one police state, only to find ourselves in another."

"I was between many other cells and all during the night drunks and drug users and those involved in fights were constantly brought in and placed into cells," says Patrick. "Much hurling of abuse by these individuals at the police. One of them irked me so much I asked the police to put him in my cell for five minutes. It was interesting, though, to observe guys brought in during the course of the night who were royally abusing the coppers. On the fourth day we had been bailed and were not supposed to contact each other.

"When we appeared in court on 20 October before the magistrate, it was behind a bullet proof screen. Even more interesting was the fact that Mr. Morris was also in court observing us with a smirk on his face. How, I still wonder, did he know we were going to be there?

"The newspapers reported Russell was the alleged mastermind behind the scheme, and he was charged with conspiracy to defeat justice. He was also charged with dealing in the 'proceeds of a crime', along with two counts of 'child stealing' and 'stalking'. For most of the hearing, he remained slumped in the dock with his eyes closed.

"The AFP told the court how the women and children were relocated and given aliases and disguises to avoid authorities. They explained in some detail how the group was able to evade authorities for four years by using fraudulent IDs, encrypted messaging apps, and an internal cash economy.

The Boys from Bulawayo

Prosecutor Christine Wilson   *Commander Justine Gough*

Commonwealth prosecutor Christine Wilson spoke of the scheme's intricacy. "The level of sophistication with this case, especially with encryption communication, is quite high," she said.

The prosecution went on to explain and speculated how Russell had bought a yacht and was planning to leave the country – "to possibly help mothers and their children start a new life in New Zealand or Zimbabwe".

Russell: "The proceeds of a crime charge was never made clear, and the particulars, if they were spelled out at all, mutated over time. The initial ploy by the AFP was to portray me to the world as the kingpin of the child-stealing network who financed the criminal operation from my reserves of gold. The gold was actually part of my superannuation and at the time of my arrest had been cashed in and invested in another enterprise, so I no longer owned any gold and the AFP knew this. They also knew the gold was from my superannuation, hard earned by a lifetime of work and taxed. The charges morphed into allegations I had financed Patrick and Tim Holt doing their exposes in Wikileaks. The charge-sheet said

5 - The Law Comes Calling

I had committed these crimes in New South Wales and Western Australia, and yet I was being prosecuted in Queensland but that seemed not to worry them."

Appearing before an elderly Magistrate, bail was granted on tough conditions aimed at silencing Russell and Patrick. Despite being granted bail, they had to remain behind bars an extra day because the police did not have the GPS trackers available. The additional problem was their phones had been confiscated and the trackers did not work without phones. GPS trackers use the 4G mobile phone network to operate, but alleged offenders must also be contactable by phone as a condition of their bail, in the event the internet fails.

They discovered later that this tracker demand rankled the Queensland police and prosecutors because there were only 100 of these devices available in the State and they were urgently needed to track dangerous criminals. As it turned out, five of these were now reserved for use on their group of 'child stealers' and they did not have enough for the 'bad guys'. They are not normally used on elderly people without a history of violence.

"I would have to wear mine for almost a year, Ann Gordon for two years. Every day I had to sit next to a charger which was a huge inconvenience," recalls Russell "This was all about intimidation by the AFP; don't mess with us when we are protecting paedophiles.

"After such a carefully orchestrated media campaign to portray us as criminals who harmed children, they could not allow the truth to come out and we were not allowed to comment on social media. We were to report daily to a police station. I was forbidden to contact over 30 people. This matter should have been dealt with in the Family Court but was elevated to the Federal Court which is a superior court and into the jurisdiction of the criminal court system and procedures.

"Outside court, our defence lawyer Mr Owens said his clients were relieved to be granted bail. 'It's going to be a long process, it was a long process up until today so the main focus was getting them out, back home and now we can deal with them as they come,' he said. 'We haven't really seen any brief of evidence because they're quite unique charges. It's certainly not a nice experience that's for sure, they weren't enjoying it in there [custody] but, like I said, they're out now and they can focus on defending themselves and making it right. They've got to bide their time and have their day in court, but it will come out eventually, the situation, and not what has been portrayed,' he told reporters outside court.

Deputy Chief Magistrate Anthony Gett who was to preside over the case (together with Attorney-General and Minister for Justice Shannon Fentiman)

"On another level my newfound notoriety did not help my personal relationships. Many people supported me; others stayed away. Few women are interested in a man facing 40 years of jail. My son was my strongest supporter, but I certainly did not want him being involved, it just makes you a target.

"I felt very targeted while wearing the GPS tracker, it is so obvious, and of course it is only given to the worst sort of criminal. I didn't manage to go to gym training, and so became weaker, deconditioned, and unfit. I avoided crowds, public places, shopped during quiet times, became reclusive. Child protection interferes with the business model of a very large industry. It is important to understand how much fear there is about protecting children in Australia.

"What came as an unpleasant surprise was that I was also charged with 'stalking David Morris', simply because Patrick phoned me while he was sitting outside Morris's house. Far from stalking him, in actual fact I had never met Morris, nor had I ever communicated with him on any medium, in any way. I had never made any threats against him, direct or indirectly. At the time of the alleged offense I was 300+ kms away. However, because stalking is a crime of violence, it was used by the police and prosecution to present me as a dangerous criminal, who needed harsher bail conditions."

The Media

"When we were released, the media were there to greet us, their nonsensical questions about whether we stole 1-200 children and whether I was the kingpin of an international child stealing network was my first insight into the AFP media campaign against me. I was also asked by the journalists why I had embezzled government funding for the Australian Anti-paedophile Party, which baffled me at the time. No AAPP candidates were elected to parliament, therefore we were not entitled to funding. There was no government money ever given to us, therefore nothing to embezzle. But it was a measure of the AFP strategy to mislead these incredibly gullible and stupid people. All the AAPP funding came from private donations, mostly from myself. I explained to anyone listening that I was looking forward to the truth coming out and repeated my view that crimes had been covered up by the very people tasked with enforcing the law. I said I looked forward to exposing the culprits. The whole exercise was a set-up, a power play, a photo-opportunity, so the whole world could see us being humiliated.

"Bearing in mind I had written to some of the highest authorities in the land over five months explaining exactly what I had done in relation to the various children, I was surprised by all this but I still, naively as it turned out, felt I had little to fear. As a result I probably said more than I should have because I was up against people who were determined to destroy my life. All they had to do was call me and tell me to report to the station and I would have done so immediately. This was clearly a well-planned event in collaboration with the press."

"I must say, the media management was neatly done. The press, electronic and print media were briefed before-hand, present at my arrest, and court appearances and extradition to Queensland in large numbers. At the arrest before television cameras and reporters, the Australian Federal Police trumpeted the fact that search warrants executed revealed plans to sail children overseas, and that they had broken a child-smuggling ring. The narrative that I was an abductor/trafficker, with all the insinuations of me doing sexual harm to children went unchallenged: I was incommunicado in jail, and by the time I was released, charges had been laid, and the matter was now *sub judice*. The false narrative echoed through the media, and was repeated after every court hearing that followed.

"In the face of this media onslaught, I was almost defenceless, denied the right of reply because of the *sub judice* rule. In terms of this we are allowed to set aside the rule and be quoted by media, in a fair and transparent way, for things that are said, but this gives the presiding officers wanting to shut us down plenty of latitude. I was muzzled by one magistrate who accused me of 'grandstanding'. So

5 - The Law Comes Calling

no fetters on anyone wanting to scandalise us, but we were pretty much told to shut up or else. At one Directions Hearing I was not even allowed to speak at my presentation so I could be heard; instead I had to submit my points for consideration in writing. Further to this, during the Committal presentation I was repeatedly threatened with Criminal Defamation and forced to redact my evidence and submissions. These people know exactly what they are doing, and they know I know too much to be allowed a voice.

"The Australian press responded to our arrests with almost irrational excitement.

Some of the headlines:

- Network helping mums, kids hide: Aussie abduction ring planned to sail mothers and kids to NZ.
- Children hidden and their identities changed by parent abduction ring.
- Abducted Australian children sent to New Zealand, South Africa.
- Kidnapping ring which helped jilted mothers abduct their children exposed.
- A parental abduction syndicate has been cracked following a two-year AFP investigation.
- Vigilante Group that Removed Kids from Sexually Abusive Parents to Stand Trial.
- Police Bust Child-Stealing Group Operating Across Australia, Four Charged.
- A vigilante group that allegedly financed and specifically assisted two separated women in Australia to abduct their own children and keep them hidden in violation of family law court orders has been struck down by authorities.

Janet Fife-Yeomans of the Daily Telegraph wrote: *The Australian Federal Police cracked an underground parental abduction ring following a two-year investigation into the group that allegedly helped jilted mothers to abduct and hide their own children across Australia. The network managed to evade detection for a decade.* Detectives say the investigation, Operation Noetic, is ongoing and there could be more arrests.

Three men and a woman were arrested and charged for their alleged role in the kidnapping syndicate, which organised and financed the children's snatching with plans to even use a yacht to smuggle them to New Zealand. He (Pridgeon) is the founder of the Australian Anti-Paedophile Party which ran Senate candidates in the 2016 election, but he says he was 'protecting them from their abusive fathers'. He is accused of having a central role in the group's 10-person "nucleus" as the key financier, however, the *Australian Federal Police believe many more "like-minded" people assisted the group in its operation to contravene family law orders.*

The network allegedly used a collection of phone messaging apps to communicate and plan the alleged abductions, an internal cash economy, encrypted messaging applications while the children were hidden by having their hair dyed, given new names and new birthdays, and fraudulent identity documents to evade detection for a decade. Additionally, it is reported that they also turned to supporters who provided food, accommodation and transport during the kidnappings.

The Australian Federal Police said they had recovered 10 children stolen in contravention of Family Court custody orders, five of them directly linked to the crime syndicate, during their two-year investigation, but fear more could remain hidden.

'*I don't think we can exclude there are other cases,*' *AFP Manager of Crime Operations Justine Gough said.*

Police said they expected to make more arrests after executing 10 search warrants on Wednesday in Grafton, Dubbo, Townsville and Perth, where they seized a yacht, called '56 South', allegedly belonging to Dr Pridgeon.

5 - The Law Comes Calling

In the wake of all the media hubris, there were some dissenting views, mainly on social media:

- The Government is trying to control the narrative in regard to the arrests that have occurred as part of Operation Noetic. They are claiming that there is a large child abduction network throughout Australia. Don't allow yourself to be taken in by the narrative that is being provided and reported by mainstream media. They are trying to make out that the two men and their connections who have been arrested are criminals. They are not. They are heroes, every single one of them.

- The catastrophic crisis in the Family Courts and connected child safety systems has dramatically imploded. It has reached a point where these systems themselves are charging and jailing advocates and professionals who are desperately trying to protect children, after their parents find that legal remedies have hit brick walls where the abuse of their children is often disregarded through inadequate investigations and misconduct.

- Being an advocate myself I have heard first hand from parents the immense trauma the courts are inflicting on children and families. 'It is now so bad I consider that it to be purposeful.' We do not have any justice in Australia. We have a legal system that processes cases in the favour of the state. There is little oversight to the criminal conduct occurring in these courts by court staff. Anyone who speaks out is quickly shut down.

- Let's be quite clear here. The children who were allegedly abducted were NOT abducted. They were removed from situations where the courts failed to protect the children. This was as a LAST RESORT ONLY. I know this myself because I have spoken to parents on whose mind it weighed heavily as to whether they should run to keep a child safe, or allow the child to go to the perpetrator knowing full well the abuse that would take place while the child is in that person's custody. This is court- sanctioned child abuse and this is rampant in the Family and Children's Courts of Australia.

- There is substantial evidence in these cases as to the abuse that is being perpetrated upon children. I won't go into the detail as it is quite horrific. It's difficult to read, and listen to the disclosures made by these children. To ignore this evidence at trial shows a complete incompetence and disregard by the judiciary. The system is broken. In fact it's worse than broken, it's completely shattered and is no longer working at all except for those who profit financially from it.

- The Australian Federal Police in this operation can be likened to the SS in Hitler's Germany. They have been tasked with eliminating dissent, particularly in regard to stonewalling on the call for a Royal Commission into the Family Law System. Yesterday's events show that they are trying to keep a lid on it. We need to continue calling for it and loudly. Only a Royal Commission can protect our children at this point because the system is so broken.

- And finally, please throw your support behind these men and the connections in their alleged network. They are good, honourable and genuine people who have tried to make a difference in this stinking system. Don't believe the rhetoric the mainstream media is trying to get you to believe. Don't let them control the narrative because it is very biased.

5 - The Law Comes Calling

Russell commented: "I have always been a self-sufficient person, and my own harshest critic. But the media portrayal was overwhelming. It took me ages to understand what an expert job they had done of character assassination. I felt much more at peace in other towns; in Grafton it was too raw. Fortunately many good people took me under their wings and supported me."

Prime Minister Scott Morrison apologises

Interestingly, only five days after the arrest of Russell and Patrick, on the 22nd of October, Prime Minister Morrison, in response to the growing outcry against the Family Court rulings, and the Commission of Inquiry findings decided to seize the limelight with an impassioned address to parliament:

Australian Prime Minister Scott Morrison apologises

"I move that the house apologise to the victims and survivors of institutional child sexual abuse.

"Mr Speaker, silenced voices, muffled cries in the darkness, unacknowledged tears, the tyranny of invisible suffering, the never-heard pleas of tortured souls, bewildered by an indifference to the unthinkable theft of their innocence. Today, Australia confronts a trauma, an abomination, hiding in plain sight for far too long. Today, we confront a question too horrible to ask, let alone answer – why weren't the children of our nation loved, nurtured and protected?

"Why was their trust betrayed? Why did those who know cover it up? Why were the cries of children and parents ignored? Why was our system of justice blind to injustice? Why has it taken so long to act? Why were other things more important than this, the care of innocent children? Why didn't we believe?

"Today, we dare to ask these questions, and finally acknowledge and confront the lost screams of our children. While we can't be so vain to pretend to answers, we must be so humble to fall before those who were forsaken and beg to them our apology. A sorry from a nation that seeks to reach out in compassion into the darkness, where you have lived for so long.

5 - The Law Comes Calling

"Nothing we can do now will right the wrongs inflicted on our nation's children. Even after a comprehensive Royal Commission, which finally enabled the voices to be heard and the silence to be broken, we will all continue to struggle.

"This apology is for them, and their families, too. As one survivor recently said to me, 'It wasn't a foreign enemy who did this to us. This was done by Australians to Australians, enemies in our midst, enemies in our midst.'

"The crimes of ritual sexual abuse happened in schools, churches, youth groups, scout troops, orphanages, foster homes, sporting clubs, group homes, charities and in family homes as well. It happened anywhere a predator thought they could get away with it and the systems within these organisations allowed it to happen, and turned a blind eye. It happened day after day, week after week, month after month, decade after decade, unrelenting torment.

"When a child spoke up, they weren't believed and the crimes continued with impunity. One survivor told me that when he told a teacher of his abuse, that teacher then became his next abuser – trust broken, innocence betrayed, power and position exploited for evil, dark crimes.

"And, again, today, we say sorry, to the children we failed, sorry. To the parents whose trust was betrayed and who have struggled to pick up the pieces, sorry. To the whistle-blowers, who we did not listen to, sorry.

"I recently met with the National Apology Survivors' Reference Group. They said to me that an apology without action is just a piece of paper, and it is. The foundations of our actions are the findings and recommendations of the Royal Commission, initiated by Prime Minister Gillard. The steady, compassionate hand of the commissioners and staff resulted in 17,000 survivors coming forward, and nearly 8,000 of them recounting their abuse in private sessions of the commission. The National Redress Scheme has commenced. It will mean that, after many years, often decades of denials and cover-ups, the institutions responsible for ruining lives admit their wrongdoing and the terrible damage they caused.

"The National Office of Child Safety was established from 1 July of this year within the Department of Social Services. As prime minister, I will be changing these arrangements to ensure that the National Office of Child Safety will report to me. It will reside within the portfolio of prime minister and Cabinet, as it should. And the Minister for Social Services will assist me in this role, including reporting to me on the progress of Royal Commission recommendations and the activities of the Office of Child Safety. The office has already begun its work to raise awareness of child safety and to drive cultural change in institutions and the community, to ensure that systemic failures and abuses of power that brought us here today are not repeated.

"Importantly, children themselves are being empowered to participate in these initiatives, because our children must be heard. And when it comes to the work of safety, it must be approachable and child friendly. They must know who they can tell. And they must be believed. And they must know where they can go. And to assist with lasting change, we recognise that there are many survivors who were abused in other settings, such as their own homes and in their communities, who will not be covered by this redress scheme. These survivors also need to be heard and believed and responded to with services to address their needs.

"We can never promise a world where there are no abusers, but we can promise a country where we commit to hear and believe our

5 - The Law Comes Calling

children, to work together to keep children safe, to trust them, and, most of all, respect their innocence. I simply say, I believe you, we believe you, your country believes you!"

A rape allegation against one of Scott Morrison's own Cabinet Ministers was referred to federal police after a letter was sent to the Prime Minister detailing the allegations. The alleged sexual assault dates to 1988, before the unnamed senior minister entered politics. The victim, who was 16 at the time of the alleged crime, took her own life last year. The letter came with a detailed statement prepared by the complainant for her lawyer and was shared with the ABC's *Four Corners* program by a friend of the alleged victim. The complainant reported the assault to NSW Police and South Australia Police.

March 26, 2021, Former Queensland MP and minister Trevor John Perrett was charged with 25 charges including eight counts of indecent treatment of girls under 16 over a two-year period in several Queensland towns, including Brisbane and Toowoomba.

The AFP responds

With the prime minister's words still ringing in their ears, the response of the AFP was disappointing for Russell and Patrick. AFP Assistant Commissioner of Crime Operations Debbie Platz addressed the press on their situation:

"The people involved with the syndicate have demonstrated a *complete disregard for the rule of law* in this country and the decision of the courts. The actions of these people are not to protect children, … [they] potentially endanger the safety and wellbeing of these children. The continual movement of children, the change in their identity, change in their location and appearances, their isolation for lengthy periods of time, has been shown to cause impacts that are long-lasting. We all know family law matters are difficult … but not agreeing to a Family Court decision is no excuse for engaging in this vigilante behaviour.

And this is really the crux of the matter, which comes first; the Family Court's legal ruling or the wellbeing of the children?

"It is alleged the group did not go by any name, but operated on a word-of-mouth basis, using a variety of encrypted phone applications to communicate and to conceal transactions.

"We believe this group has sought assistance from other people – some who may be unaware of their involvement in criminal activity – so we are urging anyone with any knowledge about these activities to come forward to the AFP. The group is also believed to have international connections in NZ and South Africa. Leads will be followed up in these countries."

"We understand that if a person has utilised the network, then they are used by the network to assist others," said Commander Justine Gough, Manager of Crime Operations who led the Operation Noetic investigation "Financing came from the members of the network ... [and] money was also derived from sympathetic persons who provided donations."

Commander Gough said further arrests were likely and confirmed that all allegations of child sex abuse made against the fathers of the children involved had been investigated and were not substantiated.

She said the ongoing investigation had found the network had links overseas, to both New Zealand and South Africa, and were also forged by the group, though the full extent of its reach has not been disclosed, she alleged, when describing the 'intelligence picture' investigators had determined regarding a yacht owned by Pridgeon.

"What we think is that vessel and the reason it was being modified was likely to be used to convey children from where it was moored

5 - The Law Comes Calling

in Fremantle to Tasmania, and then perhaps onto New Zealand."

Commander Gough explained they had reason to believe the group had assisted in other cases of child abduction, prior to those that were the subject of the charges. She said investigators could not rule out the possibility of more missing children as a result of the network and urged anyone with further information to contact police.

Russell: "Interesting that Commander Gough went on to state allegations that the children that had been abused had been investigated and found to be unsubstantiated. This despite 40 mandatory reports of child sexual abuse and an active AVO (Apprehended Violence Order) against the domestically violent father. As for the mothers who claimed they were being sexually abused by their fathers, Commander Gough said those allegations had been investigated and were also unsubstantiated.

"The clear message they and their many believers sent to the world was that I was the evil mastermind and financier of an international child trafficking ring involving up to 200 children. One report referred to '...some of the country's 'most baffling child stealing cases.

"Tellingly, despite all their inflammatory hype, right from the outset, only three children were identified. The police said they believed up to forty people were involved in the illegal enterprise and their hunt was ongoing; again this was hype designed to make them look like they were doing something useful. It is difficult to believe the press was reporting anything other than what they were being told by the police. Their lack of interest in presenting objective accounts of events is obvious and speaks more about them than it does about me.

"It was all over the news for weeks. People were jumping up and down and congratulating the Australian Federal Police for capturing this intricate network of people accused of child abduction. The media absolutely crucified us. Unfortunately, people are naïve enough to believe what they read regardless of how literally absurd the allegations are. Mothers saving their children, and people giving everything they own away to help children they never knew, went unreported."

Plankton defamation case

"Adding to my woes," remembers Russell, "I was supposed to have been in Sydney on the 22nd October 2018 for the commencement of my trial where I was to defend myself in the defamation lawsuit filed by David Plankton. I had expended most of my savings on mounting my defence and was looking forward to clearing my name. Plankton's team were proceeding confidently on the premise that Christopher would not testify but I knew by this time that he was going to; a very brave decision on his part. He had been grilled in a pre-trial cross-examination and my lawyers were positively beaming at the end of it. They were certain Christopher's evidence was damning and felt strongly that Plankton's lawyers wouldn't be able to discredit him. This was not what the police and prosecution wanted to hear.

"Now they knew the game was up and the action was withdrawn the day before the trial. This left me much poorer and denied me the chance to exonerate myself and have Plankton exposed in a court of law. I have little doubt the AFP planned my arrest with all this in mind. For me to defend myself against Plankton in front of a jury, having just been arrested for 'child-stealing' was going to be a tough call.

5 - The Law Comes Calling

"After our arrest, a triumphant Lead Investigator Sergeant Williamson had told reporters '.. the alleged syndicate acted in a clandestine way. So if parents and children went into hiding, (Pridgeon) provided his vehicle. He provided a car to move these people around the country. He's also given them provisions (like) food (and) medical support and everything suggests so far... that it was off the books.' He said police would allege all those charged were 'issue-based motivated' whatever that means?

Charges laid

"Two days after our arrest, on the 19th, Tim Holt was served with a summons to appear before the NSW Local Court with respect to the unlawful publication of an account of family law proceedings, using a telecommunications service to harass/menace/cause offence and dealing in the proceeds of crime."

"In all, ten search warrants were carried out in Grafton and Dubbo in NSW, in Perth and in Townsville, Queensland. The seven people arrested were Ariel Johnson, Joyce Fazldeen, Ann Gordon (Christopher's grandmother), Patricia Plaisted (the 78-year old grandmother of a child victim of CSA), Lizzie Weber, Arthur Weber (a 83-year old grandfather of the twin child victims), together with me and Patrick, as well as a Tim Holt."

The Charges

Dr Russell PRIDGEON

- 2x Conspiracy to defeat justice, contrary to section 42(1) of the *Crimes Act 1914;*
- 1x Deal in the proceeds of crime to the value of $100,000 or more, contrary to section 400.4(1)(a) of the *Criminal Code 1995;* and

- 3x Child stealing, contrary to section 363(1) of the Criminal Code 1899 (Qld).

Patrick O'DEA

- 2x Conspiracy to defeat justice, contrary to section 42(1) of the *Crimes Act 1914;*
- 3x Child stealing, contrary to section 363(1) of the *Criminal Code 1899* (Qld);
- 1x Unlawful stalking, contrary to section 359E of the *Criminal Code 1899* (Qld);
- 1x Illegally publish Family Court proceedings, contrary to section 121 of the *Family Law Act 1975*;
- 1x Using a carriage service (Facebook) to menace, harass or cause offence, contrary to s474.17 of the *Criminal Code 1995*.

Other people charged:

Tim HOLT was 37 years old, an unemployed/'paedophile hunter' from Townsville who was served court attendance notice for role in alleged criminal activity. Allegedly helped mothers and their children, and was paid to defame fathers and investigate them,

- 2x counts of dealing in the proceeds of crime and aiding abetting the illegal publication of Family Court proceedings.

Patricia Ann PLAISTED was aged between 73 and 77 at the times of the alleged offending.

- 2x Conspiracy to defeat justice, contrary to section 42(1) of the *Crimes Act 1914*.

Other syndicate members who were subsequently charged:

Ariel Josephine JOHNSON was aged between 72 and 75 at the times of the alleged offending.

- 1x Conspiracy to defeat justice, contrary to section 42(1) of

5 - The Law Comes Calling

the *Crimes Act 1914*.

Joyce Evelyn FAZLDEEN was aged 67 at the time of the alleged offending.

- 1x Conspiracy to defeat justice, contrary to section 42(1) of the *Crimes Act 1914* ;
- 1x Child stealing, contrary to section 363(1) of the *Criminal Code 1899* (Qld).

Lizzie Lee WEBER (also known as Lizzie Lee Morris) (the mother of twin child victims of CSA) was aged 45 at the time of the alleged offending.

- 1x Conspiracy to defeat justice, contrary to section 42(1) of the *Crimes Act 1914*;
- 1x Child stealing, contrary to section 363(1) of the *Criminal Code 1899* (Qld).

Arthur Ernest WEBER was aged between 79 and 82 at the times of the alleged offending.

- 2x Conspiracy to defeat justice, contrary to section 42(1) of the *Crimes Act 1914;*
- 1x Aid and abet the publication of an account of proceedings, contrary to section 121 of the *Family Law Act 1975;*
- 1x Deal in the proceeds of crime to the value of $10,000 or more, contrary to section 400.6(1) of the *Criminal Code 1995*;
- 1x Deal in the proceeds of crime, contrary to section 400.8(1) of the *Criminal Code 1995* charged with two counts with dealing in the proceeds of crime and one of aiding and abetting the publication of an account of proceedings.

Ann Kathleen GORDON (the grandmother) was aged 56 at the time of the alleged offending.

- 1x Child stealing, contrary to section 363(1) of the *Criminal Code 1899* (Qld).

The key points

- Russell was accused of financing a child-stealing syndicate and stalking and has been granted bail.
- The syndicate allegedly had up to 40 members and was linked to as many as five child abductions, helped mothers who had taken children from their fathers.
- A two-year investigation by AFP led to the charges.
- Australian Federal Police said the women and children were hidden in locations around the country, using aliases and disguises to avoid authorities.
- Investigators claim several of the mothers approached the network because they feared the children were being sexually abused by their fathers.
- In breach of court orders, they then went on the run with the help of the network, police allege.
- It was alleged that Russell sold his house and most of his possessions and bought gold bullion, at one stage totalling 11kg, worth about $750,000 in storage in Sydney.
- That he used the bullion, along with state funding diverted from the AAPP, to finance the operation for up to 10 years.
- Police further alleged that he had also bought a $140,000 yacht, which he allegedly learned to sail so he could spirit the women and children away to New Zealand or Zimbabwe to start new lives.
- The court further heard Russell allegedly ran a Facebook page where women would send messages asking to escape

5 - The Law Comes Calling

from men they claimed to be paedophiles.

- He allegedly wrote prescriptions in different names to give mothers drugs – also performing surgery on one of the women.
- Pensioners and professionals are believed to be part of the syndicate, which allegedly used encrypted messages in order to avoid detection.

In summary, the police charged a total of nine people in relation to a 'parental child abduction ring' – a sophisticated operation which enabled parents to abduct their own children, in order to stop the other parent from having access or visitation contrary to the Family Court ruling, which is a crime in Australia.

One of these persons, an 84-year old Queensland grandfather of the abducted children, Arthur Weber was then sentenced to an 18-month good behaviour bond in relation to payments made to this parental custody child abduction ring.

The court heard that over a six-month period, Arthur transferred $1,500 to the group, which included his daughter, thereby helping disgruntled parents to abduct their children and also facilitated the publication of private Family Court documents on the internet. This was the service the 84-year-old man had paid for.

He was convicted of dealing with money that would be an instrument of crime, which is an offence under Queensland law. Dealing with property that subsequently becomes an instrument of crime, with 'property' meaning money or other valuables.

Likewise, Holt was convicted of publishing an account of court proceedings, contrary to the Family Law Act, and one count of dealing in the proceeds of crime. He was found to have published material relating to proceedings before the Family Court, as well as other harassing and offensive material. For these services he was paid more than $28,000 and was sentenced to two years in prison.

AFP Commander of Crime, Paul Osborne, said the men sentenced committed serious criminal offences intent on undermining the judicial system:

"Laws such as these are designed to safeguard the integrity of our judicial system and to protect those vulnerable people who are involved in proceedings before the Courts, including the Federal Court of Australia. The AFP will not hesitate to act on criminal offences that ultimately deprive children of the opportunity to lead a normal life, regardless of their particular family situation."

In the case of the Morris twins, despite 40 mandatory reports of child sexual abuse and an active Apprehended Violence Order against the domestically violent father, the police saw fit to inform the Family Court that the abuse was 'unsubstantiated' and the child was ordered back into the custody of the father.

Russell: "So in a nutshell, Police alleged that for the past decade, I and the group I headed was responsible for abducting children from their allegedly abusive custodial fathers and unlawfully returning them to their mothers. I had operated a sinister syndicate of 'like-minded people,' who used 'clandestine' and 'sophisticated' methods, with links 'internationally,' to abduct and move children around the country or overseas, sometimes sending them on to New Zealand or South Africa. All in violation of Family Law Court orders. And in the process I had also dyed their hair, changed their names and altered their dates of birth. In this nefarious endeavour I was the 'key financier'.

"Initially a preposterous figure of 200 children was mentioned, then 35, then 10, then 5, yet I was only ever charged with three, and

5 - The Law Comes Calling

remember that was after I had written to the police, agencies, and government ministers admitting to this. This admission included assisting a grandmother in lawful custody of a minor.

"In all, I was charged with two counts of conspiracy to defeat justice, three counts of child stealing, and dealing in proceeds of crime worth $A100,000 or more. Police further added stalking and child stealing to the charges on October 19.

"I faced up to seven years jail for aiding and abetting child stealing, and up to 15 years each for conspiracy to defeat justice and dealing with the proceeds of crime. So there Patrick and I were, we had helped a woman shelter her children with the best will in the world, at considerable personal cost, and we were looking at 40 years in the slammer. I thought ruefully about my decision to leave Africa; I had come to the 'land of the free' and erred. It was hard to believe I would have managed to get into this sort of trouble in Mugabe's Zimbabwe; one of the most undemocratic countries on the planet.

"There were also allegations that I received money from women. This is rubbish, at no time did I receive any money or other considerations from anyone for doing what I considered my duty. I never accepted a cent, although I was offered money for food."

The Yacht Saga

"Much was made of me hiding children in my $140,000 yacht. That a search of the vessel had revealed my University Long Range Signal qualifications; and marine navigation books and charts showing the mark up of journeys from the West Coast to East Coast of Australia and then on to New Zealand and Tahiti. This, it was alleged, proved I was formulating strategies to use the vessel to covertly sail children around the country, with the possibility of kidnapping and sailing them to New Zealand and even on to Zimbabwe. The fact

The syndicate allegedly plotted to transport women and children yacht (pictured in Fremantle, Western Australia) from Australia to start new lives in New Zealand or Zimbabwe. Photo / AFP

that Zimbabwe is a landlocked country was obviously not known to these fantasists.

Medical License Withdrawn

"It never rains, it pours; on 23rd October 2018 a letter of complaint from the NSW HCCC (Health Care Complaints Commission) at the behest of the AFP was sent to my solicitor. I received the complaint from him on 24th October and was given until 26th to respond, but the Medical Council made a cock-up so they gave me until Sunday 28th to respond. Midday the next day, Monday 29th, I received a fax from them advising me that my Medical Registration had been suspended.

"So they took no more than three hours, from start of business 9.00 am to noon, to read a large volume of correspondence from me, assess, discuss, reach a determination, write the orders and write

5 - The Law Comes Calling

a notification to me informing me that I was suspended. I would have thought the least they might have done was give me a hearing and a chance to tell them my story but they were not interested.

"As the NZ Medical Council had done, the NSW Medical Council revoked my medical licence less than two weeks after I was charged, pending the outcome of this case.... for protecting those little girls. I tried to appeal this, but the Medical Insurer that I have been using for 15 years refused to fund the appeal. I sought further legal advice and was told appealing the ruling was pointless.

"The Council made no finding of guilt, stating that was a matter for the courts. Obviously the interests of the abused children were not much on their minds. I was now bereft of any opportunity to work and earn a living at a time when my legal bills had left me virtually penniless.

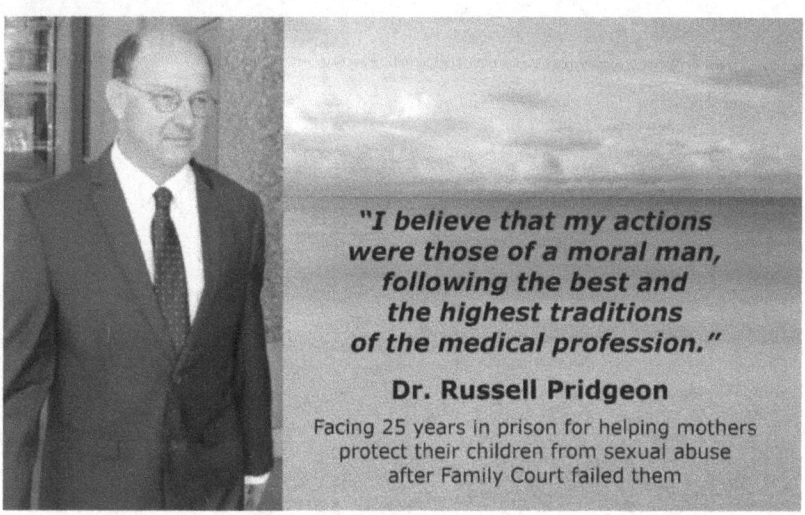

"*I believe that my actions were those of a moral man, following the best and the highest traditions of the medical profession.*"

Dr. Russell Pridgeon

Facing 25 years in prison for helping mothers protect their children from sexual abuse after Family Court failed them

In an effort to defend my actions and get the truth to my medical colleagues following all the negative media coverage, I forwarded them a letter explaining the circumstances:

As well as the letter, I sent an email to The Minister of Police in Queensland, and to Hon Christian Porter, the Federal Attorney General.

"It was a major source of grief and loss not to be able to work. My work always stabilised me, distracted me from my troubles and has given my life meaning and validity. Needless to say savings vanished quickly when my revenue was reduced to nil."

CHAPTER 6 – THE LEGAL ARGUMENTS

Trials

On Friday, 7th December it was reported that the 'abduction ring', including Dr William Russell Pridgeon appeared in Brisbane Magistrates Court alongside co-accused Patrick O'Dea, Joyce Evelyn Fazldeen and Ariel Josephine Johnson. They were charged for their roles in a network that eluded authorities supposedly for a decade. Patricia Ann Plaistead still remained at large.

Mr Owen, appearing for Dr. Pridgeon, said his client had been severely impacted by the allegations because his medical license had been revoked and he had been living with 'extremely onerous' bail conditions.

"They've just changed the types of GPS trackers. They used to be able to home charge it and take it off so they can walk around the house," Mr Owen said. "Now they have to plug it into a wall and sit there. They can't take it off their ankle. It takes about two and a half hours to charge. So bail restrictions are extremely onerous and they've been on for six months."

The high bail was set as a warning to others, although Magistrate Annette Hennessy relaxed Russell and Patrick's bail conditions so that they could access social media, travel from NSW to Queensland to meet certain people and report to police three days a week instead of daily.

At a committal hearing in the Brisbane Magistrates Court, crown prosecutor Lincoln Crowley alleged Dr Pridgeon and Mr O'Dea were the "central persons involved" in the network which helped a mother abduct her twin girls – who were under a Family Law Court order – from a school in Townsville in April 2014. He said the trio allegedly travelled out of Queensland through Western Australia and then to northern New South Wales to live for four years until they were found by authorities in May, 2018.

The prosecution alleged it was during this time that Mr O'Dea and Dr Pridgeon set up a website and social media accounts about the twins where information was published that breached the Family Law Act. Mr Crowley said it was also during that time another woman became aware of the network. She allegedly engaged with the group to help abduct her grandson from Townsville and take him to NSW via Brisbane in 2018.

"With the assistance of some of the same people, she'd been able to take her grandson from Townsville, knowing that proceedings were afoot in respect of parenting orders," Mr Crowley said. He told the court Joyce Evelyn Fazldeen – who is charged with child-stealing and conspiring to defeat justice – helped keep the woman and her grandson hidden from the boy's father for two weeks.

Defence barrister Alex Nelson, who represented Ms Fazldeen, said his client had no knowledge that the boy had been taken or that a Family Court order had been breached.

He drew the court's attention to the fact that "there's an allegation of a conspiracy, in the big scheme of which it's said this boy was forcibly or fraudulently taken away from the father in Townsville and was to be spirited off to Western Australia – and that a number of people, including my client, were a party to that conspiracy," but he contended that she was not a party to that agreement, had no idea this boy had been taken ... and was subject to Federal Circuit Court orders. It was pointed out the evidence shows Ann GORDON had lawful custody of the child and therefore could not abduct him. It also showed she had never met some of the other defendants which then begs the question as to how she could have been part of a 'child trafficking syndicate'.

Outside court Russell thanked police for their courtesy and kindness, whilst he made an impassioned statement in defence of himself and the co-defendants.

"We believed these children and we protected them," he told a large group of supporters and reporters outside a court. He <u>insisted</u> that he and Patrick were trying to rescue children from sexually abusive homes.

Flanked by two women in suits, Pridgeon accused police of deliberately ignoring evidence of child sex abuse that his group had collected from the children. "They (the police] say that abuse did not occur. It's absurd. This is a very dark moment in the history of the Australian Federal Police."

"I'm looking very forward to the truth of this matter coming out because the crimes involved here are horrendous, and the crimes have been covered up by many people who shouldn't have," Pridgeon told reporters. "I'm looking forward to exposing that and I intend to."

Friday April 5, 2019 Russell made another brief appearance in the Brisbane Magistrate's court. Greeting him while walking into the court were a number of supporters who had flown in from around the country. A red carpet was provided for him to walk down on his way into court as an obvious sign of appreciation. There were a number of banners calling for a Royal Commission, protection of children, and a standout banner reading, 'Operation No Ethics', an obvious dig at the Australian Federal Police.

Operation No ethics. A banner from a supporter

But in what appears to be a delaying tactic, Prosecutor Dearne Firth told the court that the amount of information being investigated was enormous: "The amount of forensic material is the most seen by the Commonwealth DPP," she said. "I have over 40 gigabytes of evidence already on a USB stick about 80 per cent of the brief of evidence." It was explained to the court that a forensic investigation into computers still needed to be done. Ms Firth said prosecutors needed another month to gather that information and distribute it to the accused parties' legal teams before the case could progress through the courts.

Mr Owens said the GPS monitors Dr Pridgeon and Mr O'Dea had to wear took two hours to charge and could not be removed, meaning they are forced to spend long periods of time sitting next to a power point. He also revealed that despite Dr Pridgeon having permission under his bail to visit friends in Queensland, police had pulled him over four times and threatened to arrest him when he drove across the Tweed.

6 - The Legal Arguments

Patrick O'Dea, left, is seen with supporters as he leaves the Brisbane Magistrates Court in April. Picture: AAP

Accused child abduction ring mastermind Dr William Russell Massingham Pridgeon (centre) is seen leaving the Brisbane Magistrates Court in Brisbane. Picture: Darren England

The case against Dr Pridgeon was adjourned for another four weeks to May 3 after a successful application from the prosecution to be granted more time to gather forensic information from Dr Pridgeon and O'Dea's computers.

Dr William Pridgeon (centre) has gone to court saying he doesn't like his GPS tracker

On his way out of court, Russell was met by a small barrage of reporters along with his supporters. He addressed them thus:

"This case is not about child stealing; it is about child protection. It's about the desperate efforts of good people, good law-abiding Australians, desperately trying to protect children from the worst sort of sexual abuse. We are not criminals. There is no law in Australia against protecting children from rape. We have a right to protect our children. We have a right to protect our children even against court-ordered child sexual abuse. Family Court ordered child sexual abuse. We have a duty to protect our children. If we didn't protect these children, we would be breaking the law.

"The criminal code, section 260 I think it is [note SECT 286], demands that we protect children, keep them safe, and we've done that, yet we are being charged with crimes. The people who have abused these children are not being charged, they are being protected,

6 - The Legal Arguments

they are being protected by the AFP. The AFP are denying this abuse, even though they know that these children have been abused. This denial is absolutely blatant. Raping children is a crime. It is an abomination. Ordinary decent Australians regard it with horror and disgust, but the AFP apparently do not. And the public servants who were supposed to protect these children did not. Apparently, they don't regard child sexual abuse as a problem here. The child protectors, we, the child protectors, are being prosecuted by the very people who failed to protect these children in the first place. This is a crime to hide a crime.

"The AFP knows the full effect of these children's abuse. They have access to the police databases. They have taken our computers, they've taken all our documentation, and that documentation that was leaked with the description and evidence of the children's abuse. Yet they do nothing, yet they continue to lie about the children's abuse. They say the abuse did not occur – it occurred! The descriptions that we have of the children's disclosures are graphic; they are horrendous. They know this, and yet they lie. The AFP know what we know. They know that these children have been sexually abused. We protected these children from abuse. Whatever we've done, we can say that we have given these children four years of freedom from rape. These children made 40 plus disclosures to 13 different adults. When they were between the ages of four and five, over a period of about 18 months, only one of those adults was ever interviewed by the police. This wasn't an investigation, it's not a bonafide investigation. It was a cover up. Those witnesses were excluded from testifying in the family court, which then gave custody of the children.

Medical License Appeal

"28th August the child-stealing charges changed: The CDPP advised my new (for financial reasons) lawyer Kerri Fredericks that they intended to change the child stealing from s364(1)(a) to s363(1)(b) at the committal hearing on 8/10/2019. So the wrong charge was used for longer than a year. The CDPP continued to refer to the (1)(b) charge as child stealing even though it is harbouring a stolen child. The Committal Hearing, as it turned out, did not eventuate because the CDPP said they were not prepared. This was to be the first of many such delays. You have to wonder why the CDPP were deliberately stalling.

"Unfortunately my new lawyer said she believed the AFP narrative that I had salted away money and required $150,000 down in order for her to continue. I again informed her that this was not a remote possibility. Given my financial circumstances and no legal aid, I now knew I had to represent myself. Trained as a doctor, I would henceforth apply my mind with renewed vigour to learning about the law.

"On 30th August the prosecution indicated they were going to withdraw the stalking charges against me. They knew all along it was rubbish but had used it to peddle the idea I was dangerous.

I then applied again to the Medical Council to reverse the decision to suspend my licence to practise and earn a living. In contravention of the rules and basic fairness I was not offered or given a hearing, it was done ex parte and on the papers. I did not receive orders, only a letter from John Nicolson dated 13 February 2020

"The October Panel noted that Dr Pridgeon was entitled to defend the charges and is innocent until proven guilty. In the Medical Council's own words: "We consider it was reasonable for the Appellant to believe the twin girls had been

6 - The Legal Arguments

the subject of sexual abuse and that the abuse probably came from their father. None of that however, in our view, for the reasons set out above, can be accepted as justification for the Appellant engaging in the action he did."

"The declaration he really wanted from the Tribunal was that it was never illegal to protect a child from harm. The action taken by the Appellant, in our view, has the potential to undermine the fabric of our society which is dependent upon the rule of law being effective and complied with by the citizens of this country. Challenges to decisions of our courts must be taken through the processes which are available. To take action which is motivated to defeat the ruling of a court is such a challenge to our orderly existence that this Tribunal must treat the action as extremely serious"

The Panel's duty was to assess the charges made against Dr Pridgeon in light of the public safety and public interests tests as set out in the National Law. The Panel determined that given the seriousness of the charges, it was in the public interest to suspend Dr Pridgeon's registration. Additionally, the Panel decided that it was also necessary to suspend Dr Pridgeon's registration to protect the public's health and safety, given that Dr Pridgeon may consider acting in similar ways to the alleged behaviour which gave rise to the charges against him."

"Meanwhile, the Medical Council of NSW nevertheless suspended my medical registration indefinitely. These findings against me were extraordinary insofar as the action taken by the Medical Council against me had no foundation in a complaint made by a patient or another medical practitioner. The 'complainant' was the AFP and they had no *locus standi* in this issue. This was part of their ongoing vendetta. The Medical Council based its decision on "public interest" grounds.

"I appealed this decision on the basis that I hadn't broken any law based upon the provisions of s286 of the Queensland Criminal Code, and that the trial was yet to take place. My bail conditions did not prevent me continuing to work as a medical practitioner pending my trial. Also, I reminded them I was complying with my obligations under the provisions of s286 of the Queensland Criminal Code: the law to protect children from abuse and fulfilling a moral obligation to protect children from harm. Further, I had supporting evidence to verify the children's and the mother's assertions that the children had been sexually abused and was not simply relying upon the mothers' word. Finally, I did not assist the grandmother and her grandson to breach any court orders or laws, as the child was lawfully in her care at the time.

"Unfortunately, my appeal failed. Not only that, but the appeal costs were awarded against me. At this point I was defending myself as I could not afford a lawyer. Below is a summary of their finding:

"They determined the provisions of the National Law must operate to send a message to the practitioners of Australia that such action, as taken by me, had to be regarded as very serious, and had the potential to bring the medical profession into disrepute. They were of the opinion that they had to demonstrate to the public at large that bodies that control the medical profession do not sanction that action. Accordingly they concluded that suspension of my registration as a medical practitioner is necessary in the public interest and should be imposed pursuant to s 150 of the National Law.

"Such suspension should continue until Dr Pridgeon has concluded his trial and then makes another application pursuant to s 150A of the National Law, which he may make as of right and as provided for in the National Law. It will then be for the Medical Council to determine if any further action is necessary."

Mary Maxwell at Gumshoe News website had this to say: *"This is a doctor who had to trudge around with an ankle bracelet, and who got stripped. I mean stripped, of his medical licence, by an obsequious — you can't get much*

6 - The Legal Arguments

more obsequious than this – New South Wales board of professional ethics. I wonder, will they apologise when they give it back? What will they say? 'Sorry, we don't have an ounce of integrity, ol buddy. Or Sorry, Sir, we should have listened to you.'"

"I again appealed these decisions to the NSW Civil and Administrative Tribunal (NCAT) on 30 June 2021," recalls Russell. "It was dismissed and my licence to practice remained suspended with costs awarded against me. Did any of those adjudicating ask themselves what does a decent person do when placed in the situation I was in?

"They stated further that there is the risk to the 'public interest' insofar as the erosion of the public perception that only medical practitioners who 'exhibit traits consistent with the honourable practice of an honourable profession' would be permitted to be registered by the regulatory authority. The term 'honourable practice' must include 'to act lawfully at all times'.

Given that Dr Pridgeon is facing two charges of conspiracy to defeat justice, contrary to s 42(1) of the Crimes Act, which are serious criminal offences, that insufficient change in circumstances had occurred to warrant the Medical Council setting aside or further reviewing the suspension order which had been made in 2018.

Should Dr Pridgeon be acquitted of the charges, it may nevertheless still be reasonable to suspend the order under s150. On the other hand, an acquittal would not necessarily mean a complaint could or would not be brought against him by the HCCC, seeking suspension or cancellation of Dr Pridgeon's registration as a medical practitioner.

His action in assisting a parent and grandparent to defeat or frustrate the lawful orders of an Australian court, no matter how morally sound his actions might have been to him, could be seen by the Tribunal as being the actions of a person "unsuitable to hold general registration as a medical practitioner in NSW".

So I was back to square one, even though further charges had been dropped. And from what they were saying I would remain off the register until after my trial and even if found innocent they left open the possibility I would still not get my license back. It was very difficult to find the stamina to keep going at times.

Russell requests for evidence withheld

On 3 February 2020 Russell emailed the Federal prosecutor Peter Botros, the Commonwealth Director of Public Prosecutions (CDPP) requesting evidence withheld *(redacted)*

Dear Mr Botros

......once the Prosecution becomes aware of critical evidence, it is their duty to place it before the court. Not to do so will be to deceive or knowingly or recklessly mislead the court (Queensland Barristers Rule 26).

You have written that the Prosecution intends to deny that the abuse of the children occurred. If you are aware that there is evidence of abuse, it would be "failing in your duty to the court to fairly assist the court to arrive at the truth, must seek impartially to have the whole of the relevant evidence placed intelligibly before the court, and must seek to assist the court with adequate submissions of law to enable the law properly to be applied to the facts". (Prosecutor's duties, Barristers' Rule 82).

I submit to you Sir, that your stated intention to deny the abuse of these children will bring you into conflict with these rules. I am certain as the honourable man I know you to be, you would wish under all circumstances to avoid this. I believe that Barristers Rules 83, 84, 85, 86, 87, 91 is also relevant here.

I would also ask you to consider as an honourable man, a good citizen, that these children: (Christopher Hussein and Jane & Charlotte Morris) are in the custody of their fathers, the very persons whom the children have disclosed as their abusers. To deny the children's abuse is to ensure that these children remain

6 - The Legal Arguments

in this abusive custody for the remainder of their childhoods. I am quite certain, once you acquaint yourself with the evidence of the abuse that you would wish to avoid this at any cost.

I also note that the CDPP would have been aware of this evidence since I alluded to it in my letter to the Queensland Ministers of Police and Child Safety, and the Federal A-G on 30/5/2018.

Thus I request again that the CDPP seek and find and present the court with all the evidence/documents:

Particularly we ask for the multiple reports of the disclosures of sexual and other forms of abuse made by Jane and Charlotte Morris by the father and his associates to the Court Ordered Supervisors at the Contact Centre where Lizzie had Court Ordered contact with her children after she lost custody of them.

We also ask for the Mandatory Reports which must have been made by the ICL (upon receipt of these disclosures) of the ongoing abuse of the Twins by the father and his associates. We ask for the Independent Children's Lawyers file on Lizzie Weber/Morris, David Morris and Charlotte and Jane Morris and their Family Court matter and all correspondence related to this.

Please may we request the report that Prof. Freda Briggs made after examining the disclosures of Child Sexual Abuse by Charlotte and Jane Morris.

William Russell Pridgeon[13]

6 February 2020 Danielle Buckley, Courier Mail, reported:

"GP in alleged child abduction ring is living off 'charity'"

A NSW doctor accused of financially backing a child abduction ring has claimed he is broke and living off "the charity of others" while he fights the charges. William Russell Pridgeon is accused of being part of a network that helped mothers snatch their children they claimed were being sexually abused

---

13 Subsequent to my letter, prosecutor Peter Botros resigned. Shortly thereafter I mysteriously received a video of Christopher's (Gordon) disclosures to the Townsville CPIU in the post.

by their fathers. Dr Pridgeon and six of his co-accused appeared in Brisbane Magistrates Court today ahead of their committal hearing in April. The self-represented GP told the court he had been refused Legal Aid and had no prospect of getting a lawyer.

"I don't have the resources," Dr Pridgeon said. "There has been a concerted strategy against me to drain my resources. While I started out in a reasonable position, I now depend for my board and lodging on the charity of others."

Dr Pridgeon also requested he face a separate committal hearing. The hearing will determine if there is enough evidence for the alleged ring to face trial in a higher court.

"We have received what the AFP purports to be the largest brief in Australian legal history (including around 450 photos of tarmac), which is basically mixed up like shuffling a deck of cards," he said. "So none of us have the resources to get our legal representatives to trawl through that vast amount of information.

"The Commonwealth DPP produced the largest brief of evidence in this case than any other case in Australian history," stated Russell. Well over 13,000 pages and still growing. This excludes the thousands of pages of Family Court material that will also be introduced. One wonders why so much public money is being spent to prosecute someone who has protected children rather than prosecuting those who harm them.

Co-accused Ann Gordon, who is charged with conspiring to defeat justice, also asked for the committal hearing to be split.

"I don't even know half of the people they are saying are co-accused," Ms Gordon said.

This was followed on 23rd February by an update concerning Lizzie posted by Patrick on his website: 'Two Brave Girls'.

"Yes, Lizzie still has criminal charges (maximum 50 years jail) for daring to protect her children when the police, child safety and the

6 - The Legal Arguments

Family Court refused to do so. She wears a GPS tracker, signs into a police station seven days a week, has a curfew and travel restrictions among other things. She has matters in the Supreme Court, District Court, Magistrates Court and Family Court. All for protecting her girls. To say that this is a very stressful time is an understatement.

"She has refused to be silenced though. She is still strongly advocating changes to the Family Court and state agencies and has been guest speaker and support for groups of victims and individuals currently being victimised all over again by our broken systems. She continues to meet with politicians asking them the hard questions. She stands up to the men's rights extremists who see her ex-husband as a poster boy and her as the devil.

"This is the ninth year of their fight. The girls were four years old when the father was awarded sole custody and sole parental responsibility at an interim hearing with no testing of evidence by the then FM Coker. There has still never been a full final Family Court trial.

"1st November, 2021. It has been over five months since Morris stopped one of the twins from being allowed to see Lizzie in direct opposition and deliberate contravention of Family Court orders. In direct opposition to the wishes of the child.

"Question: Will he receive criminal charges for being in contravention of orders for this long, or is it the case that Lizzie is the only parent who is expected to comply? Will the ICL act, or remain in complicit silence?"

For Russell the frustrating routine continued:

- 2nd March 2020 a Committal Brief deadline was met.
- 5th March our Application for Directions hearing was cancelled.

- 9th March I attended a Mention for Committal in Brisbane.
- 12th March there was an Application for Directions hearing again in front of Magistrate Gett.
- 16th March another Mention for Committal hearing.
- 16th April I was in court for judgement for Directions hearing.
- 17th April another Mention for Committal hearing.
- 20th April our Committal Hearing was cancelled for the second time.
- 22nd June was set down of a 'judgement' but judgement of what was never revealed.
- 6th July another Committal Mention.

Plankton: Health Care complaint

Russell: "As previously explained, Plankton had laid defamation charges against me which were withdrawn at the last moment when it became known that his son Christopher was going to testify. As the Defamation Hearing approached however, I received a letter from the Health Care Complaints Commission on 2 July 2018, informing me that David Plankton had made a complaint against me.

"The complaint contained a multitude of accusations, a large volume of untruth, partial truth and misinformation, most of which was unrelated to medical practice. Most of the matters complained about were actually part of the Family Court proceedings between himself and Debbie as plaintiff and defendant, as Debbie desperately tried to save her son from harm. I was not directly part of the court proceedings, although Mr Plankton presented his complaint as though I was. I played my part by supporting Debbie and Christopher and financing the legal costs, which were considerable.

6 - The Legal Arguments

"I wrote back to the HCCC stating that Plankton had never been my patient and explained the history of Plankton's abuse towards his son, and the significance of the forthcoming Defamation Trial. I submitted that these many complaints against me, stretching back for many years, were vexatious and malicious, and were simply a tactic to distract me and waste my time in the lead up to the Defamation hearing.

"Further, that my actions, as a man trying desperately to protect a woman and a child from violence and every sort of abuse, far from being immoral and unethical, have been in keeping with the best and highest traditions of the medical profession. I asserted that without me Debbie would have been overwhelmed and her son Christopher (my stepson at the time) would have been lost to years of abuse.

"I submitted that the decision the HCCC needed to make is whether they wished to become the vehicle for Mr Plankton 's ongoing abuse, vengeance and malice, or not. Clearly the HCCC have been very enthusiastic about being a vehicle for Plankton's abuse. They have maintained the prosecution until the present day, October 2021 that is 3 1/2 years later. During this time I have not received advice that the HCCC have a shred of evidence about the complaints in this matter.

"When I was arrested, and my registration suspended the HCCC and the NSWMC 'held over' any investigation of this complaint: the legislation does not allow them to do this! In fact there is a large body of case law that sets down that 'Delay totally invalidates an administrative decision'.

"Plankton's complaint was an admixture of untruth, partial truth and misinformation, almost nothing to do with my professional conduct. It was, to the best of my knowledge, completely without evidence. I wrote a letter to Rebecca Moynihan of the NSWMC advising her of this on 30th May 2021, and did not receive a reply.

"When I made my second appeal to the Medical Council, their submissions referred to Plankton's complaint, saying that the complaint alleged that I had been accused of child sexual abuse. Yet there was no such allegation made in Plankton's complaint, not even obliquely. This malicious allegation poisoned the submission. Accordingly I sought information about the status of this complaint.

"On 8th April 2021 I received a letter from Jennifer Ratcliff of HCCC saying that the complaint is still being investigated. This was shortly followed by an email from Mr Timothy Rochford, Senior Investigation Officer of the HCCC on 12 April, advising that the complaint was definitely closed. Mr Rochford repeated that advice on 24 June.

"At the same time I sought clarification from the NSW Medical Council. On 28th April Ms Moynihan advised that this did not accord with their records, i.e. the complaint was still open. She was to investigate it, but at time of writing, I have heard nothing. I sent a follow up letter, asking again that she follow up with the HCCC to seek documentation of the closure. 'Please advise if you have done this and advise me whether you are going to dismiss this case immediately or whether you are going to prosecute me,' I wrote.

"Plankton wrote his letter of complaint on 29 June 2018, whilst I only received notification of the complaint on 2nd July 2021. At the time of writing this complaint has continued for 38 months.

"Clearly this complaint has been held in reserve against me awaiting the outcome of my criminal trial. If I win, I am certain that this complaint will be re-activated to run interference in my life. Like my prosecution, it serves to remind anyone who seeks to protect children from harm that they will face years of consequences: Who benefits from this?"

Serena Teffaha and Ann Gordon

On the 2nd February 2021 at a Committal Hearing presided over by Deputy Chief Magistrate Anthony Gett to face the remaining charges involving two counts of 'Conspiring to Defeat Justice' and two counts of harbouring a child that was stolen. Russell spoke to the press and called the charges 'absolute nonsense'.

In addition to charges of Child Stealing and Conspiring to Defeat Justice, Patrick was accused of contravening a restriction on the publication of court proceedings, 'using a carriage service to harass, menace or cause offence and of unlawful stalking.' This was in connection with messages that had been posted on Facebook.

"Several years ago I became aware that [victim twins] had alleged serious sexual assault by their father. I was also aware that the Family Court had ordered that they live full-time with their father," Dr. Pridgeon claimed in court documents.

"I also became aware that (the victim twins') mother had breached a Family Court order and taken them into her protective custody and went into hiding.

"I also became aware at a later date that (male child victim) had disclosed that he was a victim of sexual assault by his father. I further became aware that [male child victim] disclosed this abuse to (the Queensland Police Service). It is my belief that no action of any type has been taken.

"(During my committal hearing), I raised the abuse of the (victim twins) before Magistrate Gett as part of my defence and was repeatedly stopped by Magistrate Gett and repeatedly threatened with criminal defamation if I continued.

The Boys from Bulawayo

Outside Brisbane Magistrates Court, Ann Gordon, the grandmother, Renae Leeza protective mother and supporter, Belinda Paris HUGE supporter and who gave testimony re abuse in institutions

"I was forced to redact large parts of my defence statement because of this threat. I could not understand how I could be charged with criminal defamation if everything I was saying was verifiable fact, which appeared in the prosecution's brief of evidence."

The reality was that Dr. Pridgeon has now "exhausted" his funds, he cannot work because his "ability to practice medicine has been taken away", and he cannot afford lawyers to defend himself against these charges.

6 - The Legal Arguments

He also criticised Mr Gett's decision to commit him for trial.

"Clearly Magistrate Gett had no basis for making this threat against me and by doing so, denied me the right to a defence at the committal," Dr. Pridgeon claimed in court documents.

But the hearing took an unexpected turn with regard to Solicitor Serena Teffaha, who was appearing *pro bono* for Ann Gordon. Teffaha stated in court that one of the children allegedly taken by the 'syndicate' had been 'let down' by the police and judiciary and the court was 'enabling' his abuse. This prompted an angry response from Magistrate Gett: 'In my view Ms Teffaha ... (those comments) may be prejudicial to or diminish the public confidence in the administration of justice. There may be a breach of your fundamental duty as a solicitor practising in the state of Queensland.' Gett then referred Teffaha to the Legal Services Commission in Queensland over submissions she made that he believed 'may be prejudicial to or diminish the public confidence in the administration of justice'.

Solicitor Serena Teffaha

'Gumshoe News' is a Melbourne based investigative news website, managed by Dee McLachlan, that encourages contributions from freelancers reported on the matter: This is an extract of a letter sent by Russell to the Legal Services Board in response to Gett's actions:

"Solicitor Teffeha brought this to the attention of Magistrate Gett in a private communication. This Magistrate used [the details] to publicly excoriate and humiliate Ms Teffeha, revealing the contents of Ms Teffeha's private communication, to the public, in open court, while accusing her of bringing the administration of justice into disrepute.

"I was present in the court room when Magistrate Gett attacked Ms Teffeha and threatened her with legal action. Ms Teffeha responded that she had a legal obligation to the court to tell the truth".

"Magistrate Anthony Gett struck out separate no case submissions made by Dr. Pridgeon and two other co-accused." stated Gumshoe News.

Senior member of the Family Court of Australia, Deputy Principal Registrar Virginia Wilson, then sent a letter to the VLSB (Victorian Legal Services Board) complaining about Ms Teffaha's conduct in Gett's courtroom which prompted Justice Kirsty Marion Macmillan to take the unusual step of restraining Ms Teffaha from representing her own client in the matter before her.

Ms Teffaha also went on the record stating the Family Court had 'many corruption issues', which prompted condemnation from the Australian Bar Association and the Law Council. They said her comments were 'baseless, inappropriate and undermining' of the criminal justice system and warned there was no place for them.

The Victorian Legal Services Board then wrote to Teffaha in March to provide her with a 'notice of proposed cancellation of practising certificate' but did not specifically indicate the conduct under scrutiny by the board. The notice was sent to her immediately after she filed a class action on behalf of thousands of public housing tenants subjected to the hard lockdown by the state government and confined to their homes in July 2020.

Teffaha pointed out, 'They are not attacking me on the basis of any professional misconduct or any client complaint. They are attacking me on the basis that I am diminishing public confidence in the administration of justice based on ongoing cases before the court involving serious issues of covering up child sexual abuse disclosures and family violence. They allege that by me speaking out to protect my clients, and these children, is offensive to the administration of justice. This is nothing short of psychopathic. They understand and know we are close now and they have now completely exposed how threatened they are. This is complete sabotage and bullying. I am seeking protection as a whistle-blower for myself and the most vulnerable clients, specially two clients seeking protection against the Crown for our livelihood, safety, and our financial integrity.'

On the basis of the complaints from the two judges, Teffaha's license to practice law was cancelled on the 16th April by the VSLB. Ms Teffaha responded to the VSLB's decision, labelling it 'unlawful' and said her clients 'do not accept any government regulator intervention'. She said losing her licence would not affect the class action, and that she had written a whistle-blower complaint against the legal watchdog for what she considered to be the targeting of her litigation.

"We have filed a formal whistle-blower complaint for my grandmother client who is being targeted falsely by the Australian Federal Police, Commonwealth Director of Public Prosecution, the Queensland Police, the Family Court of Australia, the Victorian Legal Services Board and Queensland Legal Services Commissioner. State-sanctioned violence will not be tolerated. We are asking for the intervention of Morrison, Dutton and the new Attorney General and the Victoria Ombudsman. Enough with this trauma. Child sexual abuse will not be accepted, and the grandmother must be repatriated and reunited with her grandson.

"The Australian Law Reform Commission (ALRC) has made an extensive report recommending that the Family Court of Australia be abolished – that's right – be taken down, completely removed, completely shut down; it and the family court judges it hires! Now I didn't say that, the ALRC did. The show will go on despite all attempts of Government and its regulators to stop and sabotage our actions."

"Meanwhile, the court continues to stalk and terrorise Ann Gordon," says Russell. "They are focusing the hearing on Gordon despite Teffaha informing them that she is going to the High Court and doing a section 72 Constitutional complaint and Peoples Commission. As Teffaha states: 'They are starting a large action to bring the end of the Family Court as we know it. Thousands of pages have been collated against them and their collusion with Police and Child Protection amongst many other organisations. And they know this, hence the targeting. They want to take me out of the legal fraternity.

"I tried to hand the magistrate my affidavit as to the reason why Sergeant David Miles swears Christopher Gordon never mentioned abuse, that is, despite him disclosing this three times to the police during forensic interviews, which were recorded and which are in our possession, and in the possession of the CDPP, yet the magistrate would just not accept the evidence.

6 - The Legal Arguments

Graeme Bell and Pastor Paul

"My experience with lawyers in the criminal justice system has been very disappointing," says Russell. "My first lawyer was also Patrick's, and I gave up on him because he kept procrastinating – 'don't worry, we will deal with that at trial' was a familiar refrain. Of the second lawyer I engaged, the less said the better, except to note she spent the last of my money available for legal fees. It is worth remembering that the only time we managed to get any charges dropped was when we were in court without any qualified legal representation. A friend suggested that I join her at her law lectures, to understand what I was in for. I did so and am continually amazed at how much it has helped me. We fought them every inch of the way, and absolutely did not let them get away with anything. Having a committed and capable lawyer at my side would have been a Godsend but I have had to be prepared to go it alone.

"Making it tougher, I couldn't get Legal Aid as Lead Investigator Williamson alleged in an affidavit that I had transferred $1,3M overseas and that he had the documentation to prove it. Despite requests, no documentation has been forthcoming. But the magistrate would not see or hear about it. To qualify for free legal assistance, a person must comply with a 'means test' (a maximum monthly or no income) and have a legal problem with merit. So here I was, destitute thanks to the machinations of a vindictive state apparatus and denied any legal assistance. They were clearly planning on inhibiting my ability to mount a credible defence but maybe they did not take into account I had been studying the law very closely and had learned a lot and had the help at this point of some wonderful people, including Pastor Paul and Graeme Bell, who have been heaven sent.

"I met Graeme and Pastor Paul through my friend Mishka, in Melbourne, who told them about my plight after I started doing my own legal work. They had involved themselves in assisting people who had found themselves on the wrong side of the law in dealing with child abuse. They immediately became very active in providing me with assistance as friends, and on the legal side. Graeme has been amazingly supportive and generous with his time and never wants money. He's a genuine crusader for the 'good guys'. He's brilliant and he's also fearless. A self-confessed 30-year career-criminal, now a legal expert, he has immersed himself in criminal law and become something of a legal savant.

"I was flogged as a kid, I had a good upbringing from a loving family but there was violence and this was normal for my family and it appears a lot of other people," remembers Graeme. "My grandfather was a Starting Price Bookie back in the 30's and 40's when things were hard. Pop was a hard man. He told me to be nice to everyone, pay the bills, but if they show violence to you, you respond ten times worse. Show them what real violence was like, and not back off. So I grew up wild. Violence was the answer to everything.

"When I was 13, my father said he was going out for half-an-hour. There were some 15- and 16-year-old boys with my brother in the house. They were unwanted guests causing trouble and not supposed to be there. My father said that when he got home, he expected them all to be off his property. He told me to use my 'initiative'. So I told the blokes my father said they must be off the property before he arrived home. Without a word, one of them stepped forward and punched me in the face. Blood was coming out of my mouth, my tooth had punctured my lip, and they were all laughing. I went inside and grabbed a gun, cocked it, and jabbed it into the boy's mouth.

'I'm 13,' I explained, 'so I can't do a day in jail. I'm going to count to three and you all be gone. One...two...,' they were gone! It was

6 - The Legal Arguments

then I realised that violence worked.

"At 15 or 16 I walked into a churchyard full of people, I was there for a rehearsal of a school play called "Lil Abner". I had a block of wood and beat a boy my age. There had been a disagreement, some thought was trivial. This boy had started it, so I hit him back. This was after a few run-ins where he kept telling people he had bashed me, but he hadn't. I decided next time I will beat him so he can't say he beat me at school. I will do it in front of everyone. So I caved his head in with a block of wood, knocked out his teeth, kicked him in the testicles. Slammed his head into a fence, then returned with a gun. Slammed it into his mouth. Held up the gun and warned the people if they start, next time I will do it well, do it really good; 'I will kill you...!' From there it went downhill, it was a wild ten minutes.

"I found the more violent, the more likely people would pay attention. Later I got into more trouble with the law. Threatened judges and witnesses, but I was never sent to jail. I had two contracts placed on me, one by the NSW Police, and one was by a couple of idiots that were reputed to work for the Mr Asia drug gang.

"In the early 80's I had a disagreement with the nephew of a bloke stated to be the manager for the Asian arm of the gang, over a $50 bet in a card game. Later, walking down the street, I see these idiots pointing at me. I sat down at a pizza shop and an old Sicilian fellow came out and says he will buy me coffee. I asked him, 'who's that?'

'He manages the Mr Asia syndicate.'

'Who are the other two idiots with him?'

'They his bodyguards, his heavies.'

'What are they here for?'

'They have come here to kill you!'

'What for?'

'Over his nephew.'

So I said, 'you want to go break the news to these imbeciles or should I do it?'

He replied, 'you drink your coffee, I'll do it.' He went down and I saw his arms waving.

They shook hands and walked away. When he returned, he said, 'I'll get you another coffee my friend.' I asked what happened?

'I told them the truth. You come to annoy a psychopath, he's insane. He's going to kill you all, and then he's going to Malaysia to find your family and kill all of them'.

He turned to his nephew and said, "You got yourself involved with a psychopath? You on your own!'

"Then one night in 1989 I got pulled up by the police. They said, 'what you got in there?' I replied a sawn-off shotgun. They told me to get out of the car and took me to the police station. There they asked whether I got anything on me? I said, 'yes meths, LSD, cash.' So they charged me.

'Where did you get it?' they asked.

'I found it in a bin, and was just on my way to hand it in.'

They wanted to know where it came from because it was 100% pure but I refused to explain. I was charged with seven offences including possession of a shortened firearm, carry and use of a firearm with disregard for safety, deemed supply, goods in custody, and possession of an un-licenced firearm. The police helped themselves to some of the gear.

"They tried to get me convicted and took me to court. I was the first person in NSW to have a judge-only trial; I was acquitted. People

6 - The Legal Arguments

have to understand NSW is the most corrupt state in the country; crooked from top to bottom, it's been like that from the beginning.

"The senior Cop then threatened my family. I explained to him that if he threatened my family, I would kill him and his family. 'You think this is a game, it's not a game!' I told him. He was totally flummoxed. Another cop in attendance responded that he would keep him on a leash.

"Years later, on appeal, in another minor matter, a Crown Solicitor was asked why he remembered this case. He explained that it was unusual because despite compelling evidence, I was acquitted, and it happened very quickly. No one testified except my wife, and I gave unsworn evidence from the dock.

"Around 1990 cops from Internal Affairs came to my dad's pub to tell me there was a contract on me. When I heard this, I laughed, and the police office said, 'This is a serious matter, they're going to kill you!'

'No they're not' I said, they're idiots they won't do anything'.

"The Internal Affairs police gave me two numbers, one a direct line to the commissioner.

Some seven years later I was in my back yard and the phone rang. It was a police Inspector who told me our 'mutual friends' wanted me to back off because they were still having a tough time. I reminded him it was them who started this when they said they were going to have me killed and I assured him I was not finished with them. He said I had effectively destroyed their lives and their careers and asked me if I would do it as a favour to him. I said I would on condition he told them I was doing this for him and not for them.

"Those cops had lost the will to fight; they come out swinging and then realised what they were up against. The same situation with Russell and Patrick; they're big bullies but they did not realise they're not scared of them either. They picked a couple of tough nuts and unfortunately for the police there is still some semblance of the law in this country; they know how to bend it much of the time but have learned you can't do it all the time. Since the arrest of Russell and Patrick the prosecutors have lost virtually every legal confrontation and I believe they know they're beaten in going after Russell and Patrick, they just don't know how to make it all go away.

"Some years after my acquittal I got a letter saying they had forgotten about other charges including possession of a firearm, possession of a firearm with disregard for safety, possession of amphetamines, LSD, and goods in custody, and that these outstanding matters had to be resolved.

"I came back to court, and pleaded not guilty, but the magistrate convicted me of five of the six charges. So I appealed. That's when I figured out, I needed to start understanding the law better and applied to go to university to study law. I got halfway through the degree when in 1996, I finally managed after seven years to get acquitted of the charges. Always acquitted, I never got convicted, and never finished the degree.

"It was in 2010 that I got my first whiff of something being rotten in the state-funded apparatus operating around child welfare. A friend got in touch with me and told me that child-care was to be privatised and there was a business opportunity for us. The more I looked into it the more promising it looked. To become operational it was mandated that we would be in partnership for a year with one of the established child-care agencies and providing we, six of us, performed at the required standard, we would then be entrusted 10 children for whom we would provide foster care. That number would then increase rapidly as long as we maintained the required standards.

"It was all looking very positive when, in the course of an online presentation an image flashed up on my screen that caught my eye before it was quickly removed. I asked to see it again, but my request was dismissed. I insisted and up it came again – there were the words 'monetary units' referring to the children. I asked for an explanation, but it was not forthcoming, and I was deeply disturbed by this. I went to a friend who was a bishop in the local church and told him. Our organisation never went ahead with the child protection business.

"One of my friends, Father Graeme, still has almost two years to go in prison having been convicted of child abuse. I was stalked on the internet for five years for assisting him fight off charges. I have known him since I was a young man and never saw him behave in any sort of inappropriate way and I never heard any chatter whatsoever. I have no doubt he's innocent. The problem for the authorities was that there was a Royal Commission on the prowl and Father Graeme was thrown to the wolves to protect others.

"When Cardinal Pell was arrested and charged, I looked at the evidence and predicted his eventual acquittal. It was extremely flimsy. He was working as a Treasurer at the Vatican. A jury in Melbourne's County Court found him guilty of child sex abuse in 2018. Pell is a big man and the prosecution claimed he pushed a child against a wall and touched him inappropriately while in his full regalia, in a hall full of people, and yet, somehow nobody saw the alleged assault. It never made any sense, and his conviction was eventually overturned. "I think the church has borne an unfair proportion of the blame for child abuse in Australia. The main culprits operate in the education system and in the disability sector which are mostly under some sort of government control.

"In Feb 2017 a complaint was lodged with the child welfare people about my pregnant daughter. They alleged drugs and alcohol, that she hadn't purchased a single thing not even a baby bottle and that she didn't go to prenatal. The first two were made up and there was no requirement for the third but at any rate she was doing everything the doctor said to. As a result it was alleged she was incapable of caring for her soon to be born baby. This was all rubbish, but they continued to harass for months even attempting to get a warrant to seize the child. Remember, a child in good health is worth about $43,000 a year to the people involved. I went to the local magistrate and police chief and told them to their faces if the child was touched, I would kill caseworkers. They assured me that the child safety mob were not listening, and I assured them I would blow their heads off. I spoke to two police inspectors and told them that if this child was touched, I would be killing caseworkers.

"Eventually a number of police from the anti-terror squad came to see me and said this situation was getting 'heavy', and that I would die or finish in prison. I told him that would be my reward because that's my ticket to the Kingdom of God.

"In many ways I have no complaints against the police involved and in fact I speak highly of them. Those last police knew we were in the right and that there was no harm to my grandchild, and they gave me their word that he would not be taken. When this was all going on a bloke came to my house unannounced to tell me he had heard I was going to kill case-workers. I confirmed this would happen if they touched my grandchild and he asked where I'd be getting the guns from. I told him I wasn't sure, but I would get them.

'No worries mate,' he said, 'I'll get you all the guns and ammo you need. We hate these people as much as you do and if we can help all you have to do is ask.'

6 - The Legal Arguments

"As it turned out, they stayed away, and the police have been true to their word. I honestly don't believe the police are the problem in this state-controlled child trafficking business. But globally, the misnamed "child safety departments" most certainly are. The truth is I have never killed anyone, but I have shown enough violence that people know I am capable of it. If my family were touched, I would most definitely kill to protect them. Particularly if the child trafficking scum from the government, the so-called child protection agencies come near my grandchildren."

Unbeknown to Graeme at this same time, early 2017, Pastor Paul Robert Burton was dealing with a similar problem.

Paul started his working life as an Electronic Technician (Technical Officer Grade 1) with a foundation in fundamental electronics, communications and computing. After four years and following a life changing significant health event, Paul gave up everything to pursue his love of music, moved from Adelaide, South Australia to Sydney, NSW and became a professional musician.

After many years of performing and not long after the passing of his grandmother, around 2000, he began an applied theological practice that aimed at illuminating the common ground between all religions and spiritual practices, and in 2004 he was initiated into the Holy Ramakrishna Order. From this time forward he dedicated his life to Pastoral work, selfless service while using his musical skills in new and creative ways to help empower and educate people.

In 2010 he turned his attention to the rapid rise of inappropriate mining and the importance of protecting the Australian environment and precious natural resources. He founded 'Our Land, Our Water, Our Future Inc' and began an intense journey of grassroots community-based education and communication through direct community engagement travelling throughout NSW, QLD and Victoria. This morphed into collaboratively restructured work to develop creative community building and community connection projects to empower individuals in 2013.

In 2016, he became active in the protection of God given, common law, constitutional and fundamental human rights, especially in regard to children, and began assisting families with Pastoral support and advocacy. Interestingly, whilst he was involved in environmental matters he spent considerable time with the Gomeroi/Gamilleroi Mob in North West NSW, and it was through his efforts to protect the sacred sites of indigenous Australians that he became aware of the vast number of aboriginals that had been forcibly removed from their families and who had also, in nearly all cases, had their own children forcibly removed. He began assisting Auntie Mimmie, a Gomeroi/Gamilleroi elder who had two grandchildren removed and who had also co-founded a large group called 'grandmothers against removals'. This group included indigenous Australian grandmothers trying to have their grandchildren returned. They were, in effect, fighting state-condoned child trafficking and child abuse. This was how he first came into contact with what was then called the NSW Dept of Family and Community Services (FACS) also known previously as DOCS. Most people are of the belief that Australia stopped engaging in Genocide around 1967, with the referendum and changes to the constitution for the Aboriginal people, however, in Paul's view nothing could be further from the truth.

'They are taking more indigenous children now than ever,' he says, 'they are actually targeted by the system and now the child removal net is growing much bigger. This was how, around late 2016 I became involved with a beautiful 4½ year old indigenous child named Chase Walker-Steven and his family.

6 - The Legal Arguments

"Chase was born healthy on August 29th, 2012, but there were complications after the birth that resulted in him being diagnosed with a severe health condition known as spastic quadriplegia cerebral palsy. This was clearly at the very least, as a consequence of hospital neglect with the most likely cause of his condition being a severe allergic reaction to a Konakion vitamin K injection followed by violent reactions to possibly one or perhaps even two Hepatitis B injections. As a consequence the child has level 5 spastic quadriplegia cerebral palsy. The parents did not know what had happened to Chase until he was about 1½ years old and they were able to obtain the hospital records through a firm of solicitors.

"They were unable to initiate legal proceedings due to limited funds so from 2013 began significant fundraising and awareness raising campaigns. They appeared in magazine articles, media events, they raised money for special equipment for Chase and they also did all this to raise awareness about his unique condition with a view to seeking legal remedy.

"Chase is fully conscious; he is highly intelligent, but he is unable to control any of his motor functions. He cannot move himself or do anything without assistance. He cannot speak or control his arms and legs. He is a very high needs child who requires 24-hour care.

"As a result of his complex intractable epilepsy and the subsequent failure of all allopathic medications to contain his multiple seizures and also because of the parents' awareness of the causes of his condition they embarked on a program of exploring alternative natural therapies to assist him and improve his quality of life. They did this with the full approval and consent of the medical practitioners they worked with regularly.

"In early 2017 the Dept of Child Protection QLD (DOCS)

Browns Plains Child Safety led by Stephen Lake, began to investigate the family with alleged concerns about their son's health. As a consequence around Jan/February 2017 the family were summoned to attend Beenleigh Children's Court before Magistrate Pamela Dowse to articulate those concerns. Magistrate Dowse found in their favour and Chase was allowed to remain in the family's care.

"Despite this, Lake, Aimee Lohrisch and Bay Gebrewold from Browns Plains continued to harass the family and threatened to remove their son. The family reported this intimidation to the Queensland Police who explained that if DOCS want your child, they continue to take you to court until they find a magistrate who agrees with them.

"Against this background I came into contact with Dr Andrew Katelaris late in 2016 as we were both assisting the family. Andrew provided medical information to the family in regard to the efficacy of medicinal cannabis in treating children with intractable epilepsy. Meanwhile I assisted the family with Pastoral and spiritual support whilst at the same time communicating with The Australian Human Rights Commission's, Gillian Triggs, the Premiere of NSW, Gladys Berejiklian, and the Minister for Health, Brad Hazzard, making them all aware of what I described as significant human rights concerns. I had observed first-hand the positive effects of the use of medicinal cannabis on children with intractable epilepsy. Unfortunately at that time medicinal cannabis was not available to the general public and access to it was so difficult that nobody could obtain it. I wrote to the government to make them aware of the forced criminalisation of many good parents who were using unlicensed medicinal cannabis as a tincture to effectively treat their children.

"Around mid-February in 2017 I arranged a meeting in QLD

6 - The Legal Arguments

with Browns Plains DOCS representatives Lake and Lorisch, Dr Andrew, Barry Futter (The President of the Church of Ubuntu) and Peter Little, at that time another staunch advocate for the family.

"By this time Dr Andrew, myself and the Church were providing considerable assistance to Chase and his family. We felt the child was in the best care possible, but the authorities had other ideas. Remember in Australia child 'protection' has now been fully privatised and even at that time this child was valuable; I call it state-condoned child-trafficking and child abuse or in short 'kids for cash'.

"When a child is taken by the state, a basic healthy child is worth about $40,000 of taxpayers' money, for starters. With the privatisation of the out-of-home care system, the department outsources the child to one of several other agencies – out-of-home care or residential care. So, when a child is taken, the department no longer looks after that child, it goes to a 3rd party. And they take taxpayers' money. So they spend around $40,000. That goes to one of these organisations. A highly compromised child such as Chase was worth around $325,000 a year back in 2016, and that is only the tip of the financial iceberg. They even refer to children as "financial units". The more compromised a child is the more valuable they become, and they pay that to these third party non-governmental organisations (NGO's) that supposedly operate in the children's best interests. This doesn't support and protect children; it puts them at far, far greater risk. Australian law place draconian restrictions around what can be reported on in regard to children in state care, so there is plenty of scope for abuse.

"It was 19th May 2017 when they came to The Church and Wellness Clinic and the trouble began in earnest. The Family and Community Services (FACS) had put out a false flag national 'Amber

Alert'[14] based on absolute rubbish, around two weeks before the 19th of May so we already had serious concerns. It was around 4.35pm in the afternoon when around six policemen barged in the Church Wellness Clinic without a warrant demanding to know the exact whereabouts of the child. When I heard the commotion, I was upstairs assisting the family in the area we used at the time for meditation with a small office area at the front, so I said to the family wait here and went downstairs. I asked the Senior Police Officer in charge for his name and reason for trespassing, to which he barked at me and said, 'I don't have to tell you fucking nothin!'

To which I replied, "well that's very different officer?"

"I later found out his name was Gerard Lawson. Whilst this was all occurring the family and child were upstairs in our communal area with a number of our community helping to guard them from now around 14 police and two FACS caseworkers who both lied and said they had court orders and they also hid their identities. I found out some time later that they were Alison Maher and Nicole Collins. Eventually we were able to negotiate with the police and caseworkers as we were prepared to fight if they attempted to separate the child from his family. The caseworkers had made an absurd claim that the child was at significant risk of harm because of low potassium levels. We argued that was demonstrably wrong but if they really felt they needed to check, they should at the very least get an ambulance, as they arrived without so much as a bloody car seat for a highly compromised child! Then, we agreed, they could allow the family together to travel to the local hospital for the child to be examined. We refused to allow them to separate the chid from

---

14 An emergency response system that disseminates information about a missing person (usually a child), by media broadcasting or electronic roadway signs.

6 - The Legal Arguments

the family and made it clear that it was NOT an option as we would have no choice other than to defend the family; four unarmed males against 14 fully armed police and two idiot caseworkers.

"They agreed that they would take the family together in an ambulance and we allowed that to happen. If I had known then, what I know now, I would have chosen instead to fight to the death if necessary so I could at least be able to get a jury trial. Basically the department and children's courts are so bad that once your child is removed (often forcibly) you have next to no chance of ever getting them back, even if there was no reason for the removal. Your best option is to do all you can to stop the people removing your child in the first instance and do everything whilst lawfully defending, but you must get a jury trial you literally have to commit an indictable offence to get any chance of justice, this is the only way you can at least tell people what is really happening.

"Later at the hospital, reinforcements arrived, so there were now 32 policemen involved in the operation and they locked down the entire emergency section of the hospital so we could not get anywhere near the family to assist and support them. Meanwhile, in all of the stress and distress Chases's two sisters had somehow been separated from Chase and their parents. Fortunately some members of our community looked after them.

"Many of us waited outside the hospital near the emergency section to hear the outcome of the hospital tests (the mother and father still had their mobile phones) and we were excited when we heard that the child was found to be well-nourished and showing no signs of neglect. Unfortunately, with FACS this makes no difference. While the father was in the toilet in the emergency section, they locked him in and then grabbed the mother. They ripped the highly compromised child from her loving arms and then dragged her kicking and screaming out to a paddy wagon. As we came to try and assist, they opened up on the rest of us outside with Pepper-Spray. With us in disarray, they raced away at breakneck speed with the mother being hurled around in the back of their van, while another group rushed out the back door of the hospital with the child, who was then of course traumatised and seizing uncontrollably.

"About six weeks after this shocking event, both myself and Dr Andrew were summoned by the Department of FACS to the NSW Supreme Court of Equity, where we were then suppressed, without a hearing, in relation to alleged offences relating to the mentioning of the child and information about his health on social media. This was despite over four million other people having witnessed the event on a social media live cast and whom were all talking about the child, his health and the disgraceful things that they had witnessed on Facebook.

"It was not long after this brutal assault and the ripping of this child from his kind loving family that I came into contact with Graeme Bell. Put very simply, after the shocking removal and the threat of court action against me in an attempt to silence me speaking truth, I began a search to find any individual who had had any success against FACS; enter Graeme Bell.

"It was also not long after this that Patrick called me in connection with Ann Gordon, who he was trying to help. Unfortunately, at the time, I was under a lot of pressure as I was being publicly defamed by international media and subjected to the harsh rigours of judicial system suppression and, not knowing who Patrick was, I thought it was quite possibly a police trap and setup, so although I was supportive of Patrick's position, I said I could not assist a stranger without first meeting her and discussing her situation. This meeting never eventuated, and I often wonder what would have happened

Pastor Paul Burton appeared as a support person for Mr O'Dea. Picture: NCA News-Wire / Glenn Campbell

if I had met Ann and become embroiled directly in their matter as well. Only later, when I read about Patrick and Russell in the media, did I make the connection and realise that clearly they had been monitored and then targeted in a very similar fashion to me, i.e. for trying to protect children from state condoned child trafficking and child abuse."

"It was when I met Paul," remembers Graeme, "that I realised I must devote myself to the children of Australia and stop these state-run child trafficking rings. I knew I was blessed by God with a great mind and a photographic memory that gives me a huge advantage over most people and every lawyer and judge I have ever come up against. I say, without any fear of contradiction, that I can take on the best legal minds in this country and beat them. But when it comes to protecting my family, I know the limitations of the law and the system and that is when I resort to violence which is all these cowards understand.

"When Ann Gordon called me to ask for help, I listened to her plea and then admonished her; 'I've been waiting 18 months for this call,' I said, 'why did you take so long?' The poor lady was desperate because they were about to transfer her case to Brisbane and that would have added to her woes. Almost immediately I advised her to seek a Directions Hearing and challenge the constitutionality of the CDPP prosecuting someone for an alleged offence that fell under the jurisdiction of the State where it was allegedly committed, without the consent of the Attorney General.

"I drew a brief up for her and told her to take it to the police station. She walked in and they were bamboozled; 'You can't do this,' they said, 'we've never seen this before!' They were completely thrown. She emailed the CDPP at 6pm on a Friday outlining her application and by 6 am on the Monday they wrote to say they were withdrawing the child-stealing charge. The police and the prosecution realised quite quickly they were out of their depth and relented. The child-stealing charges were dropped. They're bullies but when stood up to, they back off. Just as we won the Child-Stealing charge we will beat the Conspiracy charges levelled against Ann.

"Paul is like a highly organised secretary and administrator, and I started assisting him with information, case law and strong legal arguments to help support and empower the poor, hapless parents that were all contacting him for both spiritual and legal support, so we have lots on our plate. Paul, without qualified legal assistance, has probably been before more magistrates and judges than anyone else in Australia. Between the two of us nobody knows more about how this system operates and how flawed it truly is. What draws us together is the horror and pure evil of the number of children currently being abused in alleged care and how to help those poor children and other fearless people, like Russell and Patrick and Ann who are prepared to take a stand against the monster that this police state has become. And as Paul would say, we do it for God; protecting children against harm is very clear in the bible. There is a lot to do, there is more money today in selling children than drugs and firearms globally. One Australian Federal Police report showed that there are approximately 44,900 children and young people under 18 years of age living in Out-Of-Home Care in Australia. They comprise under one percent of all young people in the country, yet they made up 53% of all young people reported missing and were responsible for 77% of missing episodes during the timeframe of the study. Youth in OOHC also repeatedly went missing during the 30-day study period. They comprised 54% of all missing individuals but were responsible for 70.5% of all repeat missing youth.

"Paul has been successful in defamation actions against two multi-national media corporations, and he also successfully sued PayPal, and Paul has been compensated for injuries suffered at the behest of the police under the control of FACS when he was pepper-sprayed at the hospital. He also had two significant successes in The NSW Court of Appeal and so as a consequence we have made a considerable impact on important case-law and we are helping to lawfully expose this system in absolute crisis. Our story is not over, but as Paul said, we have made and are still making some amazing, enduring real friendships along the way and are part of a fast-growing, now international network of amazing people all striving to bring about real positive change. Ultimately this is a spiritual war.

CHAPTER 7 – THE TRUTH IS REVEALED

Trials continue

Danielle Buckley, Courier Mail, wrote:

Then finally Wednesday 24 March 2021, Patrick O'Dea was back in court. He had let fly on Facebook calling Supreme Court officials 'w — kers' and 'pedo pricks' shortly after his social media restrictions were eased, the court has heard. Mr O'Dea was allowed to have his GPS tracker removed last year after he told the Brisbane Supreme Court his ability to work had been hindered by the ankle device because he had to be plugged into a wall for two hours whenever the battery ran low. His ban on social media was also relaxed so he could contact friends, families and employees in Zimbabwe.

During a bail variation hearing in the Brisbane Supreme Court yesterday morning, Crown prosecutor Rowan Micairan argued that the 64-year-old should be banned from social media altogether while on bail. He said the day his bail application was heard Mr O'Dea posted on Facebook that he had to go to court so the '"pedo pricks' leave the GPS ankle bracelet off". Mr Micairan said his 'prolific' posts had scorned the court and Mr O'Dea had also shared and been tagged in posts that had accused courts of protecting paedophiles and Federal Police officers of perverting the course of justice.

"He cannot be trusted on social media ... he just cannot," Mr Micairan said.

Mr Micairan also argued that Mr O'Dea, who has been on bail for two years, should be made to wear the GPS tracker again and should continue to report seven days a week because he still holds 'animosity' towards a man he allegedly stalked.

7 - The Truth is Revealed

Lawyer Andrew Owens said since his arrest, Mr O'Dea had made no attempt to contact the father and had complied fully with his strict bail conditions, which included reporting seven days a week for the past eight months.

Mr Owens said Mr O'Dea had strong ties to the Grafton community so would not be a flight risk and the COVID-19 border restrictions would make it difficult for him to travel to Queensland anyway. The court was told he had reported more than 200 times since December.

"We get armed robbers and alleged murderers who don't have to report that often," said Justice Peter Applegarth hearing the matter. Justice Applegarth removed the condition requiring Mr O'Dea to wear a GPS tracker and reduced the number of days he had to report to four times a week. But he was reluctant to place a blanket ban on his social media usage.

"Let's be realistic here," Justice Applegarth said. "If he supports the Sydney Swans, he couldn't go on the Sydney Swans Facebook page and say 'go the Swannies' if the Commonwealth had its way. Is this real?" he said.

Mr Owen and Mr Micairan were left to strike a compromise about how to best manage Mr O'Dea's social media use. Since then Patrick was ordered not to publish any articles or comments concerning this protection case on Facebook.

On 28 July, the child-stealing charges against Russell and Patrick were dropped.

"The child-stealing charges were Section 363(1)(a) – that I had stolen the children using force or fraud," says Russell. "Clearly this was not the case, and they couldn't particularise the charges or specify the evidence that proved them. So then they changed it to Section 363(1)(b) – receiving or harbouring a child that had been stolen using force or fraud. The problem was Ann Gordon had lawful custody of the child and a grandmother cannot steal a child she is entitled to have in her care. With the twins they were in the custody of the father so it was more difficult but the prosecution had no evidence to show that Lizzie took the children using force or fraud so I could not have received or harboured them as defined in the act.

"This withdrawal meant of the seven original charges against me only two remained which were the two counts of conspiring to interfere with the course of justice. This prosecution has always been a criminal enterprise, which aims to hide the betrayal of the abused children and provide protection for their abusers."

Patrick O'Dea and Dr. Russell Pridgeon

Justice Clare

"On the 3rd November 2021, my application to the Brisbane District Court pleading for a permanent stay of proceedings was submitted with the help of Graeme Bell. It was presided over by Justice Clare. The thrust of the argument was that 'the course of justice' begins when a matter is brought before a court and ends when a judge or

7 - The Truth is Revealed

magistrate makes a determination or delivers a verdict and hands down a sentence. Thereafter the matter ceases to be 'judicial' and becomes 'administrative', so Ann and I could not have been interfering with the course of justice because justice had been done. If we had, for instance, interfered with witnesses prior to a hearing or trial we would have had a case to answer but that was never alleged. The prosecution argued that the 'recovery orders' were the 'course of justice' but Judge Clare opined that she was not in agreement with this, and our hopes soared. The judge had asked the prosecution to show that this was a valid prosecution which could prove intent to commit a crime. They argued that our actions in relation to the 'orders' of the court constituted a crime. And went on to say we intended to defeat future orders but failed to give further details.

"We then listened in stunned amazement as she virtually argued our case for us in a delivery that sounded more erudite and persuasive than what we had presented. Apart from that she had made frequent comments which were sympathetic to our argument. At the end of the proceedings we came away full of hope; finally fairness appeared to be showing its pretty face and Graeme was convinced we had won the day.

Graeme has long been of the view that in the case of Ann, who had lawful custody of the child, it is impossible to show viable prosecution is possible. This raised the strong possibility that if they dropped the charges against me and Ann they would have to drop them for all in our group. This would leave Patrick facing two charges that Graeme believes are easy to dismiss under Section 80 like he did with my proceeds of crime charge. He was convinced that on the basis of what she had said on the record it would be virtually impossible for her to change her opinion.

"However it was not to be; on 10 December, 2021 Ann and I were back in court before Judge Clare for her ruling. It was astonishing; she was late into court, and she looked flustered. Not the same calm, confident demeanour we had witnessed earlier. She did not take a roll call as is usual. She started talking then stopped saying she had got things mixed up. She confused the names of the applicants – Ann Gordon was the applicant and she referred to Lizzie. After a minute she restarted and abruptly reversed her earlier position.

"She dismissed Lizzie and Joyce's application for separate trials. She dismissed my application for a permanent stay, and then got Ann mixed up with Lizzie and said that Lizzie's (not Ann's, as it should have been) application for permanent stay was dismissed too.

"Then it got worse; she approved the prosecution's request to not allow the submission of the reports of the children's abuse which is fundamental to our defence. We were aghast to hear once again that the alleged crimes committed against the children were going to be concealed yet again. She was in a hurry, delivered the whole judgement in a couple of minutes and then shot out of court. Just what caused her to make this volte face we might never know but I simply cannot believe she was not under some sort of duress.

"So we now face a jury trial without being able to explain why we did what we did.

As far as the criminal justice system is concerned, we remain facing the prospect of prison.

Up against the power of the State we have our small team but Patrick is adamant good will triumph over evil. He continues to believe an honest and brave judge will appear.

"My family has been greatly stressed and affected by all of this," says Patrick. "At the start of all this, they knew nothing of my involvement in anything to do with child protection other than the

7 - The Truth is Revealed

setting up of the political party. My wife and children are fully supportive but also stressed to hell by the AFP and their attitude. Clearly domestic bliss has not exactly been shared. The police through their vindictiveness have prevented me from any sort of employment for the last three years. I have no assets and no income. As a result my wife who is now 71 has had to continue her care work to sustain us. But the pressure has taken its toll and sadly we have now separated.

At the Grafton Watchhouse my wife asked Williamson what was going on, and he stood there and, with a triumphant flourish: 'Your husband is going to jail for a VERY long time'. Pity these guys don't spend some time going after proper bad guys!

Child abuse in Australia
Russell: "The problem of child abuse is huge, involving many hundreds of cases each year. Generally, the public has not heard about this: this is because when it occurs in the Family Court, none of the details of the court case may be publicised, so the media will not touch it.

"It has been actively hidden from Australians. Secrecy emboldens, enables and empowers child sexual abusers. Clearly, transparency and accountability should be the norm. However, it is glaringly obvious that many Members of Parliament are not interested in children's issues, which cost the taxpayer around $30 billion a year, and possibly because children don't vote – there is no return on this particular investment!

"Further, Australian research suggests that boys are abused earlier, more often and by more offenders than girls, and this is not recognised in statistics because they don't report it, whilst victims and abusers are becoming younger and younger; 95-98% of this abuse will be perpetrated by family members or at least persons very well known to the family (stranger danger, as appalling as it is, is relatively uncommon).

"If the child's views are disbelieved the child is discouraged from further disclosures. The fact is young children do not concoct false allegations of abuse – they cannot describe sexual abuse unless they have experienced it. The failure of the courts to accept a child's testimony creates the perfect crime: intra-familial child sexual abuse becomes a crime that cannot be prosecuted.

"With the system as it is, it is almost as if the court's very purpose is to traffic children to paedophiles for this very purpose, and to protect the abusers, while leaving the child victims and their protectors totally vulnerable. Some of these children are ordered to live with abusers as a result of the 2006 'shared parenting' reforms until they are eighteen. They are only now are disclosing the abuse that was ongoing, because they are suffering from Complex Post-Traumatic Stress Disorder.

"Some boys who have had to accept abuse as the norm have themselves become abusers, directly because of the court's decisions. The grief and suffering of the children and of the protective parents whose children are handed over to their abusers is unimaginable.

"The most distressing aspect of becoming involved in trying to protect Australian children from ongoing abuse was the experience of seeking help from the authorities tasked with protecting children and being confronted with a baffling wall of disbelief, indifference and, eventually, people using excuses not to act.

"Clearly the police had not been trained as to how they should respond to such complaints, so it was the 'whining Sheila against my mate'. Who do you think these male macho police choose to believe?

"No matter how compelling the child's disclosures, they appear to

7 - The Truth is Revealed

refuse to prosecute the offender; the child is too young: we cannot rely on his testimony; the child will never stand up to a barrister's cross-examination in court; the child's testimony is contaminated; you should not have spoken to him; we believe the child but his testimony will never stand up in court; the excuses never end, so they also refuse to protect the child from ongoing abuse by exercising their lawful power to do so. This allows the abuser's solicitor to claim in Family Court that the child was not abused, and that the 'protective parent' is maliciously alienating the child from the abuser. The 'protective parent' is invariably characterised as emotionally abusive, and the child is removed from that person.

Liberal Senator Bill Heffernan is an anti-paedophile crusader

"This reminds one of the Aboriginal children removed from their parents; the reason given at the time that they needed to be re-educated in the 'white English Australian way'. This was often to the detriment of the child, they had to forsake, family, language and culture and all beyond the control of the biological parents."

19 October 2015 Allegations of the elite paedophile ring surfaced in Parliament, with Liberal senator Bill Heffernan claiming he had obtained a police list containing the names of 28 prominent people. Senator Heffernan wouldn't name names on Tuesday but called on Attorney-General George Brandis to expand the child abuse Royal Commission to include the legal fraternity, including a current judge, as well as a former prime minister. He said he had provided the Commission with documents, one naming the alleged paedophiles including "a whole lot of prominent people." There is enough detail in Senator Heffernan's allegations to make them very credible. Some of the details are:

- The list *"formed part of police documents that had been 'signed off' by Gary Crooke, QC, the former senior counsel assisting NSW's Wood royal commission into police corruption in the 1990s. Mr Crooke declined to comment when contacted by Fairfax Media on Tuesday."*

- *"Every Commonwealth attorney-general since Philip Ruddock had seen the list".* This seems to have been confirmed by Philip Ruddock and Former Labour Attorney-General Mark Dreyfus.

- Senator Heffernan *"accused former royal commissioner Justice James Roland Wood of refusing to investigate lawyers who had allegedly attended a Kings Cross boy brothel Costellos, which was known to be attended by members of the Sydney legal fraternity."*

- Former Royal Commissioner Wood denied the allegations by Senator Heffernan, but not outright. *"Mr Wood could not recall if the alleged list had been raised at the 1995 commission but said: "I reject that we failed to investigate anyone that fell within our terms of reference."*

'The reason the Australian government gave for not releasing the report of the paedophile investigation was because they said it would cause people to lose faith in the system," says Russell.

There is a report from a lawyer who went to a party and when a woman, a caseworker, discovered he knew about my case, she told him of an incident that occurred when she was with one of the children and she said she was quite happy to back this allegation with a signed affidavit. At some point she recalled, the TV was turned on and the child immediately recognised the face of a former prime minister. The child pointed and said, 'there's Uncle J...' and went on to explain 'we are taken to see Uncle J... a lot.' The Heffernan inquiry was probably shut down because he had evidence to hand pointing in the same direction.[15] I think it is being privy to information such as this that has triggered the response we have faced; they set out to terrify us into submission and send a signal to likeminded people that the punishment for interfering in their schemes is severe. We have been made examples of."

Relief At Last: Medical License Returned

On 18 February 2022, Russell, acting for himself, with the submissions written by Ange Hearns (paralegal advisor), took the Medical Council of NSW to the NSW Court of Appeal. For the first time since their ordeal began, justice and fairness showed its pretty face.

Some pertinent excerpts below:

The appellant, Dr Pridgeon, was a registered medical practitioner. On 29

---

15 This is very similar to UK Labour MP Tom Watson making similar claims in October 2012. Watson stood up in the British House of Commons and told the Prime Minister that police had – or used to have – a file of evidence containing "clear intelligence suggesting a powerful paedophile network linked to Parliament and No. 10. The Jimmy Savile scandal showed he too was protected at virtually every level in the BBC, by the media in general and by the relevant authorities.

October 2018, the respondent, the Medical Council of New South Wales, determined pursuant to s 150 of the Health Practitioner Regulation National Law (NSW) to suspend Dr Pridgeon's registration, after he was charged by the Australian Federal Police and later the Queensland Police with offences against the respective criminal codes of the Commonwealth and Queensland.

The charges related to Dr Pridgeon's role in harbouring and/or supporting a woman and her twin daughters. The children had been removed by their mother from a place in Queensland and not returned to the custody of their father, who was named as a residential parent by order of the Family Court of Australia and the parent with whom the Family Court had ordered the children to live. At the time when the mother took and secreted the children, she only had a right of supervised contact with them. Dr Pridgeon maintained that she had informed him that the children's father had sexually abused them.

Dr Pridgeon sought a review of that decision pursuant to s 150A. On 2 December 2020, the Medical Council affirmed the order for suspension of Dr Pridgeon's registration as a medical practitioner. Dr Pridgeon then appealed from these determinations to the New South Wales Civil and Administrative Tribunal. On 30 June 2021, the Tribunal upheld Dr Pridgeon's suspension on the ground of public interest and dismissed his appeal. Dr Pridgeon sought leave to appeal from that decision.

The principal issues before this Court were:

(i) whether the Tribunal exercised its power "in the public interest" by purporting indefinitely to suspend Dr Pridgeon's registration as a medical practitioner pursuant to s 150 of the National Law;

(ii) whether the Tribunal erred in law by acting without any factual basis upon which the exercise of the emergency power contained in s 150 depends.

The court found that:

In the context of Subdivision 7 of the National Law, the reference to the "public interest" should be understood as a reference to the public interest in *the protection of the public's health and safety. The content to be given to that protection must take its meaning from the conduct of the practice of medicine in respect of which a medical practitioner's registration is granted: at [68].*

It was not in the public interest to suspend Dr Pridgeon as it could not (yet) be said that Dr Pridgeon's alleged defiance of the court's orders undermined the rule of law. Dr Pridgeon's guilt was not a foregone conclusion. Although the Tribunal paid lip service to the presumption of innocence and did not make findings of guilt, its conclusions were patently infected by assumptions of guilt: at [69].

Later it was added that: *The public interest is not obviously served by the suspension of a competent and experienced doctor whose medical skills are not in question and whose services are in demand simply because he has been charged with offences in respect of which he would appear to have a good arguable defence.*

On the matter of urgency:

The context of s 150 of the National Law suggests that it should only be invoked as an emergency power where the circumstances are urgent.

It was decided:

There was no urgency in this matter at any time before or during the Tribunal hearing. As such, the Tribunal erred in exercising the emergency power contained in s 150 of the National Law where the circumstances did not warrant its exercise: at [70].

On the question of whether Russell actually broke the law:

The Tribunal's indication at [202] and [207] that the term "honourable practice" in the phrase "honourable practice of an honourable profession" must include a requirement that members of the medical profession act within the law at all times is in our view problematic, and begs the question in light of s 70NAE of the Family Law Act and arguably s 286 of the Criminal Code (Qld).

Meaning of reasonable excuse for contravening an order

(1) The circumstances in which a person may be taken to have had, for the purposes of this Division, a reasonable excuse for contravening an order under this Act affecting children include, but are not limited to, the circumstances set out in subsections (2), (4), (5), (6) and (7).

...

4) A person (the respondent) is taken to have had a reasonable excuse for contravening a parenting order to the extent to which it deals with whom a child is to live with in a way that resulted in the child not living with a person in whose favour the order was made if:

(a) the respondent believed on reasonable grounds that the actions constituting the contravention were necessary to protect the health or safety of a person (including the respondent or the child); and

(b) the period during which, because of the contravention, the child did not live with the person in whose favour the order was made was not longer than was necessary to protect the health or safety of the person referred to in paragraph (a).

...

286 Duty of person who has care of child

(1) It is the duty of every person who has care of a child under 16 years to–

(a) provide the necessaries of life for the child; and

(b) take the precautions that are reasonable in all the circumstances to avoid danger to the child's life, health or safety; and

(c) take the action that is reasonable in all the circumstances to remove the child from any such danger;

and he or she is held to have caused any consequences that result to the life and health of the child because of any omission to perform that duty, whether the child is helpless or not.

(2) In this section–

"person who has care of a child" includes a parent, foster parent, step-parent, guardian or other adult in charge of the child, whether or not the person has lawful custody of the child.

The court accepted that Russell believed on reasonable grounds that the actions constituting the contravention were necessary to protect the health and safety of the children. In fact, S286 also states that it is the duty of a person who has care of a child to take precautions to avoid danger to the children's health and safety and remove the children from such danger, and this includes an adult in charge of the children whether or not he had lawful custody.

The court also noted that the Council and Tribunal acknowledged that Russell was not concerned with whether the order was "right" or "wrong", but only with what he feared would be the inevitable consequences for the children of complying with the order. And went on to declare that the Tribunal's interpretation of "honourable practice" was given a very narrow interpretation rather than a wide interpretation such that it allows members of the medical profession to act outside of the law in exceptional circumstances, and it is only the courts, not the Medical Council or the Tribunal to determine guilt or innocence.

So Russell's suspension was lifted and the orders of the Tribunal of 30 June 2021 and Medical Council of NSW of 29 October and 2 December 2020 were set aside. Further the Medical Council of NSW was ordered to pay Russell's Appeal Court hearing costs.

Russell: "The barrister appearing for the respondents, Alexander

Rose, was the same lady I had been up against at the Tribunal hearings and she had it in for me there. I later laid a formal complaint about her. This came about as a result of the requirement that in order for my license to be suspended I had to have been the recipient of one of the complaints listed below:

The following complaints may be made about a registered health practitioner–

(a) A complaint the practitioner has, either in this jurisdiction or elsewhere, been convicted of or made the subject of a criminal finding for an offence.

(b) A complaint the practitioner has been guilty of unsatisfactory professional conduct or professional misconduct.

(c) A complaint the practitioner is not competent to practise the practitioner's profession.

(d) A complaint the practitioner has an impairment.

(e) A complaint the practitioner is otherwise not a suitable person to hold registration in the practitioner's profession.

Russell: "After the Tribunal had heard the submissions, and it was clear no complaints of this nature had been received I was summoned by Ms Rose to present myself for psychiatric examination. Clearly the plan was to find someone to certify me as mad. I had no option but to attend, but on arrival I identified one of the 'shrinks' as someone with a reputation for 'following orders' when people needed to be certified. To protect myself I immediately asked him if I might record the discussion which threw him. When he answered no, I asked if there was any law against this and he seemed uncertain. I then said I was going to go ahead with the recording regardless and that was really the end of that 'examination'. Their plan to neutralise me had been thwarted. Needless to say I have not been called in for a re-assessment.

"In my case, the Council relied on the AFP as the complainant but the court dismissed this thus:

During this appeal submissions by the Medical Council of NSW included that the Council stated it had received information that Russell had been charged with offences and that the AFP alleged that he was involved in and had material support to a child abduction ring in contravention of orders made by the Family Court. Russell had in fact not been charged with this.

The Medical Council did not identify any reason why the AFP had provided its information to the HCCC to be passed on to the Medical Council. The AFP had no obvious or apparent interest in Dr Pridgeon's right to continue to practise. No complaint had been made against Dr Pridgeon by anyone under S144 of the National Law.

"An important point is this successful appeal would not have happened without the help of amazing people who have come forth to help, none of whom, it needs be said, were qualified lawyers. Prior to this hearing I was absolutely exhausted physically and emotionally and felt I had lost the will to fight on. My lady-friend who wishes to remain unknown, saved me; she applied her mind and identified no less than 14 grounds for appeal which were crafted for the court in the most elegant legal prose and none were rejected. I'm not a religious man but I do believe God had a hand in this victory.

"What has become clear to us is the 'emergency' clause has been repeatedly abused by the Council to circumvent the procedural requirements and strike 'troublesome' doctors off the register without due process. In the normal course of events I should have been notified of a complaint against me in writing and then given a chance to attend a hearing and defend myself but because the 'threat' I posed was considered an 'emergency' this fundamental right was denied me.

"In this way practitioners who have prescribed Ivermectin for Covid and others who have presented as 'vaccine sceptics' have also been summarily dealt with. Our win now opens the doors for a multitude of possible class-actions as this procedure has now been exposed for the false flag it clearly is.

"At the end of the day, what should concern every decent Australian is the Medical Council and the Tribunal have been shown clearly to believe that child protection constitutes professional misconduct, and they will use their powers to destroy lives and careers in pursuit of this policy."

Graeme Bell 23rd May 2022

"What is important about this ruling is the court has pointed out quite clearly that they do not believe that Russell's conviction on the remaining charges is the forgone conclusion the authorities seem to believe it is. And they have accepted that he truly believed he was acting in the best interests of the children.

"We're going to win this it's just a matter of time. We played them off a break, they don't know what to do. We are challenging the fact that there is even a need for a trial because we can prove the initial committal to trial was flawed; you can't have a trial following a void committal. After Russell's horrible committal we appealed immediately to the SC but the prosecution rushed off to the lower District Court which is not permissible; they should have waited until the SC heard the appeal but they were desperate to try and push it through so they went to another court in the same jurisdiction before a different judge. We blocked the indictment twice, so they went and got a judge in chambers to sign the indictment without telling him there was an appeal pending in the Supreme Court. This has been noted as 'irregular' by the SC.

7 - The Truth is Revealed

At this point the Supreme Court has adjourned the case indefinitely so nobody can move until the SC makes a decision.

"Another issue I will raise relates to the High Court ruling that an indigent person cannot get a fair trial unless they have a lawyer. We want this expanded to cover all the ancillary costs that go with facing a criminal trial. In Ann Gordon's case we have a woman in Townsville with no money having to attend a trial in Brisbane 1,400kms away which, if the prosecution choose, could go on for up to a year. She has no transport and no way of accommodating herself for that period of time. Russell and Patrick are not much better off.

Graeme Bell advising Russell stated: "In a criminal trial of this nature there is a rule that should be worrying the prosecution. They acknowledge their case is based on circumstantial evidence so in terms of the rules the onus is on them to disprove every reasonable hypothesis put forward by the defence. Our defence is Russell and Patrick did what they did, not to defeat justice, but to save children from harm. They now have to convince a jury that the defendants didn't believe what they say they believed, which I would say is impossible. They just have to prove on a balance of probabilities that they believed what they believed and that is easy for us to do.

Patrick still faces two charges under s121 for publishing an account of a Family Court and two counts of conspiring to defeat justice. However, Patrick was in Grafton when he committed the alleged offence and yet he's being tried in Queensland. This is a violation of the constitution, which mandates an accused person faces trial by jury in the state where the offence is alleged to have been committed.

March 23, 2023 Dr. Pridgeon took issue with the wording of "abduction" in a copy of the prosecution's statement of facts he had seen. "I have the most profound objection to that, it implies a crime, infers a crime and wrongdoing," he told Brisbane District Court.

But Judge Leanne Clare said this was not "relevant" to the allegation of whether he planned to defeat justice. "What matters is what you knew, what you believed, and why."

Judge Clare said all three had made submissions to "free" themselves from prosecution. She dismissed their applications, saying their assembled research in support was "artificially selective".

"I do not say that is a deliberate misrepresentation, but a continued misreading of the law feeds the defendants' sense of persecution," she said. "Where there is a phrase or a portion of a section of an act of Parliament which in isolation might support their argument, they have tended to adopt it as confirmation the indictment is invalid or unlawful without considering the context or qualifying circumstance in the sentence."

A further trial review for the four defendants has been listed for May 12 before the matter proceeds to trial on May 22.

The matter was then postponed further.

Following a publication of a book 'Everyone Knows' written by Russell Pridgeon, publisher unknown, Judge Clare agreed to a separate trial for Ann Gordon and Lizzie Weber. This meant that the video of Ann's grandson disclosing abuse – the video that was concealed by the police – will not be shown to the jury of the two men.

When Patrick finally got to speak, he objected stating that he wanted the prosecution video of the boy to be brought before the jury as this goes to the credibility of the officer. Judge Clare replied, "this is not a trial of the police officer… you are the one on trial"

When Russell questioned why Judge Clare had denied all his

7 - The Truth is Revealed

avenues of defence, she replied "you have to understand this is an adversarial system"… "You are allowed" or you have the defence "of what is in your head". Russell wanted the jury to see what he saw – the documents and reports from Professor Briggs etc., that informed him and others that the children were abused and needed protection. These will now not be shown to the jury in their case.

Meanwhile, on 15 September 2023, after all that went before, having been charged in 2018 with one count of Conspiracy to defeat justice, contrary to section 42(1) of the *Crimes Act 1914*; and one count of Child stealing, contrary to section 363(1) of the *Criminal Code 1899 (Qld)*, **Joyce Fazldeen**, after pleading guilty, was convicted without sentence being passing, and ordered to pay a good behaviour $1000 bond, suspended, subject to one year good behaviour.

Subsequently at her trial, Lizzie Weber pleaded guilty and was sentenced to 3 years, but she can be released by August 2024 for good behaviour. Her solicitor stated she will not appeal the sentence.

Meanwhile, Ann Gordon has now rejoined Russell and Patricks' trial, likely around the first-half of 2024, having booted her barrister and solicitor into touch.

Review

Russell, Patrick, and five others were arrested by the Australian Federal Police in the so-called Operation Noetic. The arrests were made by no less than 28 policemen and women, and the event was widely televised in a multimedia frenzy. The message sent to the world was that Russell was the evil mastermind and financier of an international child trafficking ring involving up to 200 children, earning loads of money helping to smuggle hundreds of children away from the authorities. Tellingly, right from the outset, only three children were identified.

They called it a 'parental' child abduction ring because it was parents who had taken their own kids, hiding from alleged abusers, and no, it's not abduction if it is your own kid (obviously). Russell had bought a family food, school supplies, toys, etc. and driven them around during this difficult time.

The police had found evidence that he had helped two parents and extrapolated that there could well be hundreds. Meanwhile, the Prosecutors are actively hiding the evidence of the children's abuse from the court.

The Police and the Commonwealth prosecution are well aware of the children's sexual abuse: they are in possession of all the evidence that was seized from Russell and Patrick at the time of their arrests. Yet the prosecution is brazenly concealing the evidence.

The AFP brought forth seven charges against Russell: three counts of child stealing, a stalking charge, a proceeds of crime charge and two charges of conspiracy to defeat justice. The stalking charge was dropped because he had never approached, followed, contacted online or in person, or even laid eyes on his alleged victim, so there was no evidence. He had to wear an ankle bracelet for over a year, though, because stalkers are dangerous.

The proceeds of crime charge (where you earn money from crime) was dropped due to lack of evidence. It was originally justified by the statement in the brief of evidence that he had transferred $1.3mil into overseas accounts. This allowed them to close his bank account and seize assets. Russell pointed out he has never owned that much money before in assets, let alone cash, and certainly didn't transfer anything overseas. After this falsehood, it was later admitted that this was a 'mistake', although it was never removed from the brief of evidence.

The child-stealing charges were dropped too. In both situations it was the mother who took the children, Russell had nothing to do with it, so it was never going to hold up. Both mothers even had the child-stealing charges brought against them (although briefly) before they realised they had no hope of convicting a mother for stealing her own child. Grandmother Ann Gordon actually had full lawful custody of her child at the time, and then lost that custody because of that child-stealing charge!

7 - The Truth is Revealed

In the case of the Morris twins, despite 40 mandatory reports of child sexual abuse and an active Apprehended Violence Order against the domestically violent father, the police saw fit to inform the Family Court that the abuse was 'unsubstantiated' and the children were ordered back into the custody of the father.

Australia's pre-eminent expert on child abuse, Prof Freda Briggs AO, had investigated the allegations, and wrote a damning report about the Police negligence but she was prevented from testifying in court about the facts. Briggs was utterly horrified by the Family Court orders that gave sole custody to the father. She used her status as an Order of Australia recipient, to appeal to every possible minister or state attorney general, but she was ignored. Similarly, the 13 witnesses to the children's disclosures of abuse, were also prevented from testifying in court. The children's disclosures were graphic, detailed and consistent, no four-or five-year-old would be able to fabricate such things.

Hopes that those wielding the full force of the law of the land, who seek to destroy Russell, Patrick and Ann Gordon, would relent and end their torment, have been dashed. The possibility of prison looms large. The children are in the custody of their alleged abusers. Looking at the sequence of events from afar it appears it is now a crime in Australia to protect a child from rape.

5 Charges out of the initial 7 have been dropped because the evidence to prove the elements of the charges was never there. The s42 Conspiracy charges remain only because the elements are so vague and broadly written, that any action may be portrayed as a crime.

In fact, you can't even look to the brief of evidence for a clue as to why the charge exists, it's 90gb in PDF form and the AFP claim it's the largest in NSW history. There are even over a hundred photos in there of road tarmac surface.

Meanwhile Russell can't get legal aid well and no one will tell him why. Then an amazing lawyer came in to the case for some of the others involved and who also helped advise Russell. She pointed out all the ridiculous things about this case and has consequently been disbarred from practicing law. The reason given was she was 'bringing the court in to disrepute', as evidenced by a letter she wrote to a judge. The letter was about this case and outlined the horrible things happening (which actually does bring the courts to disrepute in my opinion). The judge released this private letter publicly, thus this public letter can now be said to be bringing the disrepute.

Our society demands that children are kept safe from harm at all times, especially such egregious harm as child sexual abuse. [The Family Law Act 1975, s70NAE, provides that a parent, or anyone, can contravene an existing custody order, if the child's safety is in danger]. Furthermore, the law criminalises child sexual abuse. The law makes it a crime not to protect children from harm at all times and in all circumstances. Yet the men whom the children identified as their abusers are untroubled by the law, and the people who tried to protect these children are being prosecuted in the most aggressive fashion and face decades in jail if convicted.

The system thus far seems to have utterly failed everyone, children and child protectors alike. But Russell and Patrick hope for a reversal of fortunes when the rules relating to criminal procedure will force the prosecution to reveal the copious documentation and evidence confirming the dreadful and prolonged child abuse that forced these good people to act as they did.

Some good may come of this though: evidence of the children's sexual abuse has now been made public because of this trial, which makes it available for journalists. The most damning evidence, which may now be shown to the jury, is the combination of a video interview of a child clearly alleging serious sexual abuse that he endured to the police and then a ranking policeman's sworn affidavit stating that no mention of any sexual abuse was disclosed to them.

* * *

Russell: "The supine silence of the media has been a huge disappointment during this ordeal. For the O'Dea family the search for justice and fairness remains elusive. Both Patrick and his sister Kathleen risked life and liberty on several occasions in the fight to rid Zimbabwe of the Mugabe regime. Both sought sanctuary in Australia where they believed justice prevailed. It looks more and more like Patrick should have stayed where he was.

Anybody who is familiar with the facts of this sorry saga will know that over the years almost every parliamentarian with influence has been approached for help, to rescue these children from the ongoing sexual abuse. They have all refused.

"Looking back, the only official who seems to have acted responsibly is Judge Foster who back in 2013 ruled in connection with the Morris twins that, "There is sufficient evidence for the proposition that the children were and would be in danger of being abused sexually were they placed in custody of dad.

"The facts of this case have been hidden from public scrutiny by the misuse of section 121 and more recently by Publication Restrictions on facts that have been in the public domain for years. Why are these people so desperate to hide their crimes from public scrutiny?

"The prosecution has been going on for more than four years with no end in sight. I feel certain the strategy employed by the AFP to destroy me has backfired. I am self-represented and intend to remain so. As such I can place the facts of the crimes against these children and the malfeasance of so many people in law enforcement in front of a jury and the public during the trial. I intend to do so in the most graphic way. Any publication of the simple facts of this case will be incredibly damaging to the lives and careers of those (eminent) persons whose criminal negligence has allowed and enabled these children to be sexually assaulted for years. The only solicitor, Serena Teffaha, who acted for her client without fear or favour, was immediately removed from the fray by the system. I, on the other hand, have nothing left to destroy. I am that most dangerous man: one with nothing left to lose. Neither Patrick nor I give a stuff about ourselves. We are totally committed to rescuing those children. The prosecutors and their masters know this, because I have told them many times.

This is not historical. The children have been in the custody of the men whom the children have clearly and repeatedly identified as their abusers. The twins (now age 13) are reported to be suicidal, self-harming and running away. Nobody knows what has happened to Christopher. In 2018 he told several people that he expected to be killed by his father. I believe that it was only that Christopher's abusive father was warned by outlaw bikies that if Christopher was harmed there would be consequences, that has kept him alive. As the witnesses to serious crimes these children have always been at risk of serious harm, at no time more than the present. So as you can imagine the criminals involved in trafficking these children for abuse will not welcome a book that reveals their malfeasance.

So if you are able to help, the first step is this: the immediate rescue of Charlotte and Jane Morris and Christopher Gordon and their return to the custody of the mother Lizzie and the grandmother Ann.

I ask nothing for myself

As I know Patrick, he would say the same.

CHAPTER 8 – FORWARD LOOKING

Where to now?

As for Russell, his solicitor, Peter O'Brien, has now written to the Commonwealth Director of Public Prosecutions, Morrison Daniel, seeking the discontinuance of proceedings as there is no reasonable prospect of conviction given:

1. The Commonwealth Director of Public Prosecutions does not possess the required evidence to secure a conviction, namely the defences of sudden or extraordinary emergency and self-defence are available on the evidence in the prosecution brief, capable of meeting the requisite standard for the defence.
2. There is no admissible evidence available that negates either defence to the requisite standard in a criminal matter.

Given that Russell has two defences:
1. Sudden or extraordinary emergency
2. Self defence

These defences have been raised within the prosecution evidence, namely a letter and Dr Pridgeon reading the letter onto a video recording, in which he clearly admits that he is doing what he is doing because the police and courts are unable to protect the children whose family members have complained to him.

Insofar as **sudden and extraordinary emergency,** this defence requires not just a subjective belief on the part of the accused but also that the conduct be, objectively, a reasonable response. To this end, the evidential burden has been discharged within the prosecution brief

- There are communications from the late Emeritus Professor Freda Briggs asserting the validity of the Morris's twins complaints from the vantage of expert level opinion.
- All of the evidence, taken together, points to the accused holding a genuine belief that the Morris's children and the Gordon child were being repeatedly sexually abused by the parent with dominant possession on Family Court Parenting Orders. Whether the children were actually abused as a matter of fact, is irrelevant. However, the circumstances surrounding, and leading to, the Russell's reasonable belief that the children were being abused, is relevant

In terms of the **reasonableness of the belief,** it is supported by video statements of the Morris's girls discussing disclosures they had allegedly previously made to their mother and parenting supervisors, regarding being touched by their father on the 'toushka'.

The allegations by the Gordon child are explicit, complete and on the face of it, entirely credible. Whilst not admissible for the purpose of establishing they were abused, they are admissible for the purpose of establishing the defendant believed the child was being abused.

Both the Morris and Gordon cases involve Queensland Police Service, Child Protection Unit asserting that both the Morris's children and the Gordon child were subject to coaching, in the absence of any evidence to support such a conclusion. At no point is the subject of coaching substantiated beyond the fanciful, and speculation of government employees.

8 - Forward Looking

Where a defendant discharges the evidential burden in relation to a defence, then the prosecution bears the legal burden of negating the defence beyond reasonable doubt. The prosecution has not served any admissible evidence which negates this defence on the balance of probabilities, let alone to the requisite standard such that there can be no reasonable prospect of conviction.

Further, Russell demonstrates a pattern of protective behaviour in relation to children who are at apparent risk of being sexually abused by an adult. See his statement concerning being sued by his stepson's father.

Also, he was involved in a political party called the "Anti-paedophile party".

Insofar as the defence of self-defence, Russell raises the necessity to protect the Morris twins in his video.

The improbability of nullifying either defence is extraordinarily high, when the following child disclosures are presented on the prosecution evidence.

From Russell's perspective, clearly the child is complaining of serious sexual abuse. Russell's belief was that the child was protecting his father, due to fear, and hence attributed this serious sexual assault allegation against his grandfather in lieu. Whether this can be substantiated or not is immaterial. The relevant factor is this is what he believed, and once established, the prosecution must negative its reasonableness to the requisite standard of beyond a reasonable doubt.

Further, there was the role of the lead investigator in this matter for Queensland Police Detective Sergeant David Miles. On 4 June 2018, D/Sgt Miles incorrectly informed the court that Christopher Gordon never disclosed when interviewed three times, any sexual abuse by the father when in fact these disclosures were recorded, this despite the fact that D/Sgt David Miles was responsible for the unit which performed the interviews of the child.

Was it not on the balance of probabilities, open for Russell to conclude

1. The child was being sexually abused.
2. The Family Court was being misinformed about such abuse by police and officers of the court and subsequently ordering that the child be ordered to stay with the parent who is disclosed as being the abuser.
3. An action to remove the child from the allegedly sexual abuser parent was a reasonable one.

Report from the late Freda Briggs Emeritus Professor in Child Development University of South Australia on the child rape of the Morris twins, suggest a failure to investigate, especially given the Contact Supervisor's Reports. Here she states that she has read 93 reports written by thirteen contact supervisors.

Having served this document, which describes the existence of child supervisor reports and the names of child supervisors, and the fact that there is relevant material in the child supervisor reports, it is surprising that Operation Noetic has not provided any child supervisor reports nor statements from police describing attempts to obtain statements from the above persons. The CDPP is *obligated to disclose this material.*

Further to that, when Russell attempted to address the Court he was rebuked and threatened with criminal defamation. How can it be said the Magistrate considered all the evidence adduced when he didn't hear from the accused on the issues because the accused didn't speak up in fear of and in obedience to the perceived threats of the Magistrate.

At the end of the day, the CDPP must disprove beyond any reasonable doubt his defences which they cannot prove.

- The charge of conspiracy to defeat the course of justice cannot be proven.
- There is no reasonable prospect of conviction, as the prosecution has no evidence to negate the defendant's statutory defences.

It would now seem that pursuant to the CDPP's policy in respect of the decision to prosecution, the standing charge ought be withdrawn.

This Family Court abuse and child abduction case is only one of many such cases, the latest reported by Dee McLachlan, in Gumshoe News on 11 October 2022: *"We have written much on Operation Noetic – and how the government tried to cover up child abuse and prosecute the child protectors. It seems this is a repeating narrative."*

This follows the Independent newspaper's headline on 11 October: "Police searching for missing mother and five-year-old daughter".

Pastor Paul Burton: "Just like with Russell Pridgeon, Patrick O'Dea, Ann Gordon, and many others, it would suggest that the family court like the children's courts are not courts but are actually child traffickers and abusers – continually returning them to sexual predators. The business of taking children from one state (i.e. from the care of his mother) and changing that state to another state (i.e. being put under the care and control of the state) is clearly child trafficking".

At least other bodies have acknowledged what is transpiring and taking action as 3rd November Australia's Cricket Board apologised to survivors of child sexual abuse who were involved in the sport and called on its members to join a national redress scheme. The apology comes weeks after jailed former cricket coach and convicted paedophile Ian King had nearly three years added to his sentence, over an historical sexual offence involving a teenage boy.

Operation Noetic had the AFP trumpeting that they had smashed the largest child smuggling ring in Australia in one of their costliest exercises where they had compiled the largest volumes of evidence, slapping Russell Pridgeon and Patrick O'Dea with charges carrying a 50-year sentences while also taking aim at pensioners as old as 83. Further, they co-opted the media's involvement and influence the Medical Council to withdraw Russell's medical license.

At the same time, Townsville's Child Protection Unit did not disclose evidence in court, nor did they tell the truth in court, and refused to believe the mothers, alleging she coached the children with no evidence to this effect, whilst disbelieving the children, and eventually handing them back to the alleged abusers. The courts also refused to hear Russell's evidence and refused him legal representation.

This is the same country where Prime Minster Scott Morrison apologised to the nation for not believing mothers and children insofar as sexual abuse, something that appears to have fallen on deaf ears where the AFP is concerned.

Is this the Australia we want?

AFP Assistant Commissioner Debbie Platz, Assistant Commissioner Crime Operations, said investigators had disrupted an organised and well-resourced group of people demonstrating a complete disregard for the rule of law and decisions of the courts. 'The actions of this group do not protect children. What it does is potentially endanger the safety and wellbeing of them,' she said."

8 - Forward Looking

According to the AFP the O'Dea, Pridgeon, and Gordon case is the biggest criminal case in Australian legal history – and the Commonwealth Director of Public Prosecutions (CDPP) has charged these persons with "Conspiracy to Defeat Justice" etc. **Despite the clear disclosures of sexual abuse by the children, plus the evidence of police misfeasance** "reasonable excuse for contravening an order; (4) A person is taken to have had a reasonable excuse for **contravening a parenting order (putting the kid in a different home that the one on the order)** … if (the person) (a) believed on reasonable grounds that the actions constituting the contravention were necessary to protect the health or safety of a person (including the respondent or the child)…"

The mother was acting within the law, protecting her children and herself. They went with her more than willingly, and I've heard her describe how seriously malnourished they were, and how, over time, they slowly began to heal from the infections and rectal bleeding.

The AFP's Conundrum

Now interestingly, when the AFP raided Dr Pridgeon, O'Dea and the others, computers were seized. On those computer was evidence regarding the mandatory reports, letters to the QLD Child Protection Minister, etc. All this suddenly became exculpatory evidence. The moment they seized the evidence, an obligation fell on prosecutors to consider the material on those computers.

The CDPP are presently fighting tooth and nail to prevent the evidence of the childrens' abuse being brought before the court. But the prosecutor is obliged by law to present all exculpatory evidence – whether it exonerates or incriminates the defendants. It appears that those accusing Pridgeon and O'Dea for "Conspiracy to defeat justice" are now the very perpetrators of that crime. They are caught in a *conundrum*. If they reveal the exculpatory evidence as they are supposed to, then authorities would be obliged to investigate the very persons the AFP officer are protecting.

By separating the trials this will no longer be the case insofar as the twins' video recorded and oral evidence where Russell and Patrick's trial is concerned.

As for Russell, "I do not understand why I am charged with conspiracy in relation to [male child victim], when the allegation is that [male child victim's grandmother] 'abducted' the child, when [she] had court-ordered custody and is not charged with abduction.

"I don't understand how I can be charged with harbouring the [victim twins] when the law states that I must do all I can to protect a child in my care, whether I have lawful custody or not."

As stated, according to the AFP, it is the biggest criminal case in Australian legal history.

This case has now been on foot for around five years – spending tens of millions of dollars but has refused to investigate why this all began. They have ignored the 40 or more reports of egregious sexual abuse and turned a blind eye when a police officer concealed the interview.

Dr. Pridgeon, a Family Doctor lost his medical practice for years; Patrick O'Dea has been unable to work because of draconian bail conditions and without the support of his family would be homeless, and another kind loving grandmother living in Townsville has also had her life decimated. All this has happened to these people because they have been persecuted for trying to protect children who had all disclosed sexual abuse.

So far, thanks to their strength and courage to self-represent, and thanks also to the tireless work of a very small dedicated team

8 - Forward Looking

of individuals, 21 charges have been dropped.

Politicians, police, prosecution and the media turned a blind eye to the allegations of the children. The Family Court then returned the children to the sole custody of the very people they accused of abusing them.

We can only hope there will be introspection insofar as the Family Court, the Townsville Child Protection unit, and the respective magistrate courts, and that these ills are rectified.

Meanwhile, what of those accused, brave Ann Gordon, and Lizzie Weber? Do they deserve not only an apology, but maybe 'Mum of the Year' for doing what is expected of all Australians by protecting their children, or are they in fact the culprits? Does the Family Court ruling supercede the rights of children?

Patrick and Russell, who believed they were doing the right thing, stood up and were counted, protecting Australian children when no one would help. Who gave their all and huge amounts of money for no reward. Who have been hounded by the AFP and vilified for protecting these children in line with the constitution and the rights of children even when the AFP knew they were in the wrong, and for showing Australians how we should act. If they are found to be innocent, then an apology will not suffice. At the very least, possibly, they should be named 'Australians of the Year'.

On the other hand, despite believing they were doing the 'right' thing, were Patrick and Russell actually helping the children? Afterall, after weighing up the facts, the Family Court had made judgements insofar as custody. Likewise there are rules of evidence and whether they must be followed in this case even if we may not agree.

There may well be a strict legal interpretation that you cannot defy the Family Court's ruling such that the AFP were simply following due process, however unfair the facts may seem to the lay person. The twin's mother pleaded guilty, so what will the boys' defence be? Will Russell's medical licence be withdrawn? As for Patrick, he also has additional social media charges. Their media person, Tim Holt, already pleaded guilty and received a jail sentence.

However, this story is not about Russell and Patrick. It is possible they may have overstepped the bounds, but maybe not, and if that's the case don't expect them to receive any compensation for pain and suffering, loss of income or reputation. But either way, they may be a catalyst for future generations insofar as the clarification of the law, which may actually set International Law, namely which takes precedent, the Family Court's ruling or the Rights of Children, and what of a doctors' duty in terms of their Hippocratic Oath?

8 - Forward Looking

Showdown with The Devil

Australia needs more "Superheros" like Russell, Patrick and Ann.

In 2018 The devil whispered in their ears---

"You are not strong enough to withstand the storm"

Today on Thursday 8th February 2024, the three superhero's whispered in the devils ear----

"WE ARE THE STORM"

(Sandra Harrison)

Winners are grinners

Patrick O'Dea, Russell Pridgeon, Ann Greer, Mash Jewell

On 05 February 2024 at the SC Court of Queensland the trial began concerning the final two conspiracy charges where Ann Gordon, Patrick, and Russell were the defendants with the Commonwealth Director of Public Prosecutions (CCPP) appearing before Judge Loury.

The Boys from Bulawayo

Patrick O'Dea, Russell Pridgeon, Pastor Paul Burton, Ann Greer

Pastor Paul Burton and Patrick O'Dea downing a victory beer

8 - Forward Looking

Immediately the CCPP tried to blindside Patrick stating there was no basis for Patrick to believe that he was going to have separate trials for the 2 conspiracy charges and the other minor six charges. Obviously Patrick was not prepared and ready to defend the six minor charges.

Clearly this was untrue as judge Clare and the CDPP previously discussed the separate trials on a number of occasions and at no stage had it been mentioned that the two trials had been joined

Judge Loury raised the issue that charges had been brought together in the Indictment equating this to joined trials, but there was no precedent for this.

Patrick argued that according to the wording of the case presented by the CDPP he is charged with a conspiracy and that the CDPP had not obtained the consent of the attorney general as they should have.

After two days it was determined that Patrick was to be tried with Ann Gordon and Russell Pridgeon on the 2 conspiracy charges and have a trial for the 6 other charges in a separate trial, exactly as judge Clare had ordered and what Patrick wanted.

Day 3 of Trial

The 3 defendants: Patrick O'Dea, Grandmother AG, and Dr Russell Pridgeon stood trial for section 42 Conspiracy to defeat the Course of Justice charges.

Robert Size, Barrister, representing Dr Russell Pridgeon sought immediately to make an application for a Stay of the Trial on basis of an Application to re-open a Pre-trial Ruling:

The prosecution alleged that the defendants' actions in removing the children from the custody of the father and assisting the mother to evade the authorities was conduct that had a tendency to obstruct, prevent, pervert or defeat "a Course of Justice[16]" as previously ruled by Judge Clare in 2021. In the case of the Mother: the Course of Justice was over and completed: orders were made.

In the case of the Grandmother: the Course of Justice was still on foot, because the grandmother had an application before the Court.

(The CDPP had chosen to ignore that the Police in the Brisbane watch house prevented the grandmother from attending the hearing at which her grandson was given into the custody of his father: the man whom the child had clearly and repeatedly identified to the Police as his abuser. Furthermore, the Police in the Brisbane Watch house, and the Commanding Officer of the Townsville Child Protection Unit, lied in their statements to the Court, thus causing the Judge to be misinformed about the facts in the case. The Independent Children's Lawyers Counsel then informed the Court, in direct answer to the Judges question, that there were no issues of abuse in this case, which he knew to be untrue. As a result the judge made orders which were catastrophic[17] for this defenseless child, while the grandmother was prevented from reaching the court by the Police, and prevented from revealing the truth of the matter to the Judge.

Clearly it would appear that the Police and other parties were acting in a Conspiracy to pervert the Course of Justice: exactly the charge that the CDPP were now prosecuting the defendants for.

The difficulty for the CDPP is that the "Course of Justice" that

---

16 Perverting the course of justice is an offence committed when a person prevents justice from being served on themselves or on another party.

17 This child has been forced to live for the past 6 years with his abuser. There has been no supervision or welfare checks, despite the fact that the father had a long history of violent criminal offences, meanwhile this child has attended hospitals with injuries on any number of occasions.

they identify as being obstructed by the defendants is the contravention proceedings. However no contravention proceedings were ever initiated, and the CDPP had no evidence that the fathers ever intended to bring any Contravention Proceedings.

Furthermore, the conduct that they allege obstructed the "Course of Justice" (hiding the children) is the same conduct which would have caused Contravention Orders to be taken out in the first place, if the fathers ever intended to do so.

Judge Clare of the District Court had previously rejected the argument that the conspiracy was to obstruct the making of recovery orders, because the removal and concealment of the twins "would ground the application for, and issuing of" contravention proceedings.

In her Judgement she concluded that it is not open as a matter of law for the Crown to allege that conduct which gives rise to the possibility of a course of justice is at the same time conduct with a tendency to obstruct that same course of justice

Barrister Size's clear and coherent presentation concerning Judge Clare's conclusion revealed a compelling legal argument, which the CDPP had to consider seriously. Justin Hannebery KC, the Senior Prosecutor asked for time to take this to the CDPP for instruction, and the court adjourned.

08 February 2024: Trial day 4

The CDPP response to Robert Size's application was to Stay the trial permanently.

The CDPP was not able to respond to Mr Size's application because they had not received instruction from the Director of the CDPP. Again the matter was stood down while the advice was awaited.

Mr Justin Hannebery KC began immediately with a motion of discontinuance for Counts 1 & 2 (section 42 conspiracy charges) for the grandmother Ann Gordon, Patrick O'Dea and Dr Russell Pridgeon

The defendants were to be discharged,

And in a moment it was all over,

The trial was finished.

Dr Pridgeon dropped to his knees immediately to give thanks and the judge Lourey J began to scream "get out, get out, get out" and continued until the defendants left the court.

Barrister Size appeared to rise and Her Honour continued screaming at him as he left the court.

It wasn't until the defendants left the courtroom that they were able to reflect upon the magnitude of Mr Size's achievement.

Charges for conspiracy to defeat justice against Russell, Patrick, and Ann have been discontinued, now only the remaining 6 other charges against Patrick are listed for further mention on 29th February remain.

This investigation and prosecution had been going for 5 years before their arrests in October 2018. And for 5.5 years after the arrests with strict Bail conditions including GPS ankle trackers. It cost tax payers millions of dollars

The prosecution was a farce, especially after it became apparent that the defendants were neither paedophiles or child stealers, but instead of admitting to their error the AFP tried to cover up their mistake, and never anticipated the defendants would fight back, such that the 3 defendants had been able to whittle back the charges one by one using the superior legal arguments brought by Graeme Bell and others, with Pastor Paul ably assisting, whilst in the process, magistrate Anthony Getts had Serena Teffah, who stood up against the corrupt practice, maliciously struck off the role by the Victoria Legal Services Board while representing the grandmother pro bono.

Graeme and Paul and another unqualified person were able to get 5 out of the 7 charges faced by Dr Russell Pridgeon dropped by extraordinary efforts and the legal mind of Graeme Bell. The other defendants charges were dropped because of this.

Against this background, Mr Robert Size, a young man, acting for Dr Pridgeon pro bono, showed how a defence should be planned and run. His level of organisation, his diligent reading of the largest brief in Australian legal history, his strategic planning of how he was to run this highly unusual case, and his superb knowledge and understanding of the law, was an object lesson in excellent legal practice.

On the morning of day 3 of the trial a lightbulb with an idea lit up, and he sat down to write the legal arguments out in a sitting

In 3 paragraphs of concise, elegant and compelling legal arguments which he presented in a few minutes he destroyed the largest criminal case in Australian legal history. An incredible legal feat.

The defendants recognised his merits as soon as they met him and held him in a kind of awe.

The magnitude of this victory over evil is breathtaking.

6 defendants had pleaded guilty to criminal charges seemingly because they were badly advised and simply gave up.

The protective mother languishes in jail for the heinous crime of protecting her children from rape, sentenced to 3 years.

The question now is whether the three innocent defendants will be taking out a malicious prosecution and damages for the loss of earnings (including loss of Russell's medical licence and reputation) against the State, the AFP, and privately against those deemed culpable.

And what about the children, how will they now be protected, and compensated? Will the grandmother get custody of her grandson? Will they recover?

This is the same country where Prime Minster Scott Morrison apologised to the nation for not believing mothers and children insofar as sexual abuse, something that appears to have fallen on deaf ears where the AFP is concerned.

Is this the Australia we want?

We can only hope there will be introspection insofar as the Family Court, the Townsville Child Protection unit, and the respective magistrate courts, and that these ills are rectified and those who crossed the line are held accountable.

Likewise, the disgraced gullible media, who should check their facts and not believe everything these bodies in authority tell them, should reflect on the damage they caused.

As for Patrick and Russell, who stood up and were counted, protecting Australian children when no one would help. Who gave their all and huge amounts of money for no reward. Who have been hounded by the AFP and vilified for protecting these children in line with the constitution and the rights of children even when the AFP knew they were in the wrong, and for showing Australians how we should act. An apology will not suffice. At the very least they should be named 'Australian Day Honours Roll'.

BIBLIOGRAPHY

- Child abduction accused to stand trial | The West Australian
https://thewest.com.au/news/crime/child-abduction...2021/02/02 ·
- NSW doctor is one of seven people to face trial over ...
https://7news.com.au/news/qld/child-abduction...021/02/02
- AFP bust alleged child-stealing ring in NSW, Queensland ...
https://www.abc.net.au/news/2018-10-18/afp-arrest...
- Doctor accused of masterminding child-stealing syndicate ...
https://www.abc.net.au/news/2018-10-19/child..
https://www.dailymail.co.uk/news/article-6369809/...2018/11/09 ·
- Operation Noetic - AFP Arrests Patrick O'Dea and Dr ...
https://gumshoenews.com/2018/10/18/operation...2018/10/18 ·
- Child abduction accused to stand trial
https://au.news.yahoo.com/child-abduction-accused...2021/02/02
- Child abduction accused to stand trial | Newcastle Herald ...
https://www.newcastleherald.com.au/story/7110179/...
- Child abduction accused to stand trial | Newcastle Herald ...
https://www.newcastleherald.com.au/story/7110179/...
- Abduction accused doesn't like GPS tracker
https://www.brisbanetimes.com.au/national/...2019/04/05 ·
- Doctor accused of financing child abductions says crimes ...
https://www.theguardian.com/australia-news/2018/...2018/12/07 ·
- Doctor accused of financing child abductions says crimes ...
https://quinnfamilylawyers.com.au/doctor-accused...
- Parental abduction ring smashed after two-year AFP ...
https://www.smh.com.au/national/parental-abduction...2018/10/18 ·

https://www.dailyexaminer.com.au/news/f-k-him-up...
- Child abduction accused to stand trial | The Kimberley Echo https://www.kimberleyecho.com.au/news/crime/child...
- Child abduction accused to stand trial. Cheryl Goodenough AAP. 2021 12:33
- Child abduction accused to stand trial | Newcastle Herald ... https://www.newcastleherald.com.au/story/7110179/...
- Abducted Australian children 'sent to New Zealand, South ... https://www.stuff.co.nz/world/australia/107962410/...2018/10/19
- Investigating A Nationwide Child Abduction Ring | Family ... https://justicefamilylawyers.com.au/domestic...2018/11/08
- Children hidden and their identities changed by parent ... https://www.smh.com.au/national/children-hidden...2018/10/18
- Dr Pridgeon, On Federal Police, Calls a Spade a Spade ... https://gumshoenews.com/2019/04/07/dr-pridgeon-on...2019/04/07
- Doctor accused of financing child abductions says crimes ... https://www.theguardian.com/australia-news/2018/...2018/12/07
- Parental abduction ring smashed after two-year AFP ... https://www.smh.com.au/national/parental-abduction...2018/10/18
- 'F--k him up': Accused child abductor's threat to dad ... https://www.dailyexaminer.com.au/news/f-k-him-up...
- Doctor accused of financing child abductions says crimes ... https://quinnfamilylawyers.com.au/doctor-accused...
- Child abduction accused to stand trial | Broome Advertiser https://www.broomead.com.au/news/crime/child...2021 12:33
- Child Stealing Operation Busted Across Australia, 4 ... https://www.theepochtimes.com/child-stealing...2018/10/20
- GP in alleged child abduction ring is living off 'charity ... https://www.dailyexaminer.com.au/news/gp-in...
- Abducted Australian children 'sent to New Zealand, South ...

Bibliography

- https://www.stuff.co.nz/world/australia/107962410/...2018/10/19
- Investigating A Nationwide Child Abduction Ring | Family ... https://justicefamilylawyers.com.au/domestic...2018/11/08
- Family court kidnapping: AFP Police believe more kids are ... https://www.dailytelegraph.com.au/news/nsw/network...2018/10/18
- Child stealing accused granted bail - 9News https://www.9news.com.au/national/child-stealing...2018/10/19
- 'F--k him up': Accused child abductor's threat to dad ... https://www.dailyexaminer.com.au/news/f-k-him-up...
- Australian Police Break Up Child Abduction Ring https://ww.nationalparentsorganization.org/recent-articles?id=24194
- Patrick Finbar McGarry O'Dea accused of being part of ... https://www.couriermail.com.au/questnews/bail...
- Child Stealing Operation Busted Across Australia, 4 ... https://www.theepochtimes.com/child-stealing...2018/10/20
- Three women charged for assisting two mothers to abduct ... https://www.smh.com.au/national/three-women...
- Accused parental abduction ring organisers released on bail https://www.brisbanetimes.com.au/national/...2018/10/19
- Police Bust Child-Stealing Group Operating Across ... https://www.ntd.com/police-bust-child-stealing...2018/10/20
- Parental abduction network facing string of charges https://www.theaustralian.com.au/nation/nation/...
- Dr Pridgeon and Patrick O'Dea have been... - Fighters ... https://www.facebook.com/facaaus/posts/2113922151986668
- Kidnapping ring that allegedly ... - Yahoo News Australia https://au.news.yahoo.com/kidnapping-ring-helped...2018/10/18
- Accused parental abduction ring organisers released on bail https://www.brisbanetimes.com.au/national/...2018/10/19 ·
- NSW kidnapping accused released on bail | The North West ...

https://www.northweststar.com.au/story/5712415/nsw...2018/10/19
- Parental abduction network facing string of charges
https://www.theaustralian.com.au/nation/nation/...
- Police Bust Child-Stealing Group Operating Across ...
https://www.ntd.com/police-bust-child-stealing...2018/10/20
- Australia: Did you know a network exists helping mothers ...
https://www.divorceresource.com.au/resources/in...2018/12/18
- Family court kidnapping: AFP Police believe more kids are ...
https://www.dailytelegraph.com.au/news/nsw/network...2018/10/18
- Parental abduction ring smashed after two-year AFP ...
https://www.adelaidelegalsolutions.com.au/parental...2018/11/01
- Child stealing ring allegations: Five accused to face ...
https://www.couriermail.com.au/news/queensland/...2019/05/03
- Accused child stealers want GPS trackers removed ...
https://www.sunshinecoastdaily.com.au/news/accused...
- Kidnapping ring that allegedly ... - Yahoo News Australia
https://au.news.yahoo.com/kidnapping-ring-helped...2018/10/18
- Family court kidnapping: AFP Police believe more kids are ...
https://www.dailytelegraph.com.au/news/nsw/network...2018/10/18
- AFP bust alleged child-stealing ring in NSW, Queensland ...
https://mensrights.com.au/family-law/afp-bust...
- Child stealing ring allegations: Five accused to face ...
https://www.couriermail.com.au/news/queensland/...2019/05/03 ·
- Parental abduction ring smashed after two-year AFP ...
https://www.adelaidelegalsolutions.com.au/parental...2018/11/01
- Doctor accused of masterminding child-stealing syndicate ...
https://www.emow.com.au/doctor-accused-of...2018/10/19
- Latest Topic Section articles | Topics | Coffs Coast Advocate
https://www.coffscoastadvocate.com.au/topic/patrick-o'dea
- News Mail

Bibliography

- https://www.news-mail.com.au/search/?tag=committal hearing
- Attempted child abduction caught on CCTV | Herald Sun https://www.heraldsun.com.au/news/world/attempted...
- Abducting Your Own Child Can Amount to a Crime in Australia https://www.sydneycriminallawyers.com.au/blog/...
- Vigilante Group that Removed Kids from 'Sexually Abusive ... https://www.vice.com/en/article/g5b3x7/vigilante...
- NSW kidnapping accused released on bail | Bendigo ... https://www.bendigoadvertiser.com.au/story/5712415/...2018/10/19
- News Mail
https://www.news-mail.com.au/search/?tag=committal hearing
- Australia - Australia - William Tyrrell, 3, Kendall, Nsw ... https://www.websleuths.com/forums/threads/...2018/10/24
- NAASCA - Nov 2018 - week 2 - Recent News | NAASCA.org www.naasca.org/2018-NAASCA-news/11Nov18-2-NAASCAnews.htm
- Queensland Times
www.qt.com.au/search/?sort=latest&all-sites=on&tag=doctor&perpage=50
- Queensland Times
https://www.qt.com.au/search/?sort=latest&category=...
- *"Australian Antipaedophile Party"*. Australian Electoral Commission. 7 March 2016.
- *"Rename Australians Against Paedophiles Party"*. Australian Electoral Commission. 7 March 2016.
- ^Jump up to:a b *"Australian Antipaedophile Party"*. Australian Electoral Commission. 25 November 2016.
- *"Meet the AAPP"*. *Australian Antipaedophile Party*. Archived from the original on 21 March 2016.
- ^Olding, Rachel (15 May 2016). *"Founder of Australian Anti-Paedophile Party sued for accusing man of paedophilia"*. The Sydney Morning Herald.
- *"Candidates for the 2016 federal election"*. Australian Electoral Commission.

11 June 2016.
- *Prosser, Candice (28 June 2016). "Election 2016: Senate hopeful Ron Waters seeks to make amends for link to Valentine's Day murders"*. Australian Broadcasting Corporation.
- Australian Anti Paedophile Party (AAPP) http://www.australianantipaedophileparty.com/ https://www.9news.com.au/2018/10/18/10/09/four-facing-court-over-alleged-australian-child-abduction-ring
- VICTORY! Russell Pridgeon Reclaims His Medical License https://gumshoenews.com › Australia
- Comparative Trials of Russell Pridgeon and Jahar Tsarnaev https://gumshoenews.com › Australia
- Voir Dire, Part 5: How Many Lies Can the AFP Tell, Using ... https://gumshoenews.com › News
- *"Everybody Knows":* New Book by Doctor Who's on Trial for ... https://womenscoalition.substack.com › everybody-know...
- REUNION. Judging the Family Court. by Mary W Maxwell, ... https://docplayer.net › 138864347-Reunion-judging-t...
- The AFP Arrested The Wrong Man -- Dr Russell Pridgeon
- A Letter From Dr Russell Pridgeon – The Man Who Fulfilled ...
- Dr Russell Pridgeon... - Department of Community Services NSW
- 29 May 2023 — www.rumormill.news/223404 ... Reunion: Judging the Family Court, and my series of articles about Russell Pridgeon at GumshoeNews.com.https://www.smh.com.au › National › Courts

www.ingramcontent.com/pod-product-compliance
Lightning Source LLC
Chambersburg PA
CBHW011149290426
44109CB00025B/2542